SHOULDER

SHOULDER

by

Moya Hession-Aiken

ELBORO

SHOULDER Copyright © 2020 by Moya Hession-Aiken

All rights reserved. No part of this book may be used or reproduced in any manner whatsoever without written permission except in the case of brief quotations embodied in critical articles and reviews.

ISBN: 978-1-7379274-7-1

Published by Elboro Press

Elboro Press books may be purchased in bulk for educational, business or sales promotional use. Please address enquiries to:

office@elboropress.com

CONTENTS

Preface
1

Part One
5

Part Two
77

Part Three
137

Part Four
199

Shoulder

The morning of the funeral the limos are lined up outside the house. My three-year-old son, Liam, is at a neighbors with their daughter. I don't want him to attend the service. We journey into Manhattan from New Jersey. We pull up outside the Cathedral and somebody says, "Bill's here."

For a split second I think they mean my husband's standing there waiting for us. But they didn't mean that and he's not.

People enter the church. Police are organizing traffic. There's a cop on horseback and people are hanging out windows looking to see what's going on.

The sun is shining.

Entering, I think about the day we were married here and how the empty church, then, made everybody look so small. But today the church is filled to capacity and it's the building that looks so tiny. I follow up the aisle behind Bill's casket, propped up by our friends, and sit in the front pew. I look over and wonder if I can reach out and rest my hand on it, just like we were holding hands. It's the first time in my life I'm not terrified by a coffin.

The service is a blur.

The priest says the Mass. We leave. I stand outside for two hours greeting people.

What do you say?

There's a lot of: "Hi, how are you?"

"Fine. You?"

Then the realization that it is not fine.

The guy from the funeral home comes over and apologizes for not having enough pages in the condolence book. He's getting more paper to add to it now. He didn't realize how big a funeral this was going to be and says he's never witnessed anything like it in the forty years he's worked in the business.

"Never saw police having to reroute traffic," he adds, looking around for help.

After about an hour, one of his associates comes over to me and asks if it's okay they take Bill now?

I tell him it's fine because I know Bill has already gone.

We all go back to Jersey and, just as we're getting into the house, a town car pulls up and out comes the sister, my older sister, all the way from England. She couldn't make it in time for the service. But she's here now. And then the phone rings. It's Me-dad calling from Manchester asking how the Mass was. I tell him it was beautiful. And then he asks:

"Moya, are you coming home now?"

Part One

1.

Me, Me-mum and Me-dad, just us. Our house in the corner of the Avenue, cozy and warm. Nothing fancy, just enough. The kitchen with its large range, fueled by coal and, on the other side of the wall, a fireplace. All this called, ingeniously, a back-to-back. Hanging from the ceiling is the clothes rack, four long wooden poles separated at equal distances and attached to a pulley system to raise and lower it, serving its purpose admirably on those rainy, cold, days typical of the North of England when Me-mum can't dry the clothes on the line outside.

Being the end house, we have a large garden on three sides. In front, Me-dad has his flower beds, crammed with blooms of every color. And there's a concrete slab just the right size to park our family vehicle: a motorcycle with sidecar.

Like clockwork, at 5:15 every day I hear the rumble of Me-dad's motorbike coming up the avenue. On to the concrete slab he drags it. Two minutes later he comes in the back door, straight to the sink, rolls up his sleeves, washes his hands, and sits down at the table ready for tea. Just the three of us and our evening's fare. Guaranteed, the potato is the most important ingredient. Regardless of what we're served, Me-dad always has a side dish of shallots, long stemmed, washed and stripped of their outer skin.

After tea, he walks the few feet into the front room, pulls out the Manchester Evening News, and devours anything related to Manchester United. I lay at his feet, waiting impatiently for the newspaper to be cast aside so I can have his undivided attention. Occasionally, he takes a deep breath and, as he exhales, whispers the part of the sentence he's reading: "Higgins never saw the..."

Back to silence. What did Higgins not see?

This happens every few minutes, not enough to tell you what Higgins didn't see but just enough for me to know Me-dad isn't finished.

At last, he's done and we can get down to business. Me-dad pulls out an enormous piece of plywood from under the couch. Laid out on this plywood is the latest 1000-piece jigsaw puzzle of some bucolic English landscape. And off we go, snapping all the pieces into place. Me-mum joins us with steaming mugs of hot tea and something for *afters*—a piece of homemade pie, chocolate biscuits, or a cream cake from Roger's bakery. Me-mum sits and assists us in the serious business of finding the missing shapes. She never seems to get the hang of it, though, and tries to wedge an obviously wrong piece of a cow's ear into its arse.

"I can never figure this out," she sighs and gives up, leaving it to the professionals.

When it's time for bed, Me-mum says:

"Alright Moya, up the dancers."

Me-dad kisses me on the forehead and adds: "Alright, cheeky monkey, goodnight."

"Alright, cheeky monkey Charlie," I'm delighted to reply. "Goodnight!"

And I tramp reluctantly up the stairs. But I'm asleep in minutes.

Cozy, Cozy, Cozy. It couldn't be more perfect. Just the three of us.

Wythenshawe was built in the 1920s and intended as what was then called a *garden city* where the overspill population from the slums of Manchester could be rehoused. Initially, I suppose, it was a delightful place to raise a family, with the lovely clean air of Cheshire to breath rather than the dense coal smoke of one England's most polluted industrial centers. But by the 1950s, when I came into the world, the sad deterioration of Wythenshawe was firmly in place. There were many wonderful, grateful, and deserving people living there. But, as these things go, you also get the crowd who just want to, or just can't help but, bring the squalor and hopelessness with them.

So, when I'm a little kid, Wythenshawe is the largest council estate in Europe, a massive warren of identical homes, twelve miles of back-to-backs, endless streets with uniformly drab-colored doors, all of it isolated from the great metropolis of Manchester. Typically, as this is England, there's a hierarchy; a kind of beneath-the-radar class system. Better areas equal a better class of people. The lowest rung in Wythenshawe, it turns out, is a place called Benchill and our little corner of paradise is smack in the middle of it.

I don't realize we're amongst such bottom feeders, but Me-mum does. I think it's great when we get new neighbors who arrive on horse drawn rag-and-bone carts with their pots and pans and littlest kids tossed up on top of a pile of dirty old bedding. When I visit them, I'm served steaming hot tea in a jam jar which still has remnants of orange marmalade stuck around the rim. In the toilet there's always a stack of newspapers, none of which are for reading. And I'm always a little envious when my playmate Brian Walkers' dad comes home on a Friday night, so happy and full of fun, that he picks me up and throws me up in the air till my head grazes the ceiling and I nearly fall flat on my face to the floor.

No jigsaw puzzles under their settee. Actually, no settee at all.

Why doesn't Me-dad act like this sometimes, I wonder?

And Me-mum never screams like Missus Walker on a Saturday morning, wailing things like: "You lousy rotten bastard! You drank every stinking penny buying drinks for them *pillocks* in the Mountain Ash! So, how're we gonna eat this week!"

I find all this hilariously entertaining.

And there's always more drama of one kind or another.

Our neighbors often drop the newspapers through our letter slot. Unfortunately, the newspapers are on fire. We're not the most popular family in the Avenue, I come to understand, being Catholic and with a massive statue of Saint Patrick in the window to let everybody know we're the worst kind of Catholics: "Fucking Irish Catholics!"

Finally, it doesn't help neighborly relations much when my monster older brother "accidentally" shoots Tommy Walker in the stomach with a slug gun. He claims he was shooting at a target at the end of the *ginnel*, or the narrow passageway between two houses. But I know better. This sadistic bastard probably sat in place for hours waiting for somebody to walk into his line of fire.

I'm always reminded we must tread carefully around this unfortunate beast, the brother, because of his "poor heart."

Poor heart! What about poor Tommy's stomach! The kid will never walk down a *ginnel* again or go through the fabulous Mersey tunnel without experiencing flashbacks of an unprovoked ambush by that nasty *Fucking Irish Catholic*!

Tommy is rushed to the doctors. Me-mum runs to church and prays for him before hurrying over to the toffee shop to buy him a box of *Milk Tray* boxed chocolates—a big box, not the shitty little one—as an apology. But she'd probably be forgiven much more completely if she'd brought twenty Woodbine cigarettes for poor Tommy. He's not much more than seven, but he likes a good smoke.

On weekends we go visiting, sometimes to one of Me-dad's four brothers who live nearby, and other times to Me-mum's two brothers further away. Me-dad first removes the bricks that secure the big black tarpaulin he uses to cover our chariot. Then he walks the vehicle out into the street. He jumps onto the pedal repeatedly until the engine roars to life, revs it a few times, and then relaxes until it settles into a steady hum.

Me-mum climbs into the sidecar, her soft round form filling the space perfectly. When she's all adjusted and settled, Me-dad lifts me up and places me into her lap. Then he secures the clear bubble-shaped dome over the two of us and snaps it shut with a clasp on the outside. We look like two weird creatures in a mobile aquarium, my face pressed ever so slightly to the plastic orb and Me-mum's Aqua-Netted hairdo squished against the dome. Me-dad then leaps onto the seat and away we go.

Me-dad, astride the machine, looks like a super hero to me. He wears a little black beret with leather trim and two little tail-like ribbons hanging down the back, big bulbous goggles, the straps dangling from his temples, a long gabardine raincoat cinched at the waist with a soft wide belt. And there's a white silk scarf trailing from over his shoulder like a flag. As we zoom along, there's not one article of this outfit that's not flapping, fluttering, or billowing. Pure poetry in motion.

What a sight we must be! People look on in awe as we rattle along, incredulous as they pass us in their cars.

Sometimes Me-dad takes me alone for a little trip on a Sunday afternoon while Me-mum prepares the roast. It's amazing how much room there is inside the sidecar without Me-mum. I can swivel my head, look around, cross my legs—very roomy actually.

We always go to the same place: *my farm* in the country. We pull up alongside a field, Me-dad unseals the bubble, lifts me out, and sits me on a fence. We point out to one another the various crops, the sheep, cows, farm buildings, and the machinery because, after all, this belongs to me. I never really understand this perfectly, but if Me-dad says it is my farm then it is *my bloody farm*. It's not till a few years later I begin to wonder: if I actually do own a farm, then how come we're living in cheap government housing back in Wythenshawe? But at the time, I think: yes, indeed, we are living the life, aren't we? Cozy home, games by the fire, and a country estate we never set foot in. Doesn't get much better than that, then, does it?

Otherwise, I play in the avenue with all the local kids. Sometimes we play hardscrabble football or maybe a game of alleys at the worn-out patch of grass at the end of the street. Often, I go to a local pond with my fishing net to catch newts. But the best of all is a good game of *Split the Kipper.*

One of us kids runs home and asks mum for a sharp knife, the sharper the better. Standing about four feet apart, facing each other, and with legs pressed together, we take turns throwing the knife to the left or to the right of our opponent's feet. Usually, my opponent is a boy, as no girl plays such a boring game. The knife has to stick in the ground. If it doesn't that's considered a "no throw." Wherever your opponent's thrown knife sticks, you have to move your foot to that spot. This continues until you can spread your legs no further. Then, to get back to the original closed-legged stance, you have to throw the knife while trying to stay upright and hope the blade lands between your opponent's legs. The game continues until one player falls over or can't take the discomfort any longer and the other is declared the victor.

The game usually ends with somebody's mum screaming out the backdoor wanting, "me sharp knife back, ya bloody pests!"

We get visits from our parish priest, Father Malloy.

This, I'm made to understand, is a great honor for a proud Irish Catholic family. He sits for hours and chats with Me-dad about the motherland, the old country, Ireland, the greatest place God ever created. He consumes endless cups of tea and eats all the best *afters.* Before long, Me-mum says, "Right Moya, up the dancers." And off I go. No "goodnight cheeky monkey" from Me-dad. Just a "Goodnight. God bless. See you in the morning." Me-mum doesn't even stick around until I'm asleep. She leaves me staring at the worrisome plate on the wall opposite my bed, the plate with a picture of a blond little boy kneeling at his own bedside, hands clasped, staring at the words of the prayer floating up there in the air above him:

Now I lay me down to sleep,
I pray the Lord my soul to keep,
And if I die before I wake,
I pray the Lord my soul to take.

Terrifying. What child wants to hear this at bedtime? Enough to keep a child awake for fear of dying in her sleep. She might literally die from sleep deprivation.

The other religious visitor we receive regularly is Sister Bernadette. I can spot the architectural masterpiece strapped to her head from 200 yards away; white, bird-like wings, starched and clean, floating over all the privet hedges of the neighborhood as she navigates her way angelically to our house.

Our front door is very narrow and opens into a tiny hallway, the low entrance to the front room immediately to the right. But Sister Bernadette has acquired some expertise in negotiating cramped quarters with such mammoth head gear. Me-mum gets out of the way and closes the door behind the nun as Bernadette angles her head just so, ducks and weaves gracefully and with such easy precision, before coming to rest demurely on the settee in front of the window.

I like Sister Bernadette. She usually visits during the day, only has one cup of tea, and never touches any of my *afters*. She is gentle, soft spoken, and elegant. For ten minutes our humble home is as quiet and civilized as a convent.

Then the backdoor slams and we hear: "Where's me tea!"

He's home. The brother. The angry, inconsiderate, psychopath. I have no idea where he spends his time. He only comes home occasionally when he needs something or has to hide. He showed up once on the crossbar of his friend's bicycle. He was all wobbly and making funny faces, his eyes rolling back in his head. I thought that was great fun until Me-dad found out he was caught breaking into somebody's shop and, as he escaped, broke both his ankles. Another time he was leaving the house doing a funny walk that amused me no-end until the police showed up and explained he'd been caught with a loaded rifle stuffed down his trouser leg.

Not only was he a monster, he was an unclean monster. Trying to get him to bathe was an ongoing battle with Me-mum. He always had a tide mark of scum on his neck where the swill of water on his face met the rest of his body. Me-mum would draw him a bath of precious immersion heated hot water and he would sit in the bathroom for a while until the water went cold, never so much as dipping a toe into it, then let the virgin water swirl down the drain. Downstairs he would come with the same ugly tide mark on his neck. One time he was going on a school trip to the zoo, thankfully that meant he would not be home for tea. When he did arrive home after probably torturing every teacher and chaperone who had the misfortune to have him in their group, he declared he was going to take a bath. He could be heard for a couple of hours splashing away. Me-mum was chuffed, delighted at the prospect of a clean son, what a transformation. When Me-dad came home Me-mum told him of the great development in the hygiene department, so he went to check it out for himself only to find the true nature of this cleanliness regime—he had stolen a baby penguin from the zoo and it was merrily splashing and shitting in our bathtub. Time to unwrap the motor bike.

Still, everybody has to be careful with the brother as he has a bad heart, resulting from childhood rheumatic fever. And it's his meal ticket.

"Careful of his heart."

"Well, he has a bad heart, after all."

And so on.

I don't understand this at all. I think you have to have a heart in order to have a *bad* heart. And I'm not sure the brother has a heart at all. He's heartless.

I'm left alone with him twice when Me-mum and Me-dad visit an ailing relative or some other emergency comes up. The first time, he suggests he teach me karate. I'm delighted he wants to do something with me. He proceeds to throw me against the wall repeatedly and I just keep leaping up for more until it hurts too much and I realize he's not playing. The second time, he insists we play doctors and nurses. How bad can that be? Not too bad until he slices open my finger with one of Me-dad's razor blades and practices bandaging it with a dirty napkin and sellotape.

That's left a physical and an emotional scar to this day.

One evening, we see the familiar white magnificence of Sister Bernadette's headgear sailing valiantly above the hedges. Strange: it's not daytime and Me-dad is home. Of course, she's welcomed respectfully and enters the front room, sheepishly accompanied by a nervous seventeen-year-old doe-eyed blonde: my sister.

"Madeleine Cecelia is with child," the nun announces softly.

Just like that. Like she's announcing a biblical event or something. Madeleine Cecelia: the paragon of virtue, straight A student, pretty, scared of her own shadow, not allowed to wear make-up or stockings—*that* Madeleine Cecelia?

I don't fully understand what's going on before my eyes here, a situation that will cause a lot of pain and suffering for years to come. But I know it can't be good when Me-mum breaks down in tears and Me-dad looks like I've never seen him before: wounded.

It turns out Madeleine Cecelia, who is more than a decade older than me and whom I think of more as an auntie, has been allowed to go to a dance. There, she met a young *something*; calling him a young man would be giving him too much credit. A few months pass, she's missing her period, goes to the doctor and—well, the inevitable.

Now, she's six months pregnant.

A little later, the "man" of the hour shows up and even my child-sized mind knows this is a huge problem. This cocky, greasy, leather-jacketed high school dropout just stands there twitching and smirking like an idiot.

Worst of all—he's a Protestant!

God help us! (But not *him*, obviously.) Me-mum and Me-dad think through the situation and come up with three options:

1. Go to Ireland, have the baby, and place it for adoption.

2. Go to Ireland, have the baby, and we will raise the child as our own.

3. You can get married.

Madeleine Cecelia looks down, picks at her finger nails, and decides:

"We will get married."

I'm in kindergarten at the time and the playground wraps around our parish church. When there's nothing better to do, I hang on the fence and watch weddings and funerals come and go. One day, I've got my head through the iron railings, lazily studying what I take to be a funeral; sad people arriving and entering the church reluctantly. Then I start to recognize the mourners.

"Hey, that's Me-uncle Bob and Me-auntie Dorris!"

Soon, there are more relatives, each one sadder than the last. Finally, a car pulls up and out comes Me-dad and Me-sister, heads down, making for the alter like a couple of criminals.

It's Me-big-sister's wedding day!

It's my playtime.

2.

Me-Mum is getting more and more anxious to move to a better part of Wythenshawe. She goes repeatedly to the council offices requesting a transfer and, so, we're constantly going to look at other houses, most of which are even worse than our own. She's prepared to wait until she finds something that's just right and this means years of disappointment. So, life goes on. Me-dad goes to work as usual. Me-mum stays home and shops daily for our groceries since we don't have a fridge—or a car, or a television, or a phone. But none of this means much to a five-year-old who might be, for instance, busy nursing her bruised ego after a lost bout of *Split the Kipper*.

Being raised, essentially, as an only child, I'm the center of Me-mum's universe and, for instance, I'm terribly spoiled in the food department. There's only a handful of things I'll eat: beans on toast, fish fingers and beans, beans and sausage and, on Sunday, whatever is served as long as there are beans and raw carrots on a side plate.

Very picky.

Strangely, at some point I deign to incorporate liver and black pudding into this highly circumscribed diet, even though visits to the tripe shop leave me pale and mildly traumatized. The doctor tells Me-mum not to worry, though, I'll eat when I'm hungry and all will be well.

I come home from school one day to find Madelaine Cecelia sitting in the front room with a big fat baby in her lap.

"You're an auntie now yourself, Moya," I'm told.

"Madeleine Cecelia is now a mum too," Me-mum explains, "and she'll be staying with us for a while. She'll be sharing the bed with you, just like old times."

Just like old times, except that in old times there wasn't a cage in the room with a screaming baby boy in it. But I'm beyond excited to have Me-sister home. One day I run upstairs to where she's napping and, as she's sound asleep, I can study closely what I take to be blue eye shadow smeared down her cheek and along the length of her lip where it's met by a red and purple scab.

In fact, this is a massive bruise.

It's the first of many times I find Me-sister in my bed this banged up. She stays a couple of days and then returns to the "Queer Fella," as Me-dad calls her husband. Time and time again, there's hurried missions to bring Me-sister home. Countless times I wake to find her in my bed and, as daylight fills the room, see the evidence of brutal abuse on her face and arms. One time, she has the image of an iron down the length of her cheek. Another knock on the door, another frantic call to a neighbor's house, Me-mum running off to answer it, the rush to uncover the motorbike—

Then, Me-dad is off to the rescue.

I don't get it. Me-dad is a massively strong man. His hands are enormous and his biceps bulge through all his clothes. He could beat the crap out of this puny, bucktoothed, lazy, excuse of a man and put an end to Me-sister's problems. In fact, as our doctor assures Me-mum, I am myself a wildly energetic and athletic tomboy, and I'm about ready to go over and destroy this bastard myself. But for Me-dad (and for Me-mum, I guess, and Me-sister, and for that whole community) this never seems to be an option. And, so, the beatings and the rescues became another ritual in our cozy little home in Wythenshawe, as regular as Sunday Mass.

~

Meanwhile, I'm given special VIP treatment as I enter Saint John's primary school (officially, Saint John Fisher and Saint Thomas Moore) because Me-sister, that pretty, well-behaved and diligent student, has paved the way with a good example. Everyone agrees to forget the antichrist brother who also came along that way, but wielding a jackhammer and a wrecking bar.

I love the place. There are no tests or exams and we have the greatest headmaster in the world, Mr. Hanlon. He walks around joking and smiling, often with a child on his shoulders. And Me-sister has a special place in Mister Hanlon's heart. He even has a special name for her: "Pussy."

That's right, Me-sister is known as Pussy.

This is because she has a grin like the Cheshire Cat in C.S Lewis' *Alice In Wonderland*. Every time Mister Hanlon sees me, he asks:

"How's your Pussy?"

Or: "There's Pussy's little sister!"

Sometimes: "Give my love to your Pussy."

Apparently, Mister Hanlon just loved Pussy.

And then it happens: we get a car.

At least, I think it's a car. Maybe it's a truck. It's as big as a house and has three rows of seats, one of which folds out into a bed. It's called a Standard Vanguard and is a muddy blue color. Again, not the most common family vehicle of the time, but it gets us places.

We now go on day trips to exotic locales like the Mersey Tunnel, an engineering miracle connecting Liverpool to Birkenhead. Me-dad loves this trip. It takes one and a half hours to reach the tunnel, about fifteen minutes to drive through it, then another fifteen minutes to turn around and head back home.

That's what we call a day trip.

Other destinations are to, say, Mow Cop, which is not a castle but the remains of an elaborate summer house built to *look* like a castle. Because why would we visit a real castle, which are commonplace in Great Britain, when we can go and see a *fake* castle!

Occasionally, we venture to North Wales and sit on a rocky

beach for an hour. Then we head home for tea. We never eat in restaurants. That's extravagant. In fact, I won't eat in a restaurant until I'm nineteen.

The big annual journey is our trip to Blackpool to see the famous Illuminations, a colossal display of electric light and British ingenuity held each year in this seaside resort on the Irish Sea. These trips include Me-mum's side of the family and it's a pretty big and crowded turnout. Me-dad, Me-mum, Me-aunties Celia, Rosie, Biddy, Kitty, Edith, and Molly, Me-uncles Teddy, Vin, and Jimmy and Me-cousins Gail, Anne, Tony, Kathleen, Michael, and Bernadette—all jammed in nice and snug in our Standard Vanguard.

"There's not much room in this car, Charlie," Celia observes with attitude. "I thought you said it was big."

"Celia, this car is presently carrying seventeen people!"

What a sight to behold are the Blackpool Illuminations! One million light bulbs covering six miles of seafront. A light bulb attached to every imaginable object, both living and inanimate. Trams gliding by and blinking all the colors of the rainbow. Animated tableau featuring, for instance, an Egyptian sarcophagus that opens to reveal a rotting mummy. (This scares the bejesus out of me and I hunker down between some grownups till we pass by.) There are nursery rhymes, pirate ships, Ali Baba, huge billboards of famous people all outlined in lights.

"Is that the Eiffel Tower?" someone asks.

"Not the real one, no. That's over in France somewhere."

It's the most awe-inspiring thing I've ever witnessed. We never get out of the car. We just cruise up and down the promenade, hanging out the windows of the Standard Vanguard, slack jawed, and lulled into silence by the spectacle. Poor dad patiently chauffeurs and never refuses a request for yet another lap around this mind-blowing marvel.

Satiated, every blinking light seared into our corneas, we head back to the dreary monochrome land we call home.

~

But then there's another visit from Sister Bernadette which leads to yet another addition to our family.

There's a couple going through a difficult time and separating. They have a young son they're unable to care for and Sister hopes that we can take him in. Without hesitation, Me-mum and Me-dad say, "of course!" So, just like that, I have another brother, Brian, who is two years younger than me. I'm thrilled and Brian fits into our family perfectly. After several months it looks like Brian will be with us forever.

At Saint John's, when you have a younger sibling joining the school you introduce them in general assembly. I'm beyond excited to get up on the stage and proudly announce: "Today my little brother, Brian, is starting kindergarten."

I summon him to join me on stage.

There's a few titters and surprised faces when he walks over to me because Brian is Black. Actually, he's more of a purplish aubergine color it occurs to me. But, beyond that, I never think about what the color of his skin means. Anyway, we see Me-mum at the back of the hall, smiling, so Brian and I give her a little wave before we walk off to join our classes.

Though Wythenshawe in the nineteen-sixties has only a small population of Black people, Me-uncle Jack and Me-auntie Ellen adopted Black twins as soon as the kids were born. So, in our household it's nothing new to be amongst Black people. I'm very close to Brian and Me-dad is happy to have a little boy to kick a ball around with and not have to worry about him deliberately aiming for a neighbor's window—another favorite ambition of the monster brother.

After a couple of years, Me-mum and Me-dad decide it's time to officially adopt Brian. But Sister Bernadette shows up with a man and a woman who, it turns out, are Brian's parents. They've reconciled and want their precious son back. We're all devastated but there's nothing more to be said. My big tough Irish father carries Brian's things out to their car, tears rolling down his cheeks. Me-mum asks them to promise that, if they ever need someone to care for Brian again, they'll turn to us. They agree, pile into the car, and drive off.

We never hear from Brian again. Sister Bernadette has no news of him either. Several years later I see him in a schoolyard running around with a group of kids. Delighted, I run over and call his name. But he doesn't know who I am, just stares a moment, maybe remembers something, but then let's it go. In any event, he's too preoccupied with his friends to worry about it.

He runs off.

Shockingly, years later, when I begin dating a Black boy, Memum is very unhappy. I'm so mad I call her a hypocrite. She explains it was difficult when she was out and about with Brian. With blue eyed blonde me on one arm and Brian on her other, she was spat at, called awful names, and ridiculed. She says she doesn't want me to have to go through that. Being Irish Catholic in Wythenshawe is bad enough.

Saturday is the day the local kids of Wythenshawe congregate at the Forum Cinema in Northenden. After a short bus ride, crowds of unruly little monsters disembark and head into the massive brick building where we all become ABC Minors, each with a badge sporting a triangular logo that glows in the dark. When the lights go down there's a frenzy of little triangles moving in every direction.

The show opens with an organ bellowing throughout the cavernous space and, slowly, from out of the depths, appears the maestro masterfully commanding the keys. Invariably, he has all sorts of candy thrown at his head. But the dignified gent remains calm and unperturbed.

Before the main event (some kid-friendly film) the MC saunters onstage and shouts, "Hello boys and girls!" and then ignores a variety of vicious provocations:

"Fuck off! Put the film on!"

"Get off the stage, ya big Nelly!"

"Hey, show us your tits!"

The poor man continues with his routine, asking: "Do we have any birthdays here today?"

A few genuine candidates shyly walk up onstage—plus George Clancy. Week after week, George claims his birthday sweets and smiles gratefully as the whole audience sings *Happy Birthday*. It's not that nobody notices it's George's birthday every single week, we're just too scared to mention it.

There's an ABC Minors song we're encouraged to scream in unison:

We are the boys and girls all known
As Minors of the ABC
And every Saturday all line up
To see the films we like and shout aloud with glee
We like to laugh and have our sing-song
Such a happy crowd are we!

There's also slogans such as: "Good Films! Good Fellowship! Good Fun!" Lofty sentiments wasted on the three hundred or so uncouth bastards from the toughest housing project in the North of England set loose without adult supervision in a huge dark room.

God knows what happens when the lights are dimmed.

It's during one of these riotous Saturday afternoons that I hear a sound which will dominate my life for years and years: the sound of a ringing telephone. Not just any ringing telephone, though: an *American* ringing telephone. It's a sound unlike anything I've ever heard; the sound of promise, of a magical land, of happy children eating ice cream, of sunshine, of handsome fathers in suits with trousers that are cuffed a little above the shoe exposing a sliver of sock, of mothers with wavy hair and pretty dresses cinched to reveal tiny waistlines, of big shiny cars, of huge houses with lovely gardens and white fences, of people around enormous Christmas trees wearing chunky sweaters and opening millions of presents wrapped in shiny paper; homes where the occupants burst into song at a moment's notice.

This is where I will live one day—in full Technicolor.

3.

The sister has now moved into a flat of her own, another slum overspill estate called Hattersley, located at the edge of the Pennines and the Lancashire moors. She has two young boys now and is still beaten regularly by the Queer Fella. Now that Me-dad has suitable transportation we regularly make the one-hour drive to visit her at the new flat. As we still don't have a phone—nor does she—it's the only way Me-mum and Me-dad can make sure she's okay.

Sometimes they let me stay with her for a couple of days and I'm happy to do so. I love my little nephews and Me-sister gives me such freedom to play outside and visit other people's homes for tea and biscuits. She doesn't know where I am half the time. But I'm delighted with the change of scene and with not having to be the focus of Me-mum's constant concern. And, in any event, I'm probably sent to stay with Me-sister because our parents think it might stop the Queer Fella from being so violent. But it doesn't matter who's staying in the flat with them. This bastard doesn't care at all who sees the daily beatings he gives out. And it isn't reserved for Me-sister either, the boys are subjected to terrible abuse too. One night the two little lads are just out of the bath, standing, giggling, naked in front of the fire. This angers the Queer Fella for some reason. He picks up a hair brush and hits them on their backsides with such force it actually cuts them.

And I don't know what to do. Tell Me-mum and Me-dad? They'd never let me come back. And they'd lose even more sleep over Me-sister's and the boys' safety. What's even more confusing is Me-sister trusts me to keep my mouth shut. Or doesn't she worry about what's going on—about how bad this is? And how bad is it, anyway? How different than countless other homes?

I don't know. I'm just a little kid.

These are grownups, right?

Me-sister, in fact, is a very outgoing and friendly person, she talks to everybody and makes friends wherever she goes. I love to accompany her to town on market days. We walk to the bus stop, passing her neighbor, Myra's, house.

"Hello, Myra!" she calls to a stern, mannish looking women busy cleaning her grey minivan.

Myra glances up, pauses, then allows a stiff little nod.

We walk along and Me-sister continues to me, "Myra is so proud of that minivan! Always cleaning it, inside and out."

Now Me-mum gets a job. Not a day job but an evening job cleaning offices at the place Me-dad works. This means that after tea Me-dad ferries her to work and returns to pick her up when her shift is done. I'm allowed to play in the avenue all this time.

One night I wander from the avenue with a group of kids from another street and we find a massive puddle and, since I'm wearing my wellies, I'm more than well equipped to enjoy this adventure. I'm happily splashing away when I see Me-dad's Standard Vanguard cruising by. He stops abruptly, throws open the door, and yells: "Get in!"

I happily jump in and his uncharacteristically grumpy demeanor doesn't even register with me. When we enter the kitchen and I perch on a stool to take off my wellies, I feel a slap on my legs that knocks me to the floor. As I lay there in complete shock—wham!—another crack to my legs that spins me around on the linoleum.

Three more blows rein down on me and, as the welts appear on my legs and frightened tears flow down my face, Me-dad just stares at me angrily and says, "No supper tonight. Get to bed."

Shaking and confused, I run up the stairs as fast as I can. I'm still trembling and sitting with my knees up to my chest when I hear Me-mum and Me-dad down below.

Then silence.

A few minutes pass and Me-mum appears wearing her pinny. She puts a finger to her lips and quiets me:

"Shhhh. Don't tell your dad." She pulls out a jam butty (or a sandwich, for my American friends) from the pinny's pocket. I'm not that hungry as I'm still trying to digest what just happened. If Me-mum is going to keep working, I wonder, am I going to be left with this lunatic every night?

"Your dad was frightened when he couldn't find you," she explains. "A lot of children have been vanishing around Manchester, even a little girl like you is missing."

"But why did he have to wallop me, then, mum?" I demand indignantly. "Why doesn't he go beat up the Queer Fella instead!"

This is all a bit much for Me-mum. She looks away, sighs tiredly, and massages her temples. When she's finally calmed me down and tucked me in for the night, she steps quietly from the room, leaving me staring at that scary plate with the scarier prayer about dying in my sleep and thinking now, too, about some monster prowling the streets of Manchester looking for little children to abduct.

Not a goodnight all around. That's the only time I ever saw Me-dad angry and the only time he ever raised a hand to me.

I stay close to home after that.

One night, not long after, there's a knock on the door. Missus Amos from number six is standing there:

"Your daughter's telephoned. She's on the line. Come. She sounds very upset."

I guess I'll be having company in my bed again tonight.

When she returns from Missus Amos' house, Me-mum is as white as a ghost. She speaks quietly to Me-dad and I'm told it's time for bed. The next day, as soon she hears the mail slot clattering shut, Me-mum rushes to retrieve the *Manchester Evening News*. She sits staring at the picture on the front page of a pretty little girl alongside two headshots of a man and a woman. The woman looks scary but also a little familiar. Her peroxide-blonde hair styled in the fashion of the day is quite commonplace. Even Me-sister has the same doo.

But it isn't that. I let it go.

"What's for tea, Mum," I inquire, breaking her concentration for a moment. She doesn't reply. She's miles away. When Me-dad comes home he, too, goes straight for the paper and scans the main story. He turns to Me-mum in disbelief, shaking his head.

"I can't believe it," he sighs.

"Me too," I chime in, wanting to be part of this grownup conversation. "We had stew for tea last night, dad—ugh!"

I'm oblivious to what is unfolding, to what has the whole country captivated. Much later, I come to understand:

Me-sister had been woken at her flat by sirens and when she looked out the window the area was swarming with police cars. It turned out Me-sister's proud, minivan loving neighbor, Myra, was Myra Hindley, the most evil, hated, child serial killer ever to walk the face of the earth. Her and her equally demonic boyfriend, Ian Brady, were The Moors Murderers. For two years, they'd been luring children into their sick world, torturing and brutally abusing them, before killing them and burying their remains on Saddleworth Moor. They even made audio recordings and took photographs of these vile deeds. The monstrous, perverse brutality of their crimes is still a raw wound in the memory of the people of Britain.

4.

Of course, Saint Patrick's Day is a big event in our house. Two weeks before the great day, an envelope arrives from the *motherland*; actually, from Me-auntie Mary who lives in the *motherland*.

It never fails. The envelope is greeted with great excitement, even though its contents—always the same handful of Shamrock ripped from Me-auntie's farm, roots, dirt, and all—are already dead from the two-week journey. Me-mum tries to resuscitate the rotting, not-so-emerald green shamrock by placing it on a wet piece of pink blotting paper. And there it sits on the windowsill, festering until March 17th.

It's a great day to be Irish but not when you have a nasty, brown, muddy, smelly, mushy, rotting, clump of shamrock pinned to your school jumper. When I sit at my desk with my head down all I can smell is the rotting vegetation and the nasty wetness of it touching my face. All the other kids from Irish families wear a lovely medal of St. Patrick, a shiny green ribbon, or even a tricolored rosette.

Not me.

When I'm ridiculed, I somehow manage to make a convincing argument for this blob of decay proudly pinned to my chest as being more authentic and, therefore, more of a real homage to the great man himself, belittling mere decorative gestures such as ribbons, rosettes and medals.

Sometimes it works.

There are different kinds of Irish Catholics in Wythenshawe, I start to notice. There are those who say "God be willing," after everything else they say. "I'll be going to the Butcher's to get a nice pork chop, God be willing," or, "Our Tommy is getting a new pair of shoes, God be willing." Then there's the type that genuflect and make the sign of the cross when passing by a Catholic church and cross the street when encountering a protestant one. Yes, there are the ones who spend all their time drinking in the pubs and show up to midnight Mass blathered out of their minds and singing at the top of their lungs. And there are the Professional Irish Catholics, in whose home everything from the welcome mat to the tea cups and dish towel are emblazoned with a shamrock.

Despite the huge statue of Saint Patrick in our front window, we are the *go about your business in as quiet a way as possible discreetly bow your head when passing a catholic church and do not bring attention to yourself in this anti Irish climate* type of Irish Catholics.

Finally, we're moving.

Me-mum's persistence and selectiveness lands us a new house in a prime location. As word gets out that we're *flitting*, Me-dad gets a farewell gift from the neighbors. They fill his petrol tank with dirt, stones, broken glass, twigs, leaves, and sand. As usual, Me-dad says nothing. He just walks the few miles to work and spends his evenings trying to clean the gas tank and repair the damage. The Standard Vanguard is never the same again.

Our new home is a corner house with a driveway, a garage directly across from a park, and is smack in the middle of the best neighborhood in Wythenshawe. We even have an actual dining room.

The new house means a new school. This new school is Saint Peter's and is a bit of a shock to my system. I enter the world of tests, exams, and something called *homework*. This, I discover, is schoolwork you do at home. Who, I wonder, thought up this stupid idea!

Me-mum is informed on the first day that since my previous school, Saint John's, kept no academic records, there's no way to tell how bright or stupid I might be.

"Hey, don't they know I'm Pussy's sister?" I'm tempted to ask.

I'm put into the academically challenged class with Miss Rogers presiding. For the first time in my life, I excel academically in comparison to my peers. Relatively speaking, I'm positively genius material. I'm also a gifted athlete and teacher's pet. So, life is good. Though I'm horrified by the behavior of some of my classmates, especially the Clancy twins, Jimmy and George.

George is misbehaving one day. He's called to the front of the class to face his punishment. "Hmmm," I think, intrigued, "this should be interesting."

The only corporal punishment I saw at Saint John's was dished out by Missus Hogan, a sadistic old bitch who seemed to stay up late figuring out ways to inflict as much pain as possible on small children. Her chosen penal skill was to slap a child on the delicate soft skin at the elbow's crease. I was a recipient of her wrath once and can confirm: her research paid off. It hurt like hell and stung for quite a while.

I'm curious to see what Miss Rogers' preference will be. George stands there with his hand stretched out, palm down, the metal edged ruler held upright in Miss Rogers' hand. She smacks his fingers repeatedly—whack, whack, whack. George takes his punishment like a man—or, rather, like a young boy—and I watch him walk back to his desk with each hand under an armpit, his eyes welling with tears. Then, just as he turns to sit down, he spins back and yells: "You fucking cunt!"

There's an instantaneous and uniform gasp of the academically challenged throughout the room. My jaw drops, even though I don't exactly realize the severity of this insult. "Fucking," I dimly understand is no way to address an adult. But "cunt" sails over my head entirely.

Miss Rogers tells me to sit in her seat and watch the class as she marches the foulmouthed Clancy to the headmaster's office.

This headmaster is no Mister Hanlon. He doesn't walk around with kids on his shoulders and give big sisters nicknames that will traumatize little sisters for years to come. No, this Headmaster is eight feet tall and a skilled administer of the *strap*; the strap being a brown hard leather instrument forked at one end, exquisitely designed as an instrument of pain, especially to small defenseless children.

I wonder, now, and have for years, if there's a special course at MI5 where Catholic school teachers are taught how to maximize the pain and misery of children in the name of God. At Saint Peter's the strap is meted out with such frequency that there's often a line of boys and girls outside the headmaster's office waiting to be punished. Sometimes the headmaster makes *house calls* to the classroom where he can show off his masterful technique. Don't think you can fool him by moving your hand down just before impact. That will get you extra lashes. Don't ever try putting your one hand under the awaiting hand to absorb some of the impact. That will get you, at least, two more. And never move your hand out of the way of the strap as it's careening toward you through the giant wing span of an eight-foot-tall headmaster, causing him, in fact, to slap his own leg. George Clancy, trust us! The only thing to do is to accept your punishment and not scream obscenities at the bearer of this weapon!

But, poor George—he never had a chance.

That night at tea, I can't wait to tell Me-mum and Me-dad about the day's excitement. However, I don't get the reaction I'm expecting.

"George Clancy called Miss Rogers a fucking cunt!" Then, for effect, I add, "to her face."

I did detect a little bit of suppressed laughter just like the time I came home singing:

Hitler has only got one ball
The other is with his mother
In the Free Trade Hall...

No *afters* that night either.

After a while at the top of the academically challenged, I prove myself so incredibly clever I'm promoted to a class with the bright kids. Things start off well enough with an art project that's instantly pinned to the classroom wall for all to enjoy. Creative genius. Check, that's me. I'm feeling pretty good about myself. But now the real fun starts: tests and preparations for something called the eleven-plus.

Apparently, this is a very big deal. This is a test that determines your fate. If you pass, you'll continue your education for another seven years at one of the top schools in Manchester. If not, oh well, it's, "Do you want salt and vinegar on your fish 'n' chips, sir?"

A reasonable amount of pressure to heap on to a kid, I think. But I'm like that—cocky. Nevertheless, when the results come in for the mock tests (or practice tests), out of a class of thirty-two I come in thirty-second!

The two top scholars in my new class were David O'Reilly who spent most of his time kneeling under his desk smelling his new leather shoes (nothing strange about that, maybe he might like to be introduced to a nice piece of leather the headmaster has) and John Kelly who seemed to derive great pleasure zipping and unzipping his trousers when he was concentrating. These two boys scored off the charts, so the future of England is in great hands.

Thank God for the bell signaling playtime.

As usual, I'm the only girl playing football with the boys. And, as usual, I'm running rings around them. After a particularly aggressive but fair tackle, the recipient of my skilled footwork, wiping tears and snot from his face, calls me a "stupid bottom of the class idiot."

Them's fighting words. I know this even at ten. And one other thing I've learned in life thus far: if you're going to fight, never fight a girl. Girls are biting, scratching, hairpulling demons. But boys I'd fight any day of the week. This seems like a perfect opportunity. Off we go and within seconds we're in full-fledged combat, rolling around on the concrete playground. Word spreads fast and we're now the center of a massive throng of kids, fists flying. Then the shrill sound of a whistle. The crowd parts and, like Moses, the headmaster appears. He grabs the two of us by our collars, looks at me, then at snot-face, then at me again, and finally back to snot-face:

"Who won?"

"Well, sir," Snot-face mutters, "she got me down twice, but then I, then I..." And, finally, he gives up. "She won, sir."

The headmaster scowls and nods judiciously: "I hope you have learned a lesson. Never fight a girl."

Wise man, I think. I may not be the brightest star, academically, but I'm creative, can kick a ball with the best of them, and kick arse harder than anybody on this playground.

This is me at ten. The class dunce, deemed stupid by my peers. And who's to say? I just can never understand most of what I'm being taught. Sometimes in class I feel like a trapped animal and want to explode, or just walk out of the classroom. The only things I excel in are sports, art, and Irish dancing.

The testing and exams ramp up dramatically as the eleven-plus nears and my anxiety and frustration grows accordingly. We're given test after test. And to make sure there are no surprises when we take the real test, we're ferried by bus to the grammar school where the eleven-plus will be administered. On the way, we pass by Saint John's. Kids running in the playground. Mr. Hanlon playing jump rope with a group of young girls. No worries there at Saint John's. Nobody in that playground worrying where they'll be studying for the next seven years. Actually, they don't even know what studying is, lucky bastards.

We're locked in a gymnasium where we participate in the trial test. The categories: Nonverbal Reasoning, Maths, English and General Intelligence. As well as these categories, we're given a selection of titles to write an essay on, such as: The bravest deed I know (easy—George Clancy calling Miss Rogers a fucking cunt);

Eggs (I like mine fried with bacon, especially after Sunday Mass); Everest (I can see the Pennines from my house); The Gothic (The Gothic what?); Queen Salote (never heard of her, but Me-mum hates the Queen, especially Victoria, as she did nothing to help our ancestors during the potato famine); What must life be like as a cat (same as any other animal in Wythenshawe: fend for yourself); Give an account of an imaginary conversation between an eagle and an owl (hmmm, probably a lot of hoo-hoo from the owl until the eagle's had enough, rips the owl's head off, and feeds it to her baby eagles).

Done.

Still, I know this is not going to end well. No questions about how to dribble a football and then kick it with the side of your foot to make it swerve into the top corner of the goal while the goalie's going the wrong way. There's nothing about how to draw a figure looking straight at you and how to make the shoes look perfect—what this ten-year-old creative genius knows as *perspective*. How about an essay on the different styles of Irish dancing? The music, the tempo, the many categories, jigs, hornpipes, reels or, my favorite, set dances with names like *Finnegan's Wake* about how Finnegan dies in a drunken stupor and is laid out in his coffin with all his family and friends sitting around boozing. But then he wakes up, snatches a bottle of beer and dances a very wobbly jig! Now, that's a great story and ought to be discussed in one's eleven-plus exam! Right?

No such luck. My future is looking bleak. I console myself thinking I'll at least be reunited with my friends from Saint John's when we attend the distinctly disappointing local secondary modern school for losers.

And now I'm suffering bouts of chronic vomiting. Following a holy day, the priest shows up in the classroom and asks, not so innocently, "what did you all do yesterday?" Obviously, this is a ploy, as he's trying to figure out who went to Mass and who the pagans are. I raise my hand triumphantly:

"Father, I threw up seven times on the way to Mass yesterday."

He responds, thrown, but concerned: "I am glad you kept count. Did you make it to Mass?"

So, I'm taken to see Doctor Weyll, a chain-smoking, coughing-his-lungs-up doctor who spends most of my visit responding to Me-mum's polite inquiries about his own obviously bad health. His diagnosis: growing pains.

"Thank you, doctor, I hope you feel better."

She hopes *he* feels better. I'm the one who's vomiting at every lamppost on my way to school each day.

Before long, I'm dragged back to Dr. Weyll's surgery and—why should this surprise us?—he's out sick. So, we see a Doctor Leather who, within minutes, has me in an ambulance and rushed to the hospital for an emergency appendectomy.

I survive. And I'm back in school just in time for the preparations for the real eleven-plus.

I begin vomiting regularly again.

Now we know it can't be the appendix as that had been removed. This time I'm diagnosed with something called, *abdominal migraine*, an unusual illness that most people are unaware of. It's clearly brought on by stress and the enormous pressure that is being heaped on me by Me-myself.

Me-mum and Me-dad never push me regarding school. The only thing they ask of me is that I behave—probably as a result of being dragged heavy-footed to the headmaster's office so many times to hear about the demon son they brought into the world. Perhaps it's only me who thinks this way, feeling I need to compensate; to not only behave but to earn reasonably good grades. I don't know. I'm only ten. But the vomiting is real.

The dreaded day arrives and, as usual, I'm sent off with a flask of hot tea, toast, and a hardboiled egg wrapped neatly in grease-proof paper and tucked into my little plaid school bag. This is not for lunch but to eat after daily Mass before school as we are not allowed to eat before receiving communion. I've already been to confession, so my soul is nice and shiny. I'm as prepared as I'll ever be.

The actual test is a blur. I don't remember much about it. But I do remember waiting weeks for the results and wondering which of the local schools I'd be attending. I make Me-mum promise that when the envelope containing my score arrives, she'd not open it. The first post comes when I'm still in bed. Me-mum knocks on my bedroom door and asks, "Is this what you're waiting for?"

She hands me an official looking envelope. I gingerly take it and tear open the seal.

"What!" I scream. "Are you kidding me? I passed!"

I passed. Barely. But I passed. I don't qualify for any top schools but I'm guaranteed seven more years at a pretty good school, which is fine by me. Out of my class of thirty-two, we all passed. From the academically challenged class, only one child passed: George Clancy. From Saint John's not one child passed.

Me passing in our house is a big deal as I'm the only one in our family ever to succeed at the eleven-plus. Then, again, I'm the only one to have been taken out of Saint John's and put into a competitive academic environment.

The next big concern is getting my school uniform and figuring out how to pay for it. I hear so many stories all the time of "your brilliant Auntie Molly who was accepted to Lorretto, but couldn't go as there was no money for the uniform." Or then there is "poor Uncle Vinnie who wanted to be a doctor and got into Saint Bede's, but there was no money for the uniform so he became a bus conductor instead."

We never have much money but we never go without. True, we don't have a television yet, or a phone, or a fridge. But that's not terribly unusual around Wythenshawe. Me-mum is no longer working as a cleaner but somehow Me-dad manages to keep us fed, clothed, and warm. Still, the list arrives for my school uniform and it's daunting.

WINTER UNIFORM:
School hat plus rain hat to wear over school hat during inclement

weather.
Rain coat plus plastic rain coat to wear over rain coat in case of rain
At least 2 cotton shirts
At least 2 woolen pullovers
1 blue school tie
1 pleated blue and yellow plaid tunic
At least 3 pairs of beige knee high woolen socks
At least 3 pairs of beige knee high woolen socks
At least 3 pairs of hideous triple layered woolen underwear
1 pair of brown leather lace up outdoor shoes
1 pair of brown leather indoor sandals
1 pair of plimsolls for P.E
1 pair of black plimsolls for drama
1 pair of hockey shoes
1 pair of blue woolen gloves
1 aertex gym shirt with name embroidered with name on front
1 blue gym skirt
1 romper for team sports so hideous that will ensure humiliation when facing opposing teams.
1 three paneled shoe bag - ALL shoes must be cleaned every week.

SUMMER UNIFORM:
1 ridiculously large straw boater
Plastic hat to cover ridiculously large straw boater in case of rain
Really expensive barrathea blazer
At least 2 yellow cotton dresses
1 blue cardigan
1 pair of brown leather sandals for outdoor use
At least 3 pairs of hideous triple-layered woolen underwear
1 pair of white cotton gloves

Me-mum and Me-dad don't say as much but I can tell they're concerned from the way they move and look around the kitchen, silent, thoughtful, worried, but determined. Every article of clothing has to be regulation and purchased from one clothier in the most exclusive shopping area in Saint Anne's Square, Manchester: Henry Barry's.

List in hand, we board the bus to Manchester.

Me-mum grew up in Manchester city center, so she knows it like the back of her hand. The two of us get the 102 bus and head into town. She's spayed half a can of Aqua Net hairspray on herself and, with her spitting on her handkerchief and wiping my dirty face with it, I'm feeling nauseas. I need to get off the bus. But, no way. Not yet.

The worst part of the bus ride into Manchester is traveling past Southern Cemetery, which is the biggest municipal cemetery in the UK. It's massive, so large it's even got roads going through it. It seems to take forever to pass. In every direction you look, there are rows and rows of headstones, statues, archangels, and Virgin Mary's. As long as I can remember I've always had a dread of funerals, coffins, and cemeteries. Visiting Me-sister, we have to pass a funeral home that's across from a cemetery. I secretly dread that part of the journey. Weekday Masses make me very wary as they often slip in a coffin at the last minute and, *voila*, now it's a requiem mass! As the coffin is carried in on the pallbearer's shoulders, I scramble and hide under the pew. Forget communion. I'm not going anywhere near that coffin.

Having finally passed the cemetery, I beg to get off the bus and out of its foul, hair spray and body odor funk. Me-mum and I are set down at the curb and we walk the last mile or so into Manchester. We arrive at Henry Barry's with our list in hand. Me-mum stands aside as I'm measured and dragged from one rack to the next, making sure I'm going to be properly attired for life's next great adventure. I don't know how they've done it, but I get everything on the list and it's paid for in full.

The big day arrives and I'm off to my shiny new school, my uniform laid out in front of the fire so it will be nice and toasty and ready for me to slip on. But first, a suitable breakfast for a budding scholar—warm porridge with the added treat of the cream off the top of the milk drizzled over it. A nice cup of tea and away I go. No test runs, just given my free bus pass and instructed to get the 8:15 102 bus and get off at Nell Lane.

"Then walk down what?" I ask, uncertain, "Nell Lane? I don't know where that is."

Me-mum sighs:

"Course you do, you've passed it a hundred times. It's that road that goes through Southern Cemetery."

"No!" I scream, "I don't want to go down there! Can I go another way?"

"Well, apparently not. You cannot avoid the cemetery any which way you go."

Oh, why did I have to pass my eleven-plus! I could've been cruising Easy Street, literally (there was one), making a cemetery-free commute to an inferior secondary modern high school with minimal uniform requirements. I don't feel much like a winner right now. And my pleas to Me-mum are useless:

"Don't be daft, Moya! Get on with you!"

So, I trudge to the bus stop in my *buy everything a few sizes bigger with room to grow* uniform, carrying my new leather briefcase that's too big as well and practically dragging on the ground. How do you grow into a briefcase? Then there's the stupid hat that keeps falling down over my eyes and the gloves that don't help at all when trying to scratch the itchiness of my new uniform.

It starts raining.

Now I have to open my briefcase and get out the packet containing the rain hat to put over my hat and find the pouch with the raincoat to put over my coat. All the while, my books and pencil case are getting soaked. Why isn't a rain case for my briefcase part of the uniform? And, perhaps, a rain bag for my shoe bag? I feel I'm doomed and, looking back, my instincts were correct.

Southern Cemetery, the gateway to the Marist Convent School for Young Ladies, really is the gateway to hell on earth. Walking through the school gates on that first day I'm met by a gauntlet of smiling, welcoming nuns in blue and white habits. Okay, off to a good start, I think.

The actual school itself is very impressive. It's *state of the art* and I'm going to be a member of the first class to complete my education there. It has science labs, language labs, music rooms, kitchens, a drama hall and—the two most important areas for me—sports facilities and art studios. This is going to be brilliant, I think, and enter into the adventure with hope and excitement. I'm clearly the most gifted of athletes, quickly elected Games Captain, and recruited for all the sports teams.

My next mission is to get to the art room and display my budding creative skills to the art teacher, Miss Mercer. Art is my favorite subject and I'm excited to absorb all the learning she can bestow on me. I'm almost bursting with excitement. Let me at it!

I've been warned Miss Mercer is tough, stern, and has, in fact, taught at a *Borstal*, a kind of youth detention center. So, if she's capable of teaching the delinquent youth of Great Britain, then the whiney school girls of Manchester will be a piece of cake. She's certainly an imposing figure: six-foot-tall, broad-shouldered, and severely scarred by chronic acne, poor thing. As we enter her classroom she sits and sizes each of us up, scowling.

I think Mary Burns actually pees her pants.

Our first task is to make papier mâché puppets. We're instructed to decide on a character and start sketching ideas. Big sheets of foolscap paper, sharpened colored pencils, magic markers—I'm in art class heaven!

Not surprisingly, it seems to this arrogant little schoolgirl, Miss Mercer sees my promising artistic ability immediately. After a couple of passes by my desk, she stops and studies my work.

"Very good, and what is your name?"

I proudly announce my full name: "Mary Hession, Miss."

Miss Mercer takes a large gulp, squints her eyes and replies: "Do you have a brother called—"

"Yes, Miss," I declare, worried.

She raises her chin and, seething, announces: "He was the bane of my existence when I taught at All Hallows."

Panicked, I think, no, no, this can't be happening! Not in art class! Not in the only subject I've never been made to feel like an idiot in! For one desperate moment I consider adding that I'm also Pussy's sister.

No. Besides, it's too late. Miss Mercer has moved on up the aisle.

Once again, just being *related* to the demon seed flushes any semblance of happiness I might have had down the spanking new drain of the art room. My fate is sealed and Miss Mercer certainly makes it her mission to make my life as miserable as the brother made hers.

The only thing I can be grateful for is that there is no corporal punishment at the Marist. I wouldn't stand a chance at the capable hands of Miss Mercer. Nonetheless, she devises countless ways to inflict both physical and emotional pain: standing in the corner, standing in the corner on one leg, kneeling in the corner on the hard floor, standing in the corner with my back to the class and my arms behind my head, cleaning the jam jars—

"Don't look at the class!"

She's relentless in her quest to break my spirit.

The school's impressive facilities also include a common room for each year. These rooms are where we eat lunch and where we hang out when the weather is too bad for outside playtime. Each common room is laid with a carpet, a different color for each year. Red for first year, blue for second, and green for third. One of the more disgusting inventions the nuns have come up with is cleaning up after lunch. As we eat in the carpeted common room it falls to whoever is allocated clean-up duty after lunch to get down on her hands and knees and pick any food droppings from off the carpet, by hand, before the janitor comes in with a proper vacuum cleaner. Food ground into the carpet has to be scraped out with one's bare hands and, God forbid, you have a problem with any of your classmates or are disliked when you're on clean-up duty! These are opportunities for easy and thorough revenge. Such was Miss Mercer's distaste for me she was known to stop by my lunch table and deposit a big dollop of gravy and mashed potatoes by my station and grind into the carpet. I often gagged and wretched as I struggled to scratch out the food with my nails while she stood there smirking.

High school is, and will remain, the most miserable time of my life. I'm not an evil child, I promise. True, I am somewhat mischievous and a bit of a class clown. I have a lot of energy. I'm easily bored. I just forget to behave sometimes. Anyway, when you're raised in a devout Catholic family and are sent off to Catholic school, you sort of have a target on your back. Your parents are likely to believe everything the sisters say. And these sisters take great satisfaction calling my parents into the school to explain how they have given birth to and raised the Antichrist herself.

Some parents get a call explaining:

"Missus Brown, your Jane was smoking in class today."

To which the Brown's reply: "So what, she smokes at home too."

Not so with my parents.

The headmistress, Sister Sheila Mary Hunt, is a wiry, twitchy, squinty ball of energy. She guards her domain like a rottweiler, always ready to pounce. Her office is situated in its own building, away from the rest of the school, so she has a 360-degree view of her subjects at all times. Outside, there's a waiting room. On the wall next to her door is a series of lights: red means stop, yellow wait and green, of course, enter. I spend many hours staring at that red signal light, listening to the muffled sounds of Sister Sheila, the all-powerful Mary Hunt, ranting on and on to Me-poor-mum about what a horrible child I am.

The door opens and Me-mum comes out, tears streaming down her face, head hung in shame. Sister Sheila Hairy Cunt smirking over her shoulder. But no matter how hard I try, I can't seem to do the one thing Me-mum wants me to do:

"Just behave yourself."

5.

After two years at the Marist there's a couple of bright lights on the horizon—the first being the appearance of a dear friend from the old neighborhood: the brilliant Patsy Dickson.

I adore Patsy. She's a large Black girl with a lint-filled messy afro and the best sense of humor I've ever encountered. Patsy is not scared of anything, which is unfortunate for our biology teacher, Miss Saunders.

Miss Saunders is a lovely woman. But she's nervous and uncertain. And she's stuck teaching a group of uninterested schoolgirls who, for the most part, don't give a crap about biology. Rumor has it she was studying medicine to become a surgeon but, tragically, a car accident halted that ambition and left her blind in one eye. As a consequence, she wears her lovely, shiny black hair in a stylish bob that falls over part of her face, covering the damaged eye.

Not one to miss an opportunity for some good old-fashioned hilarity, Patsy takes full advantage of our teacher's *blind side* and her nervous condition. As Miss Saunders turns away to the blackboard, Patsy stands up and gestures for the whole class to lie on the floor. (Nobody ever says no to Patsy.) Then, when Miss Saunders turns back around and sees everybody on the floor she instantly panics and yells:

"Class, what are you doing on the floor!"

"Miss," Patsy leans up and explains, "you told the class to lie on the floor,".

Poor Miss Saunders, of course, protests. But she's forever uncertain and troubled even as she insists:

"But that's madness, Patsy. Why would I—"

"But, Miss, you did."

Next time, Patsy tells the class to line up outside the lab. It's pretty much the same routine:

"Miss, you told us to form an orderly line outside the lab."

"No, I didn't!"

And so on. This poor woman really endures a lot at the capable hands of Patsy Dickson. Still, I never see Patsy's mum and dad dragged into school. So, it seems Miss Saunders isn't a tattletale, probably a good egg, and certainly undeserving of our childish cruelty.

But we can't help ourselves.

One day, we're all dozing as usual and not paying any attention when Miss Saunders mentions something about the female frog's vageena.

Everybody sits upright for this.

"What did you call it?" Patsy asks, intrigued.

"The vageena."

We all turn to one another. "What is she talking about?"

"Miss, what do you mean exactly?" Patsy pursues.

Exasperated, Miss Saunders struggles on: "A vageena."

"Do you mean a vagina?"

"Yes, yes, a vageena."

Well, she explained that depends on whether you pronounce it with a hard "G" or a soft "G" and her choice was to use a hard "G". Every time she said "vageena" there was a resounding chorus of twenty-three girls yelling "vagina" at poor Miss Saunders.

The next ray of hope to enter my life is an additional art teacher, Miss Frasier-Smith. The sheer relief I feel when I find out I will no longer be under the tutelage of *Frau Mercer* of the Third Reich is unbelievable. There is a God after all, I think, and—since, for the moment, we're on speaking terms: "God, I just want to remind you about a certain relative living under the same roof. No pressure! But it would be great if you can do something about him."

Miss Frasier-Smith is a joy: sweet, gentle, and with a great sense of humor. Well, at least, she thinks I'm funny. She's a brilliant and inspirational teacher. It doesn't take long for her to recognize I have some talent. But, more than that, she sees my enthusiasm and hunger to learn all she has to offer. This woman with a posh accent and a double-barreled name believes in me, she encourages me to reach further than I ever might have imagined. If I hand in a substandard piece of work, she looks at me and says, "really?" This propels me onward and I try harder. I can't sell myself short and definitely can't let Miss F.S. down. Her classroom is my oasis and I spend any free time I have in there perusing her personal art library or the mountains of inspirational reference clippings she has in neat piles on her desk. Her room is chock-full of bits of moss, branches, leaves of every color, fish skeletons, dried flowers—all available for still life studies. I can't understand my classmates' lack of enthusiasm for art class. But even they love the warm disposition and encouragement Miss F. S. bestows on us. There's even outside school activities she shares with me. She takes me to museums, galleries, even a group show of student work deemed to be the best in the country. All this to prove, to me, that I'm capable of going far with my talent. She takes a group of us provincial northerners to London to visit the Tate and the National Gallery which prompts my interest in William Blake and Salvador Dali. When I'm in my third year she gets married and I'm terrified what changes this will bring. Will she leave? But the only difference is she's now known as Missus Edwards.

Phew!

So, I chug through school somehow only because I like Missus Edwards. Otherwise, I dread waking up each morning, realizing I have to go through it again: the nuns telling me I'll never amount to anything, that I'm a waste of time and space, Sister Hairy summoning me to her office to try on new sample uniforms for the sixth form, pinning me against the wall, getting closer and closer until I can feel her knee in between my legs.

I've pretty much checked out of even trying to succeed in academic subjects. What's the point? No matter how hard I try, I fail miserably. Besides, I have a pretty active social life outside of the Marist.

Now I'm thirteen, I'm able to get a weekend job in a local newsagents. I use the term newsagents loosely as we sell everything from a child's bicycle to a sewing needle. The shop, Fitton's, itself is located in my old neighborhood, in the middle of a group of retail establishments in various states of disrepair. The customers vary from four-year-old kids with hand written notes requesting a pack of Woodbines "for Me-mam who's still in bed," to the well-dressed young school teacher wanting a copy of *The Guardian*. It's a snapshot of working-class England in the seventies, a representative swath of people who don't have much to strive for. A can of air freshener is kept close at hand behind the counter to eradicate the awful smell of bodies that haven't bathed in weeks, a smell that goes hand in hand with a lack of hope.

Fitton's is, in fact, the center of the community's shopping needs. Besides cigarettes and newspapers, the shelves are lined with row upon row of multicolored sweets, boxes of assorted chocolates, lollipops, and everything needed to ensure that the person earning the most money in town is the dentist, Mr. Midgely. The shop itself has a large chest-high horseshoe counter that wraps around inside its perimeter. The only access is by lifting up a heavy wooden gate. The girls I work with are an interesting group with ages ranging from thirteen to seventeen. And I'm the youngest. The common denominator is that we're all local girls. Some work after school, if they bother to go, and others are full-time employees. I've been working at the shop for a couple of weeks and have settled into a nice steady routine. I no longer get flustered when the line is out the door with people waiting for their Sunday papers.

During an ordinary workday I'm going about my business with my four colleagues when, all of a sudden, they all drop to the floor and hide. A large woman, Missus McGuire, with curlers in her hair, stained, disheveled clothes, and an unfiltered cigarette hanging from her lips, approaches me.

"Hiya luv, I'm Margaret and Bridget's Mam. Are they here?"

I glance furtively over to see her twin daughters crouching on the floor behind the tall counter, shaking their heads.

"Ah, I think they're on a break," I reply unconvincingly.

"No matter, cock. You can serve me then."

She pulls out a tattered list from her wrinkled and food-stained cardigan and hands it to me.

It's a long list containing everything from cigarettes, hairspray, tights, a hair net, chocolates, teabags, and shampoo.

"Oh, and I'll take that blue bike for our Will."

By then my coworkers, except for the twins, are up and helping other customers. I find a ladder and climb up to retrieve Will's new bicycle and proudly wheel it across the shop floor. Back behind the till, I start totaling up her considerable purchase.

"That will be sixty-five pound and forty-six pence, please."

She takes a break from stuffing her purchases into her many bags, handing them off to a cluster of little unwashed kids, to retrieve her purse. She hands me her money and when I look at it I almost faint. It's a five-pound note. What am I supposed to do with this?

Sweating, I look at her and she stares straight into my eyes, hand outstretched, waiting for her fucking change!

"Excuse me," I stammer, trying to think, "I have to go check the other till for change."

I walk around to the other side of the shop, stumbling over the twins who are still huddled up and cringing beneath the counter.

"Just give her back four pound," Bridget hisses, desperate.

"What about my till," I whisper back. "I'm going to be short!"

"Don't worry about that," Margaret cries weakly. "We'll sort it out later."

Still not comprehending what kind of crime syndicate I've just been indoctrinated in to, I march back over and hand back four pound to Missus McGuire. But her large, fleshy, sweaty hand is still hanging there, expecting to be reimbursed the last pound! After a tense standoff, she turns and wobbles out the door with her plentiful bounty.

"Next."

Still shaking, I'm approached by the twins, knocking dust off their skirts. "Was that your Mam?"

"Yes," Bridget confirms, "she comes in all the time."

"Well, not on my watch."

From then on, I take to scanning the distance over the heads of the customers, constantly on the lookout for Missus McGuire. But there's a lot to be doing and, inevitably, one day everybody drops to the floor again.

"Look out! It's Claire's mam!"

And the same sort of thing. But this time it's Claire's mam who extorts free stuff.

Well, if you can't beat them, I think, join them. Me-mum shows up at my counter wanting to buy a pair of tights. Sixty-five pence, I say. She hands me one pound and I give her back eighty pence in change, only charging her twenty pence for the tights.

When I get home that evening, she's waiting for me.

"I want to talk to you, young lady," she says. "When I left that shop today, I could feel a hand on my shoulder."

"Really," I wonder, all innocence, "I didn't notice."

"Not actually," she continues, "but I could feel the hand of a policeman on my shoulder."

I'm catching on: "Oh, yeah, I see."

"Don't you ever do that again. And here's the forty pence I owe the store. I am so ashamed."

Blimey, I can't imagine what she'd do if she knew what the other mums are getting away with over at Fitton's: shopping for Christmas in July, Easter in August!

6.

All the shop employees become fast friends and it isn't long before the older girls have taught me the ways of getting served alcohol in the local pubs. Friday night, we're out and about, Saturday morning, sick as dogs, than we're back behind the counter at Fitton's.

Saturday night, perfectly recovered, the cycle repeats.

Local pubs are not that interesting, so we venture further afield to the crowded discos of greater Manchester. After work, I'm off home to change into a fabulous new outfit recently purchased at Miss Selfridge or Top Shop. Then, it's off to Chris's house to have her skillfully apply the most fashionable make up—false eye lashes included. Finally, we go to Lynne's house to meet up with the rest of the gang: Lynne, Claire, and Elaine. In all our gorgeousness, we traipse off to the bus stop to catch the 101 bus to Barlow Moor Road and "The Oaks."

Inevitably, there's a hiccup when three minutes before our stop Claire announces: "I'm not going."

Groan.

Here we go again. We miss our stop and spend the next twenty minutes trying to persuade Claire to change her mind, that we're going to have a great time, and that none of us will go without her. Our argument always wins and she always changes her mind. We get off the bus, cross over the parkway and wait for another bus to take us to our original destination which we passed thirty minutes ago.

This happens every time.

Claire clearly has issues. She's from a broken home and her mother regularly attempts suicide to coincide with Claire coming home from school. She places a pillow in the oven and turns on the gas. But it never works because she leaves a window open and, besides, Wythenshawe is, by now, using natural gas which won't poison a person anyway.

I guess she has no intention of really *going* either.

The Oaks is a large old pub located about five miles from home; just far enough away as not to run into any of the Wythenshawe riffraff or for anybody to realize that we are, in fact, the Wythenshawe riffraff. Three nights a week the large back room is a disco and usually there's a great crowd. Entering The Oaks is always nerve-racking for me. Being the youngest at fourteen, I'm terrified of not getting in with my fake ID and letting everybody down because if one of us can't get it, we'll all go home together. But I'm admitted again and again and become a regular patron of this fine establishment, a connoisseur of Carlsberg Specials.

As a group we're pretty striking and we walk around like we own the place. There's Chris, a couple of months older than me, beautiful, tall, and arrogant, striding through life with her nose in the air and her long legs leaving everyone in her wake. She takes great pleasure in seeing me struggle to keep up with her and loves it even more when I give up, watching her stride on fifty feet ahead of me.

Claire is beautiful and can be a lot of fun. But her sudden bouts of moodiness prove at times to be more trouble than she's worth. But then we know what she goes through at home.

Another important member of our clique is Missus Bailey, Lynne's Mum. Missus B. She's a rare gem with a very loud Manchester accent who always covers for me when my parents want to know where I am.

"Oh, she's down at Saint Anthony's youth club with the girls," she says, knowing full well I'm at some nightclub in Manchester, probably being serenaded by everybody in the disco for my twenty-first birthday—a favorite ploy we use to get free drinks.

Our nights out to The Oaks are pretty formulaic. We arrive at the disco, take a look around, get the lay of the land, then convene in the bathroom. There, we check out how great we all look before heading off to the dance floor. We form a circle with our handbags in the center and boogie away to Gloria Gaynor, Donna Summer, maybe some Bee Gees or The Village People. Sometimes we meet up with a gang of lads and, if there's a car, we might end up at Manchester airport or a motorway cafe for a late-night bite.

Our Saturday night adventures end up with us crashing at Missus B's. We all pile into Lynne's bed and pass out. Lynne herself rises at five forty-five to get Sunday papers out at Fitton's, works till nine, then comes back and sleeps again while the rest of us get up for the nine-to-noon shift. Then, after we close up shop, it's back to Lynne's where Missus B serves us bacon buttys and tea in bed. We rest till it's time to get up and start the process all over again. But it being Sunday, it won't be a late night as we have school the next day.

Life's almost perfect except for that damn school thing. At least I have summer holidays to look forward to. And the end of year three can't come fast enough for me.

7.

I now work full-time at Fitton's and save some money for a holiday. Chris and I first decide we'll join Missus B at a caravan in North Wales for a week. Lynne and Claire, meanwhile, are going to travel across Europe for the whole summer.

"Oh, how lucky you are," Chris and I exclaim, enviously, "to have such an exciting trip to look forward to!"

"Come with us, then," says Lynne. "Just for a week."

What a brilliant idea! But Chris and I are only fourteen and don't have passports yet. I know Me-mum and Me-dad will never let me go. Fortunately, Fitton's, being the lifeline of our community, is also a post office where you can acquire a temporary passport valid for six months. The post mistress also manages the shop and has a bit of a soft spot for Chris and I. We ask her how we should go about getting a passport.

"Easy, get two photos and have a parent sign this form."

She hands us the forms.

I summon all my artistic talent and forge Me-mum's signature—and then Chris's Mam's.

Next hurdle is that Me-mum and Me-dad will expect a postcard from me during "my trip to Wales." As Missus Bailey is now in on the fraud, she tells us to write a couple of postcards that she'll send our parents from Wales. I can only find blank white postcards, no scenic beauties of the Welsh coastline. But it will have to do. I take one and scrawl happily across it: "Having a grand time in Wales! Miss you!" I hand this off to Missus B and she assures me it'll be fine.

We don't have a clue where we're going, only that Chris and I will accompany the older girls for one week on the first leg of their European adventure. We have our luggage loaded with the latest fashions and extra makeup with separate cases for our sleeping bags. All flared trousers and platform shoes, we board the bus to Manchester, then a train to London, followed by another to Dover. Finally, there's the boat across the Channel to Calais. It's all going smoothly until Claire, as usual, starts in with her:

"I'm not going."

We begin the usual routine and try to persuade her to change her mind. Then the boat blows its horn, signaling its departure.

"Alright, Claire, see you back in Wythenshawe. We're off!"

But as we clatter up the gangway, wobbling on our platforms, flares flapping, and suitcases dragging, we hear the sound of an extra set of clogs behind us.

Claire has changed her mind once again.

It's a pretty calm voyage across the notoriously rough channel and *viola!* there we are, in France. No clue what our next step is to be. So, we decide to board a train and see where it takes us; maybe a small town or village in the countryside for a few days before the girls continue their journey across the continent. We board the first train we see. The conductor comes along requesting fare and informs us we're on a nonstop to Paris.

Paris. That's not what we're expecting. Lynne said we'd be staying in a quaint little French village hostel—lovely, chewy baguettes, stinky cheeses, and gorgeous, bucolic countryside.

No.

We pull into Gare du Nord, a busy, smelly, bustling, noisy hub right in the thick of things. Knowing we don't have money enough for Paris priced hotels we make a plan—a kind of plan-less plan. But it sounds like a plan to me.

Firstly, since Lynne is our fearless leader, the oldest and wisest, she will be responsible for all our money and passports and carry them securely at all times. Next, we decide to deposit all our belongings in the station's lockers and go exploring.

Walking down the Champs-Élysées with a baguette in one hand and a bottle of milk in the other, I look at Lynne. She's beaming.

"Isn't this fantastic," she says. "So romantic!"

I look at my bottle of milk and want to pour it all over her head.

"No, this is horrible," I reply acidly. "I wish I was in Wales with your Mam! Where are we going to sleep tonight?"

But Lynne has that figured out. We'll go back to the station and see what we can find.

At the station, dozens of weary and bedraggled travelers are unfurling their sleeping bags, ready to settle in for the night.

"See," Lynne says, pointing out our night's accommodation.

Then we're approached by a man who introduces himself as Thierry. He says he's seen us earlier at the station and is concerned about us. He has a place for us to stay, for free, and will take us there. The other girls are actually mulling this over.

"No way!" I insist. "Who the hell is this guy? God only knows where he'll take us. Plus, it's dark and we won't even be able to see where we're going!"

Admittedly, since finding out my sister's neighbor was a serial killer, I'm much more cautious than my friends. True: not cautious enough to avoid being in a foreign country with a forged passport and my family not knowing where I am. But I'm cautious enough to know not to go off with a stranger.

"Listen, monsieur," I suggest, "if you want to help us, come back tomorrow afternoon and show us around Paris—in the daylight."

It makes sense to me but, in reality, if he's going to rape and kill us all, it really doesn't matter if it's night or day. Nevertheless, he agrees. The girls do too. Plans are made, Thierry goes off, and we get ready for our first night in the glorious city of light, sleeping on the floor of the train station.

Around midnight I hear a rumpus and wake to being poked and prodded by gendarmes.

"*Alle, Alle, Alle...*"

This means we have to go outside and sleep on the street. We jump up, still in our sleeping bags, and hop through the nearest exit like a herd of kangaroos. Again, we settle in for the night along with dozens of other vagabonds. But now I'm woken by some creep trying to touch me up outside my sleeping bag. In my best genteel British accent, I yell:

"Get your greasy fucking hands of me, you dirty bastard!"

He gets the message and shuffles off, offended. I stay awake all night, on guard. Morning can't come fast enough for me. Once everybody's up and ready to face the day, we retrieve the soap, toothbrushes, toothpaste, and towels from our luggage and head to the public washrooms. Lynne and Claire go first, down the stairs to the *toilettes,* as Chris and I keep an eye on our belongings. Within seconds, they come running back up, chased by an angry little French *toilette* attendant.

Apparently, it is not *l'hotel.* And there is more about us being, "*merde, gypsier, floutage*!" Even with my little bit of high school French, I know this is not good. Exhausted and filthy, I'm already looking up the train schedule and making a plan to get Chris and I back to England. But not Lynne, no. She's loving the excitement and energy of Paris! We venture outside the station to find some inexpensive breakfast.

I must admit: once I get over the shock that chocolate filled croissants are an acceptable breakfast food in this country, I'm feeling a little less irritated by all things French.

The afternoon arrives and we head back to the station to meet up with Thierry. I'm still against about going anywhere with him even though the others argue that there's four of us and only one of him.

"Yes, but, that is... now. But, what if..."

My mind is full of horrors.

But then there he is, coming towards us, French-English dictionary in hand. We pile into his Citroen and he shows us the sights: The Seine, the Eiffel Tower. He drives us around and around the Arc de Triumph before depositing us at the bottom of the steps of *Sacre Coeur*, where he explains his mother is in the hospital and he's got to go visit her. He'll be back at nine that night and take us to our accommodation.

"Fine, no problem," the girls all seem to decide.

But my brain is stirring.

"Listen, it'll be dark again. Just like last night. I don't think we should go anywhere with this bloke. He only shows up in the dark."

It's hard to say why—night descending, fatigue, genuine fear—but everyone gradually agrees with me. At five minutes to nine, we grab our belongings and run up the three hundred steps to *Sacre Coeur* in our platform shoes. When we reach the church, there are groups of young people sitting around enjoying the beautiful view. Some play guitar and sing, which is right up Lynne's Street. She's mesmerized by the crunchy hippiness of it all. Meanwhile, I decide to mingle, hoping to find some cheap and secure accommodation for the night. One particular group of Germans seem very friendly until I explain we don't not have anywhere to stay. This one lunatic stands up and starts slapping his hands, giving us a lecture: Slap! "Vot do you mean you av novere to stay!" Slap! "Virst ven you travel you must virst vind accommodation! Slap! "Zen you make a base vor your travels!"

I wander back over to Lynne, sitting with her newfound *fabulous* people, listening to folk songs and all of them stinking to high heaven. Around eleven o'clock the crowd begins to dissipate. All Lynne's new friends are saying goodbye and the German is off to his—slap!—"very goot inexpensif hotel!"

As we sit back on the sacred steps of the sacred church and try to figure out where we're going to spend the night, when Lynne starts yelling:

"Me bag! Me bag! Somebody's nicked me bag!"

None of the retreating horde give us a second look, they just keep moving down the three hundred steps, evaporating into the night.

As Lynne is the keeper of all our money and passports, we are well and truly in deep trouble. I can't even call home because Me-mum and Me-dad think I'm under the protective custody of Missus B in Wales.

Then, pushing his way through the crowd, comes Thierry. He's panicked.

"What happened! I came back to get you and you were gone. Do you know how dangerous it is up here? There are thieves..."

Well, Thierry, funny you should mention that. Because..."

We explain what's happened and he tells us to get in his car. He takes us straight to a police station to report our loss. Obviously, nothing can be done, but we realize that if Thierry is a rapist and murderer, it's not likely he'd be hanging around the police station. So, his concern for this gang of lost English girls he hardly even knows is probably genuine.

Afterwards, he takes us to this huge apartment and explains that it's where he had offered us to stay the previous night. It belongs to a doctor friend of his who's on holiday. He gives us the keys and his phone number in case we need anything and then leaves. The next morning, he shows up with croissants and coffee for breakfast before driving us to the British Consulate to report our stolen passports.

At the consulate, Lynne and Claire are issued replacement passports so they can continue their trip. Chris and I are given papers that are valid for twenty-four hours that enable us to leave the country—which sounds great to me. I have some cash hidden in my shoe for emergencies. So, I have enough for Chris and me to get back to Calais on the train.

Thierry gives Lynne two hundred pounds to replace the money she's lost. She's very grateful and promises to send it back to him once she gets back to England. He drives us to Gare du Nord where we say our goodbyes. And at the ticket counter, Lynne and Claire decide to return to England with us, the past three days in Paris having quenched their thirst for travel.

The big problem for Chris and I, though, is that we can't go home because we're supposed to be in Wales! So, we decide to go to London with Claire and visit her dad.

Lynne goes home alone and stops in to see Me-mum. She tells her all about her adventure in Paris. She marvels at how expensive Paris is and, how "four cups of coffee cost two pound fifty!"

A few years later, Me-auntie Molly is visiting and asks if I'd ever

been abroad. I tell her no. But then Me-mum chimes in, saying:
"I think she has."

Surprised, I say: "What do you mean? I haven't."

She speaks right past me to Molly and explains: "I think she went to Paris a while back with her friends. When Lynne came back and told me four cups of coffee cost two pound fifty in Paris, I knew who the four were! Not to mention blank postcards from Wales!"

8.

Summer is over and the nightmare of the Marist is back on my doorstep. As if school isn't difficult enough, I now enter the world of O levels. O Levels are a series of public exams in various subjects that are required before moving on to more specialized courses of study, known as A Levels. Testing and revising are endless and frustrating. So, most nights I go over to Lynne's house and sit with Missus Bailey while Lynne is at night school. I take my books and sit for hours on their settee—rarely studying— and enjoy Missus B's company and banter. She tells me all the crazy shenanigans she gets up to on bus trips with the local ladies from Wythenshawe who, if they've paid good money for a night out, are going to have a "bloody good time!" Wearing Tampons as earrings, dancing all night, being locked out of the bus because the local scrubber is shagging the bus driver on the back seat. More or less the same scenario every outing. But she always has a "crackin' good time."

I remember once going to a local supermarket with Missus B and as we walked from aisle to aisle she'd ask, "jere wont a drink?" And she'd hand me a bottle of Dandelion and Burdoc, a favorite of mine. Then, "ere ave some choccy." And she'd hand me a bar of Cadbury milk chocolate. "Wont some crisps?" I munched on a packet of crisps thinking how different it was to be out shopping with Me-mum. No such extravagances with her. So I was leisurely enjoying Missus B's generosity until she stopped and glared at me: "urry up and finish wot yer eatin afore we get to the till. I am not payin for all your shite." And again, I saw I was sucked back into the lawbreaking side of everyday life in Wythenshawe.

Back at the Bailey house, there's a loud knock at the door. Missus B goes into the hall to answer it. I could hear muffled voices. Then she calls to me: "Do ya wont anyfin from town?"

"From town?"

She clarifies: "Yes, any cloves? This lad ere is going into Manchester and ee's takin' orders."

Seems Missus B has a personal shopper.

"No, thanks." I say.

The lad takes off and she comes back in, enthusing over a lovely navy wool coat she saw in Debenhams. "Gorgeous it is wiv a likkle velvet collar."

Next night, however, another knock on the door and I hear an agitated Missus B shouting: "What the fuck is this! I said navy not maroon! I don't wont it!"

She slams the door and flops down into her big faux leather arm chair: "Wot a waste of fuckin time! He got me maroon! 'Ees brover is much better."

"Can't you take it back and exchange it?"

She glares across at me, pityingly. Then she explains for this naive and uncorrupted youth: "No, cos it's nicked! You tell im wot you want and he goes and nicks it for ya."

I should not be surprised by any of this, seeing as how Missus B is a cleaner at the local hospital and every sheet, pillowcase, towel, flannel, and roll of toilet paper in her home is emblazoned with *Property of Wythenshawe Hospital*.

Me-mum likes Missus B but is a little envious that I'm spending so much time with her. I could tell her Lynne's mam is just so much fun. But it's more than that: she's completely on my side. When I tell her about another run-in with Sister Sheila, she replies, "she's a fuckin cow, take no notice." Whereas, with Me-mum, I'm always in the wrong and the nuns are always in the right.

This changes dramatically, however, when, after being summoned to Sister Hairy's office once more to try on another new uniform, I say I don't want to and go back to class. Fortunately, this is witnessed by a friend. When I get home, I learn Me-mum's already gotten the call on our new phone about my insubordination. I tell Me-mum to ask my friend what she's seen and heard. Me-mum is informed that Sister Hairy was trying to get me to change clothes in her office again.

She's troubled but, fearlessly, calls the almighty sister and asks what's going on. Ever prepared, Sister Hairy explains that she knew I had a physical with the school doctor and she wanted to make sure my underwear was fit for the doctor to see.

"What business is my daughter's underwear of yours?"

Pretty much, that puts a stop to my frequent visits to the principal's office and Me-mum is never called into the school again.

Even though the Marist offers seven more years of high school in preparation for further education, there is an option to leave after five years, after O Levels. Most of the people I hang out with, both in and out of school, are going to exercise the option of leaving after their exams and go join the workforce. Chris wants to be a cosmetologist, Lynne is going to community college to become a kindergarten teacher, Claire is going to work full-time in the shop and Elaine is *not* going to be a brain surgeon.

For my part: the only two subjects I'm good at are Art and Gym. Where will that leave me?

The O Levels are fast approaching. As usual, the results of the repeated testing and mock exams places me squarely at the bottom of the class. No matter how hard I work, no matter how much cramming I do—all this information I learn—nothing seems to make sense to my aching brain. I am enrolled to take eight O Levels in all the academic subjects plus Art. One by one we are marched into the gym. Rules are repeated, silence ordered. There will be no breaks and not even a window to gaze out of. The moderator hands out the papers, two booklets. I pick up the first of the two and thumb through the questions. Deciding I'm incapable of answering anything in it, I pick up the second booklet, hoping I might have better luck with the topics therein.

Horror above horrors: the second booklet is only blank paper to write my answers on! Shit, shit, shit. What the hell am I going to do for three whole hours? There's no point in me even pretending to answer these questions. What am I doing here, anyway?

My only hope, I suppose, is Missus Edwards and Art.

Sometime earlier, before I had to take a biology exam, she tried to encourage me, saying, "knock them dead with your beautiful illustrations!"

Good thinking. That should keep me occupied for a couple of hours, at least. My only alternatives are to sit here and dwell on my humiliation or to stand up and walk out. And I don't think they'll let me walk out.

Fuck it, I've done some impressive biological illustrations in class; the many layers of the skin, a heart, even a *vageena*! What do I have to illustrate? I page through the test. What beauty can I create to blow everybody away and maybe, later, get contacted by the British Medical Journal wanting my superior skills. Here we go!

Draw—what?

Draw a transverse section of—are they for real? *Villi*. Specifically: a membranous structure supporting *villi*.

Okay, I know what *villi* are, so I must not be a complete ignoramus. Drawing is probably the only reason I haven't failed biology yet. But come on! A fucking transverse section of *villi*? *Villi* are the small, fingerlike projections that increase the surface area of a membrane, like in the placenta or the mucous membrane coating of the small intestine.

How am I supposed to make this beautiful?

This is not happening. There couldn't be a worse or more boring subject to illustrate—not to say gross.

But if they want a *villi*, they will get *villi*, fucking transverse section and all. I set about the task at hand, figuring the light source so as to get the shadow my *villi* will cast just right. I give it dimension and a subtle but accurate amount of texture until it seems to pop right off the page. I have no doubt it is probably the best illustration of *villi* accompanying the worst test handed in to the matriculation board in Manchester's recent history.

All eight O Levels complete, my friends are leaving school for good, never to darken the doors of the Marist again. Most have—or soon will have—jobs, so their exam results are of no consequence. Unfortunately, the same cannot be said of me. I cannot work in an office, a dentists, the makeup counter in a department store, or in a mill for the rest of my life.

But why? Other people do those sorts of things. Do I think I'm different? Special?

No, I just want something else.

But what?

My uncertain future is feeling even more uncertain.

The O Levels are scored one through nine—one being the highest score or grade. Two through six are passing grades; seven, eight and nine fails—nine being the lowest and given for basically showing up and spelling your name correctly. And just to heighten the humiliation, most schools post the results in the evening newspaper. Thank God, my school does not participate in this—which I think oddly inconsistent with the Sisters' evident interest in humiliation.

Working at Fitton's, I am a firsthand witness to the frenzy of people lining up for the newspaper; that is to say, the seven frenzied parents whose kids have some kind of chance at making good. Though there are a few disappointments to be overheard.

"Our Jonathan got 8."

"Our Sheila got 9."

"Our Jen got 7."

"Our Michael got..."

I know my fate will be waiting for me when I get home. And there it is: an unopened envelope just sitting on the table ready to vomit up the knowledge that Sister Hairy was right all along. The girl is stupid, useless, and will never accomplish anything.

I lift the envelope, open it, and take out the results.

SUBJECT	GRADE
GEOGRAPHY	9
MATHS	9
ENGLISH	9
ENGLISH LIT	9
CHEMISTRY	9
BIOLOGY	9
PHYSICS	9
RELIGION	9
ART	1

Not wanting to fall apart completely, I look at Me-mum eagerly waiting for the great news. I hand her the results.

"Oh, that's shocking," she says.

I agree. Then she continues:

"You only got one out of ten in Art! I thought you would have got more than that with all your lovely drawing and so on!"

I can't believe my ears. Since I'm the first one in the family to sit these tests, Me-mum isn't familiar with the scoring. So, she thinks I passed all subjects *but* Art with flying colors. "Oh, yes, she got mostly nines," she'd proudly announce to the neighbors, thinking I got nine out of ten in all subjects but Art.

Hey, I'm not about to burst that bubble. She'll understand soon enough, though.

Deep down I know I have to face this disaster alone and that is what I'll do. I'm going back to the Marist, volunteering to hold myself back, joining classes with the younger girls, knuckling down and retaking the O Levels. But maybe not all eight subjects; just enough to get me into an art course at a local community college and then, hopefully, insure myself a job as a textile designer in any one of the big textile houses in the North of England.

My uncertain future is feeling a little less uncertain than a few days ago. But it's a big pill to swallow. I'll put that fucking uniform back on, walk through the cemetery with all the new lambs going to the slaughter, and right on up to Sister Sheila who'll say, "Well, well! I thought we had seen the back of you."

But no, Sister, you haven't. Not yet.

9.

The girls and I decide to go on holiday. Me-mum and Me-dad take a bit of persuading, but they like my friends and know Lynne is a responsible and well-behaved girl. We decide we should go away for a week. Nothing too far. Rhyl in North Wales seems like a good choice. We peruse the newspaper ads for a holiday rental and settle on a "*luxury chalet*" in something called the Sunnyvale Holiday Camp. The excitement is palpable as the six of us board the coach to Rhyl. One and a half hours later we reach our destination, the landlord waiting for us outside the so-called *chalet*.

What a shock! The place is an absolute dump. One small room with a Murphy bed and four other beds crammed together any which way. I open a door and ask:

"Is this the shower?"

This slumlord replies, "Where do you think you are, The Ritz?"

There's a small toilet. But if you actually sit on the bowl your knees will knock the door open. The only furniture is cheap aluminum beach chairs. My heart sinks. I can't stay here. It's disgusting. I find a phonebooth, call home, and tell Me-mum what a horrible place it is.

"Do you want your dad to come and get you?"

I say I do and that I'll call back later with all the info he'll need to find us. I get back to the *chalet* and see the girls have moved stuff around, pulled down the Murphy bed and opened the windows. Things start to look a little better. Our spirits lift. We put the furniture outside to make some room. Then we all jump onto the Murphy bed, tearing down half the wall it's attached to.

Laughing, we decide to make the best of a rotten situation. I call Me-mum and explain I'm staying, it's not so bad after all.

The nightlife in Rhyl is pretty lively, so we glam ourselves up and head to the local clubs. As usual Elaine is wearing one of her Mam's glamorous cabaret evening gowns with lurex threads adding some extra sparkle. Lynne is particularly taken with a local boy named Phil. The rest of us are happy to enjoy the music and a few drinks. When it's time to leave, Elaine tells us she's met a young man and she will not be coming back with us.

"See you later at the chalet!"

I sleep by the window all during our stay, so I'm a witness to a variety of events as I peer through the shabby curtains. One morning I'm awoken by the sound of the dustbin men collecting the rubbish. When I look, I see all the chalet's furnishings disappearing into the bowels of the truck! I wake everyone up and the general consensus is, "Fuck it, it was garbage anyway!"

Gradually, we realize Elaine has not come back at all and we're concerned. Just then, the door bursts open and there's Elaine standing in her evening gown, Lurex threads pulled out and snagged in every direction. She's positively disheveled.

"What happened to you," we ask, expecting the worst, terrified to hear the answer.

"I had to walk through the market to get back 'ere," she explains, fuming. "It was fucking crowded with all these Welsh women doing the shopping and my dress kept getting snagged on all their fucking wicker shopping baskets!" She throws herself down on the bed, despondent. "Me-mum don't know I borrowed this frock! She's gonna to kill me!"

Relieved, we all burst out laughing, collapsing on the Murphy bed and causing even more damage to the already wrecked wall.

In fact, my front row window seat on the comings and goings of life in this "luxury" holiday camp in North Wales is better than having a TV. I witness Elaine coming back from a date with her new love who drives a purple dune buggy. I see her legs dangling out of the low-slung buggy's door and hear her yelling, "owd de ye get out this fuckin fing?"

Then I'm startled one morning when I see a beady eye peering back at me through one of the holes in the curtains. It's terrifying until I realize the eyeball is attached to a mentally challenged young man called Bobby who has taken to visiting us on a daily basis. Nothing to be concerned about until he starts banging on the window and shouting, "I luf you! I luf you!"

He gets more and more frenzied and hits the window so hard he puts his hand through the glass. Shards scattered everywhere, Bobby so shocked and frightened he runs away. The girls wake up and figure the best solution is to cover the broken window with some cardboard.

Home improvement, Wythenshawe style.

The rest of the holiday is a blast. Lining up for showers at the disgusting communal wash rooms; hours spent prepping and preening for another night on the town; mornings spent laughing in our cramped and broken-down sleeping quarters. Laughing that kind of laugh that feels better than any other. That laugh when you're lying down and recounting the night's adventures with your closest girlfriends—that laugh is one of the most magical feelings in life.

What started as a nightmare has turned into one of the most brilliant and fun times of our lives. As we sit on our suitcases outside the blitzed-out chalet, waiting for taxis to take us to the bus station, I see a car bumping along the potholed road.

"Ere, what kind of car did the landlord have?"

"Blue Cortina."

"Shit, here he comes!"

We pick up our suitcases and take off running, platform shoes and all. We don't get very far when he catches up with us, screaming about the mess we've made of his *chalet*.

"And where's me tubular metal framed chairs!"

To which we reply: "Where's the fucking luxury chalet!"

We keep running. He tracks us down, though, and we send him some money for the damages. In the end, it's money well spent. We had a blast. And Lynne left something in Wales: her heart. This was the beginning of her great romance with Phil, the local Welsh boy.

Back at the Marist nothing much is changed other than me now attending classes with students a year younger than myself, which isn't too bad. It's not like I look older than the rest of the class. I'm not massively tall and don't have huge boobs like Moira Buxton. And I don't have masses of dark hair sprouting from my crotch, barely contained by underwear, like Margaret over there. After a humiliating first few days, it's pretty easy to fit in. I still visit the sixth form common room and have a cigarette between classes with the girls. It's commonplace to smoke in certain areas of the school as long as you're sixteen. Most girls smoke No. 6, Benson and Hedges, or maybe Embassy. But I'm privy to a library of cigarette brands at Fitton's so I always smoke something a little more special. Some days it's a St. Moritz, which is a long white cigarette with a large flashy gold band circling the filter. Other days, it's a cocktail cigarette named Sobranie, which comes in a pack of twenty and all the colors of the rainbow—pink, yellow, magenta, turquoise, lilac—and the whole filter is gold.

What a tit I must look like sitting in my school uniform with a lilac cigarette dangling from my mouth!

Such is the need for cigarettes in school that the local sweet shop sells them individually. I'm considering entering the market too with my fabulous tobacco products via Fitton's. But the gritty girls of Manchester aren't that interested in pretty cigarettes. They want maximum nicotine unfiltered for instant gratification.

The plan now is for me to take the few subjects required to help me pass the O Levels I need for the local art school. If I accomplish this, then I can go on to take the A Levels, which I'll only need in two subjects. Missus Edwards suggests that, since I passed O Level Art with the highest grade possible, and seeing that I'm going to be in school for another three years, I should start working on my A Level Art at the same time as I'm working on my O Levels. This way I can take my A Level Art while I still have one year left of school and use the following year to concentrate on my other subjects. Also, this will give me a chance to re-sit my A Level Art if I don't score high enough for the art school on my first try.

Brilliant idea. But the best part is I need art class and Missus Edwards to stop me from exploding.

Plan in place. It's time for me to get to work.

The next couple of school years are uneventful. Most of my friends are off in the big world working, getting pregnant, having babies, getting pregnant, divorcing, getting pregnant. I keep a low profile and any downtime I have—if I'm not smoking ridiculous cigarettes in the common room—is spent hanging around the art room. Often, I help Missus Edwards with a class of younger students and run errands for her.

One day she asks me to go to Miss Mercer's classroom and request two sheets of foolscap paper.

"No, no, no, anything but that!" I plead. "I'll do anything for you but please don't ask me to go to Miss Mercer's classroom."

"Don't be silly."

I reply I wouldn't do this for anyone but her and off I go.

I walk across the courtyard and up five flights of stairs, then along the corridor to Mercer's classroom, all the time going over in my head what I will say and how to follow the correct protocol. I am not going to give that bitch any reason to attack me with her viciousness.

Deep breath, knock twice on the door, count three seconds, then enter her domain. There's a class of twenty-three fourth-year students all sitting attentively, which I take into consideration. I then execute my plan:

"Excuse, Miss Mercer, I am terribly sorry for interrupting your lesson, but Missus Edwards wondered if you could possibly spare two sheets of foolscap paper."

Pretty good, I think. The right amount of respect and to the point.

Mercer stands up straight, glares into my eyes and, with seething jaw clenched responds:

"Mary Hession, do you know what I would like to do with those sheets of foolscap paper?"

Don't do it. Don't do it. But she's standing there waiting for a response, so I have to.

"No, Miss Mercer, what would you like to do with the two sheets of foolscap paper?"

Lamb to the slaughter. Why can't I be brave like George Clancy and call her a fucking cunt? No, I stand there waiting for her response and in true form she doesn't disappoint.

"I would like to scrunch it up in a ball and ram it down your throat!"

She's got a bunch of young girls as an audience who giggle and titter while I stand there in silence pinching my leg so I won't give her the satisfaction of seeing me fold up and cry. And after what seems like a lifetime, she realizes she is not going to get a rise out of me. Disappointed, she hands me the foolscap paper. I calmly leave the room and, as I walk away, can still hear the laughter. I go straight into the toilets and throw up. I wash my face with cold water to calm down and head back to the shelter of Missus Edwards' classroom. I hand her the paper and she thanks me, adding:

"See, that wasn't so bad, was it?"

10.

Outside of school I still have my job at Fitton's and still have the girls to keep me sane. There's not as much going out anymore, as I have to study and Lynne is now in a steady relationship with Phil, the boy she met in Wales. This means every Friday she gets the bus into Manchester and then a train to Colwyn Bay.

Lynne has gone from a city girl to a country girl. She spends her weekends sitting by her man as he fishes, or plods alongside him as he hunts for game in the farmlands of North Wales. No more fashionable clothes for Lynne. It's all waterproof jackets and wellies. And she loves it. It's just as well, as Phil never wants to come to the big city, which he detests. I miss Lynne so much and still go over to see her mam when I have a chance.

Finally, I pass the minimum required O Levels with the lowest acceptable passing scores. Now all I have to do is concentrate on getting a couple of A Levels and I'm free and clear of this hell hole of learning. As well as Art, I have to take A Level English language and English literature. A fresh face—well, as fresh as an eighty-year-old face can be—arrives at the Marist to teach these subjects.

Missus Hughes.

She's elegant, stern, and with a wicked sense of humor. She's come out of retirement to teach again and, as she lives miles away in the beautiful Lake District, she must be a little crazy to abandon that idyllic setting and come here to Chorlton-cum-Hardy. When she comes into class the first time, wearing her smart tweed suit, her hair in an unusual bun reminiscent of Katherine Hepburn in her later years, she asks each of us to stand and introduce ourselves. When it comes my turn, she sighs:

"Ah, yes, your reputation precedes you. I hope you don't live up to it under my charge."

Great start. I can't even blame my brother for this little black cloud I'm now under. But, as it turns out, Mrs. Hughes and I get along famously and her style of teaching is not unlike Missus Edwards'. As a result, I have nothing but respect for the Grand Dame of the Lakes.

Turning seventeen means I'm now old enough to drive. I'm ready right out of the gate. I've saved enough money for driving lessons which I start the day after my birthday. As terrible a student as I am, I have no problem passing my driving test the first time, which is not a feat to be taken lightly. An added bonus is waiting for me in the garage when I get home after my victory. Me-dad has bought me my very own car—a 1962 Mini. It's a piss yellow color with a white roof. The body is a bit rusty in parts but it only has 13,000 miles on it. And Me-dad got it for a bargain: twenty pounds.

This car is my pride and joy and it takes me everywhere—as long as it's not raining. Now, in the North of England, the chances of it not raining are ridiculously slim on the sunniest of days. Though my Mini is otherwise very reliable, if driven in the rain water gets into the distributor and prevents it from starting.

But who cares about that! It's mine! I buy a few accessories to make it just a little more special. I replace the large skinny steering wheel with a twelve-inch leather bound one that is "dropped" so it sits low into my lap. Then I replace the long wiggly gear stick with a short heavier model and, of course, a pair of bucket seats and a new radio.

No more buses for me. Now I zoom past the cemetery on Nell Lane with my radio blaring. I'm the first girl in school to have a car. So, of course, Sister Hairy has to interfere. It is decreed that I cannot park my car in the school parking lot.

Not a problem. I park right alongside the main school building where it sits all day waiting for me. Once that final bell rings, I'm out the door and in my car. No more trudging past all those graves. No more having to worry about the perverts jumping out from behind a tombstone and dropping their drawers as I walk alone on those dark winter nights after the many team practices. No, I'm free and clear. I fly past everybody, happy to be out of school. Sometimes I'm a little too zippy and as I fly along, passing a stream of slow coaches, feeling very full of myself, I discover I'm passing a funeral cortège and find myself and my Mini neck and neck with another coffin.

Under Missus Edwards' guidance I take my A Level Art exam. Unlike O Levels, the grades are simpler. A, B, and C are passes, D and E fails. I'm pretty confident I'll pass but I'm not sure what grade I'll get. The pressure is lessened by knowing if I get a low score, I can retake the test in one year and try to improve it. But the result comes in and I'm shocked to see I've earned an A. This means I can now just focus on passing my English courses.

My goal for college is a local school in Stockport, a neighboring town. I do a tour of the place and I'm impressed enough. I tell Missus Edwards about my visit and that I'm going to apply there. But she sits me down and says she doesn't think I should go to Stockport. She thinks I should aim higher and apply to Manchester University's foundation course.

Manchester!!!

Are you serious? Manchester has the best foundation course in the country. People come from all over to participate in it. I don't stand a chance of getting into Manchester!

But Missus Edwards disagrees. She says if we spend my last year in high school working on my portfolio, she is very confident I will be accepted. To boost my confidence, she even asks another teacher's son, who is currently attending Manchester, to bring in his portfolio. The young man arrives and proudly shows us his work.

What a realization! His work is very ordinary and, in a flash, I know I can do much better.

New plan: work on my portfolio and apply to some of the better Universities offering a foundation course, Manchester being the top choice.

All my applications are sent off and I have several interviews. Manchester is just a thirty-minute drive. Birmingham and Liverpool are both train rides. And, besides, the second I walk into Manchester art school I know this is where I want to be. The ancient Gothic vaulted ceilings, the creaky floor boards, the connected modern annex. I love the bustle and the paint-spattered arty kids strolling around, completely opposite of me in my fashionable striped flared pants and platform shoes. But I feel this will be a perfect fit for me.

I've been warned that some of the interview processes in art schools can be a little different. When I walk into the Dean's office, he's sitting there holding up a newspaper to his face. After a few seconds, nothing happens. I wait. Still, nothing until he says:

"Get my attention."

What a looney, I think. How am I supposed to get his attention? If he knows I am sitting here, then I have his attention, right? I take out my cigarette lighter and set fire to his newspaper.

This gets his attention.

He jumps up, drops the paper, and stomps on it.

"Very good, very good!"

He calms down, sits at his desk, asks me a couple of questions and looks over my work. Then:

"Thank you, goodbye."

Missus Edwards doesn't seem too impressed when I tell her about this interview.

"You actually set fire to his newspaper?"

My other interviews are much more straightforward: a look at my portfolio, a couple of questions, done. English results come in and—thank God for the wonderful Missus Hughes—I pass both language and literature. No A's, but a respectable B and C. Enough to get me out of the Marist and, hopefully, into a decent art school.

The letters start arriving. I'm accepted to Birmingham, then Liverpool but nothing yet from Manchester. Maybe they're thinking they didn't want a pyromaniac in their fine establishment.

But at least I'm accepted to a couple of programs, I remind myself. But they are not what I want. I'm also not ready to leave home and all me mates. I'm unsettled. Day in day out, no news from Manchester and I'm going mad. Then—plonk—the post comes crashing through our letter box. A big manila envelope with the Manchester University logo in one corner. I'm scared to open it. Maybe it's a bill for fire damage in the Dean's office. I take a deep breath. I rip it open and—yes, I'm accepted.

I'm accepted to the best foundation course in Great Britain.

I'm accepted.

Part Two

11.

There's an Irish saying that if you ever want to return to a place, look back over your shoulder when you're leaving it. So, walking out through the gates of the Marist high school for the last time I hold my head rigidly facing forward, not wanting to risk being dragged back into the hell hole I've inhabited for the past eight years. Me-mum has one final gesture for Sister Sheila, though. She sends flowers with a card that reads: "Thank you for all you did for Mary. And you know what that was."

Goodbye, goodbye, goodbye. I know the rest of my life can only be an improvement and I'm ready to move on. First order of business is to seek full time employment for the summer and take advantage of the fact that, as a student, I will not have to pay income tax. The plan is to work as many hours as possible with as much overtime as I can lay my hands.

It pays to have friends in high places and it just so happens that my sister works, for many years now, at a large meat factory called Walls. Walls is an enormous operation which produces pork product sausages, meat pies, bacon, black pudding—all vital to the North of England's discriminating palette. There are four thousand employees that work 'round-the-clock shifts to fill the vast appetite for these savory delights.

The nearest town is Hyde—or as the locals pronounce it, "eede." Whole families work alongside each other and the operation begins with the arrival of endless trucks filled with squealing pigs to be dropped off at the slaughter house, only to emerge in neat packages of breakfast fodder.

Me-sister guarantees me a position in the main factory and assures me I'll be given one of the cushier jobs. Feeling very confident due to my rosy future, I'm eager to begin work. I'm told to arrive half an hour before my 6:30 a.m. shift so I can be trained for the task at hand.

I show up in my racy little souped-up Mini, freshly showered and hair perfectly coiffed, and report for duty. I'm introduced to my supervisor who is happy to meet me as I'm, "Madeleine from wages' sister." I'm given a locker and my uniform. It consists of a very large drab green coverall over which is worn a plastic full-length apron, shiny white wellingtons and, to cap it all off, a huge white hair net.

This is certainly a shock to my system. But I stuff my Farah Fawcett hair into this hideous hair net and am led onto the factory floor. All is quiet as there is a shift change in progress, massive pie making machines and rows of ovens roaring in anticipation of the work day. The job I'm given is to be a part of the Grovesnor Pie department.

I've seen Grovesnor Pies in the butchers all my life but have never put much thought into where they came from. Basically, a Grovesnor Pie is a long brick shaped pie with an outer crust. The contents are chopped pork. And the crowning glory is a hardboiled egg in the center of the meat. Served in slices, the desired result is a piece of pie with the crust, meat and a slice of egg. The part of the assembly line I'm assigned to is the boiled egg department.

I'm sat down at a garbage can and my instruction begins. First, you reach behind yourself and retrieve a hardboiled egg from a three-foot-tall container. Next, you tap the egg on the metal bar, peel the egg, rinse it in a bowl of water and then throw it into another large black container. It is all a question of rhythm: grab, crack, rinse, throw, next.

My supervisor is duly impressed with how I master this so effortlessly and I wonder why I've been allocated thirty minutes for the training that I conquered in five.

A siren bellows, signaling the beginning of the shift and I sit there waiting for my egg peeling colleagues to join me. In comes an avalanche of workers all attired in identical clothes. As they all walk past me, I wonder who is going to join me at the egg table. Then I hear tap, tap, tap, and look over to see a dwarf leading a blind woman with a white cane. They take their places beside me. The blind woman, Hilda, on another chair and the dwarf, Vera, standing on a box. I introduce myself and make what I think is a witty comment about us having matching names, Moya, Vera, and Hilda. That goes down like a bucket of hardboiled eggs on a factory floor.

Another siren, the signal to commence work.

There's a frenzy of egg peeling, rinsing and throwing. I keep up with my associates and think my sister, true to her word, got me a cushy job. Apart from the smell of ten thousand eggs being peeled, it isn't so bad.

Then it happens. Thwack—a boiled egg right in the face. Two minutes later: thwack! Another one.

Hilda, the blind woman, is tossing eggs every which way. And every time she hears an egg slap me in the face, she says in a squeaky little voice, "emmm sorry." If she isn't hitting me in the face with an egg, she's missing the barrel. Unsuspecting workers are slipping and crashing as they come into contact with these slippery orbs.

The frenzy of the eggs continues until my face is becoming raw. The water splashing around creates another hazard. I hear a crash and see Vera lying on her back on the wet floor, her little arms and legs wriggling as she tries to right herself, her box kicked aside. I run over to help and try making light of the awkward situation by joking, "Good job you didn't have too far to fall!"

That does it. She jumps up, fist clenched, and snarls: "Who the fuck are you! Do you want to take it outside!"

Obviously, I don't want to fight her as I don't fight girls or woman. Plus, I know she'd beat the shit out of me. Thankfully, the siren sounds for the first tea break. I run to the offices, looking for my sister. When she sees me her first question is: "What's the matter with the side of your face?"

"Oh! That would be the side that Hilda sits on."

Me-sister, in her usual, wonderful, everybody-loves-Madeleine manner, says: "Ah, Hilda! She is a sweetheart."

"Actually, Madeleine, she is a fucking egg throwing terrorist! You have to get me a different job before I have no flesh on the right side of my face!"

I go back to my station, trying to position myself out of the way of this blind heat-seeking egg thrower.

Next day, though, when I report for duty, I'm informed I've been relocated to the pork pie department. Again, some training is required and this is far more complicated. There are four women to a machine. A tray of small pie dishes are filled with dough and lined up on a rolling sloping shelf. The object is for the first woman to grab the pie dish with her right hand and put it on a circular base that rotates so that a hammer-like mechanism can squash the dough into the form of a pie base. Then, with the left hand, she takes the pie base and puts it on a conveyor belt where the next woman slaps a dollop of mushed pie filling into it. And then on it travels to the next woman who places on the pie's top. Finally, it's onto the conveyor belt again to complete its journey into the enormous fire breathing dragon of an oven.

The skill here is quite demanding, coupled with the pressure being put on me by my fellow pie makers. I'm told in no uncertain terms that, as there are bonuses allotted for pie production, they're not happy to have me, a novice, on their machine potentially slowing them down.

I'm a nervous wreck. It's not an easy task keeping up with these women who have worked together for more than twenty years. And there are a couple of attempts to sabotage my progress. The men who load the dough into the pie tins think it's hysterical to form the dough in the shape of male genitalia to shock the little school girl. I get great satisfaction placing the dough penis on the machine and glancing over at their snickering as the hammer squishes it into a pie crust.

After a couple of days, I'm up to par and become a welcome addition to the group. We have rivals on the other machines whom we cream with our speedy and prolific out lay. A couple of times I'm asked to fill in over in the sausage department.

Again, a group of male coworkers can't wait to see my reaction when I'm put in charge for the first step of the sausage production. I'm told to stand at the feeder machine and just make sure the skin of the sausage doesn't twist. Basically, it's like placing an enormous condom onto a tube. It seems pretty straightforward until the feeder is turned on and an enormous sixty-foot sausage is between my fingers, much to the delight of the men. And as if this isn't bad enough, I then have to control this monster sausage and slam it onto a table where twenty women are waiting to twist it into links.

I'm happy to return to my pie makers.

I become close to a group of women at Walls. I meet some of the greatest people there whose attitude is not unlike Mrs. B. If they put the time and effort into a night out, they are going to have the best possible time they can, regardless of if it's down the local or off to the labor club. I never hear on Monday morning that a night was a wash out. It is always the greatest night ever.

There is Doreen and Doris, two huge West Indian women who work the ovens. When they're particularly hot, they stand in front of the massive industrial fans, lifting their overalls up and wailing "WHEEEEEEEE!!!" If I don't have any overtime, I often give them and their friend, Sidney, a ride home. Sidney is an equally large West Indian man with one large gold tooth, plucked eyebrows, mascara, and a penciled in mustache above his full lips.

After our shift, we change and wait for Sidney, who totters over in stiletto sling-backs. He bursts into a loud soprano and announces the day is done. Then they all squeeze into my Mini and the car is filled with a variety of sweet perfumes. Sometimes we stop at a red light and Doris returns the stare of a car full of people alongside us and says: "Lukka all dem peeples lookin at us! They be wundering why is dat little white gurl drivin dem bunch."

I love to see Doris walking with her best friend, Vera—Doris six feet tall and very round beside Vera who's just three feet high and keeping up with her. Doris with her huge belly laugh, brightening any day.

The work is hard and the days are long but the characters are the salt of the earth. And once they get to know me, I'm admitted into their circle. I'm even invited to a lunchtime birthday celebration for which there is extensive planning: who is bringing what delicacies ("no Walls products!"); who will supply a cassette tape player with an extension cord and suitable music? The venue: the ladies locker room and toilets. This means that anybody not invited needs to find alternative washroom facilities. The extension cord is draped over the tops of the lockers and plugged in to an outlet near the door. The actual party is literally in the toilets. Trays of food placed on all available surfaces, including the sinks and the toilet bowls. The music is cranked and ten women—who have all changed clothes for the thirty-minute celebration—dance and sing their hearts out. These wonderful women make a party in a Victorian era meat factory toilet seem like it is the best disco in town.

The siren blows. Lunch is over in five minutes. And with tremendous efficiency the toilets are back to normal and there is no sign of the festivities that have just occurred.

12.

Early mornings and as much overtime as Walls can give me, means I have funds for art supplies and some new clothes. I apply for a grant, too, but because I'm living at home and Me-dad is still working, I'm awarded only a small amount. But that's fine with me as I have every intention of keeping my various jobs, which now includes four nights bartending at Me-cousin's pub, "The Spread Eagle." Me-dad very proudly announces that his company is aware of my further education and they are going to award me a scholarship of five hundred pounds! Five hundred pounds is more than Me-dad makes in six weeks! He's delighted.

After enduring eight years at the Marist, I have no idea what college life will entail. I board the same bus I'd taken to school all those years but this time I'm not wearing the blue and gold uniform. And as I sail past the Marist bus stop, I'm overwhelmed with relief that the nightmare is over.

My main class at Manchester University is situated in the old Gothic wing of the school. My homeroom tutor is Katy. Yes, Katy. No Miss, no Missus, no having to stop when Katy passes me on the stairs, no having to watch my mouth, no raising my hand when I have a question, no being made to stand in the corner, no getting Saturday detention and having to sew dust rags for the nuns. This is nothing like school. And I love it. But the classes are tough and the standards high. I know instantly that my talent is average and some of my contemporaries are exceptionally talented. I'm intimidated.

The foundation course is a requirement I must fulfill before going on to obtain a bachelor's degree. This course introduces you to the varying disciplines of art before you decide what to specialize in. Classes in graphic design, ceramics, fine art, textile design, fashion, industrial design, and photography are required. I'm sure I'm going to study textile design but experimenting in the other subjects is fun.

The tutors are a mixed bunch of characters, some of whom hang out at the student bar after class. This, again, blows my mind, having just come to terms with the idea that you do not have to be a sadist to be a teacher. Our fine art tutor, Stan, has a wooden leg just like Long John Silver. He can be heard all over school as his leg thumps and echoes through the hallways.

My first class on Wednesday, drawing, is with Stan. He shows us how to sharpen pencils with a surgeon's scalpel and how to sharpen the scalpel's blade. Stan is very proud of the fact that he has been using the same blade for twenty years. I don't have the heart to tell him he can buy a pack of a dozen blades for under a pound at the school shop.

I get to class early and wait for the others to arrive when this gorgeous young man comes into the room.

"Is this Drawing One B?"

"Yes," I reply, thinking: thank God! New blood!

Because our class is comprised of twelve girls and one boy interested in textiles and fashion, we're short on good looking blokes. His name is Greg and he's very pleasant. We're chatting for a while when, though it's not that hot in the room, he starts taking his clothes off.

"You want me to open a window?"

"No, thanks," he replies. "I don't like drafts.

But, holy shit, now the pants are coming off! He's down to his drawers. What the fuck is going on? Thankfully, I hear the clunk, clunk, clunk of Stan approaching.

"Ah, I see you have met Greg."

Met him? I am practically engaged to the man!

Now he is completely naked. A couple of girls from class walk in, spin around and leave, saying they're going to grab a cup of tea and will be right back, giggling their way out of the room.

Well, the class begins and we are taught to hold out our pencil towards the part of the body we are drawing. Stan clunks around and observes that the drawings seem to have a void and negative space where Greg's ample manhood should be.

What do you expect? We're all fresh out of high school and here we are sitting with a naked man, legs akimbo, staring into our eyes while we measure the proportions of his willy! I know one thing: I am not taking this drawing home. The priest will be around in two seconds flat, armed with a *Brillo* pad to scrub away the massive purple splotches on my soul!

Art school is more than I ever hoped for. Sometimes it's a little strange but it's interesting to see the metamorphosis of some students once they become comfortable with their new surroundings. One young man, Pete, comes from a remote village in Wales. He's wide eyed and nerdy. But within a few weeks he's transformed into a crazy and wild avant-garde artist who believes everything he touches is a masterpiece. I pass his room one day and he's rigged up a crane kind of thing which hoists him ten feet in the air while he eats a bowl of baked beans.

Genius art, apparently.

Another time, I see Welsh Pete come in from the cafeteria with a carton of milk which he throws against the wall. He watches the liquid splatter all over the place. Studies how it drips.

Hey, genius, who's going to clean up this mess!

Nothing is off limits in Pete's pursuit of Art. His *pièce de résistance*, which he proudly shows to everybody, is his ability to put a toothbrush up his arse and make it go in and out.

I'd say his parents must be so proud until I run into some of his friends a few years later and learn that Welsh Pete, having gone home for Christmas, found his parents had moved out without having told him where they'd gone to. Imagine sending your child off to a prestigious art school and he comes back and shows you what he can do with a toothbrush. Oh, and do you have any milk, Mam, because you will love what I can do with that!

Anyway, I've got my own issues. As much as I'm enjoying college life, I'm definitely struggling with the work. I'm not comfortable creating pieces in front of my peers and open class critiques are terrifying. My work is way below standard, which is obvious to all. My tutor, Katy, asks to meet me and says in her brash northern manner that my work's crap and she can't tell how I was even accepted into the foundation course.

"Forget about going on to get your degree. You won't even get into a community college." Still, she's willing to help me in any way she can. "But you've got to put what little talent you have to better use."

Wow. A hard blow. But I'm still standing. My biggest problem is how self-conscious I am about my work and being exposed to people's criticism. Nevertheless, according to Katy, I do have *a little* talent I can make better use of. So, the first thing I do is stop working at the pub. The next is trying to figure out what my inspirations are. I spend time in the library, go to museums and galleries, and meet with Katy as often as I can. She encourages me.

Christmas vacation for me is working back at Walls. It's great to see all my old colleagues again. But working on the assembly line of a meat factory also reminds me I've been given a great opportunity in being accepted to the foundation course at Manchester and I cannot let it slip away. After the holidays, I'm back in class, working hard, making friends, my confidence growing, and my skin getting thicker during class critiques. The next two semesters are all about developing skills and honing a portfolio that can get me into a decent art school. I have no clue where I'm going to go but I know I should probably move away from Manchester. There are many brilliant art colleges in England, the most desirable being in London, which I assume is clearly out of my league.

But Katy's is frankly surprised when she sees what I'm now capable of. My work is improving. My critiques are generally positive and, at last, I'm comfortable standing in front of my peers while they discuss my work. Appointments are scheduled with personal tutors to discuss where one should go to study for one's degree. My jaw drops when Katy suggests I apply to Central School of Art and Design in London.

"Are you serious," I ask. "I don't have a chance! There's only thirteen places available and hundreds of people apply every year."

"If you keep going in the direction you're going now, I think you might have a chance."

Still not convinced, a little woozy, I say, "I'll give it a try."

But now I've got London on the brain. Most of my classmates are applying to Northern schools. That doesn't appeal to me now and I forge ahead, sights set on the capital! I fill out my application and send it off. The next few weeks are a frenzy of new work, most of which is done on the pine table in our tiny dining room. Me-mum is very patient as I completely take over the room and fill it with all kinds of materials. She's constantly coming into see me with mugs of tea and biscuits. She looks at my work, puzzled, but always says:

"Oh! Aren't you clever!" (Just like the time she saw my drawing of the male genitalia for a biology class in high school: "Hmmm, is that a tree?" "Yes, Mum. It's the tree of life.")

Katy and I go through my work, sorting what's going in the portfolio and what I still need to work on. Weeks of organizing, mounting, and cleaning finally comes to an end and I'm ready for my interview at Central School.

13.

I'm a complete wreck as I board the bus into Manchester, then the train to London's Euston station. And now the terrifying last step—the Tube.

I'd only visited London once before, with Missus Edwards and my high school class. That time, I managed to get separated from everyone when the Tube doors opened and I stepped in. I turned back as they shut again and I see Missus Edwards and the class still standing on the platform. Panicked, I nevertheless had the sense to get off at the next stop and head back to where I thought my class would be. My instincts were correct and Missus Edwards said she was happy that it was me that got lost as she knew I'd figure out how to deal with the situation.

Well, here I am again with another situation.

Map in hand, I manage to navigate my way to St. Holborn's Station. Thankfully, my appointment is in the early afternoon because there's no way I could make it through London's rush hour with my ridiculously large portfolio. At last, I am standing outside the venerable Central School of Art and Design feeling very overwhelmed. I see there is a public toilet so I decide to go and check myself in the mirror. There's a bathroom attendant who can see I'm nervous. I smile at her and explain:

"I have an interview at Central."

She smiles back and nods: "Good luck. You look terrible. You should have worn something better."

What a cow! I think I looked pretty great, myself, in my navy and white pinstriped jeans, tucked-in granddad shirt, a pair of cool braces and smart brown wedged brogues—all inspired by the high fashion pages of the shiniest teen magazines of 1976!

Sitting outside the dean's office, there's couple of super trendy girls waiting ahead of me. I sit patiently as each girl goes in and out, quite rapidly. My name is called and there's this crew of arty looking people looking so fabulous. I'm invited to sit down and show my work. As I unzip my portfolio, I'm asked about my unusual name. What's its origin?

I take a big gulp and say: "It's Swedish."

Instantly, I'm ashamed. But not ashamed enough to take back the lie and make a joke about it. I'm not sure being Irish is okay in London.

They peruse my work quite indifferently and ask a few mundane questions.

"Have you ever had a job of any kind?"

Bingo! The doors of my personality open and I regale them with stories about peeling boiled eggs with Vera and Hilda, about being on a sausage assembly line, about all the brilliant characters I'd met at Walls. They're wide eyed with amazement as they enter the world of a working-class girl from "up north."

Interview over, I set off on my journey back home.

Back in school, things are less fraught and, overall, the atmosphere is much calmer. My friends and I spend more time at the Union Bar hanging out with the other students and faculty. Everyone's been through the same thing: work hard on the portfolio, get the appointment, go for the interview, show the portfolio.

And now it's all about waiting.

And then I see the most gorgeous man I've ever seen in my life. He's tall, lean and with long straggly blonde hair. Every girl has a crush on him. I watch from afar as he appears with a different girl on a daily basis. I learn his name is Mark and he's from East Africa, a mature student of twenty-five. Our eyes meet a couple of times but we never speak.

One day, I'm running up a flight of stairs, trying to get to class, when I see him coming towards me. I blush and smile. He makes some cocky remark about me rushing and then says:

"There's going to be a party Friday night and everybody's going. You should come too."

My insides are doing cartwheels but I calmly reply like I have tons of things to do on Friday: "Sounds like fun. I'll see."

But of course, I'm going. I literally count the seconds until Friday night and persuade a couple of girls to join me. But at the party there's no sign of the gorgeous Mark. I sit on the floor with my head down, thinking about how I'll get myself home, when I notice a familiar pair of ratty sneakers standing there before me. I raise my eyes up over the long legs, the shirt front and, finally, to Mark's smiling face.

"Glad you made it!"

Well, that's that. We start dating immediately and are hardly ever out of one another's sight. He meets my parents, is comfortable in our home, he's not horrified that I live in Wythenshawe and that I'm not posh.

This is turning out to be the greatest year of my life.

And even though, dating Mark, I'm often gratefully distracted from the anxiety of my application to Central, there I am again waiting impatiently for another letter of acceptance to plonk through our letter box. Mark, too, has applied to a college just outside London. So, my head is also crowded with all of life's rich possibilities: school, maybe a job, and a boyfriend in London!

Unless, of course, I don't get accepted.

But I do. I get accepted.

I watch the familiar manila envelope slide in through the letterbox and tumble to the hallway floor. I walk over and look down at the unfamiliar London post mark and the Central School of Art logo, carry it in to the dining room and sit at the table, opening it slowly. Delighted and terrified at once, I read I'm one of thirteen students accepted to study Textile Design.

Me-dad is set to retire during my year at Manchester. His company sends him to a retirement course to give him ideas of how to spend his time when he stops working. He comes home after his day of instruction and has us in stitches explaining what he's learned.

"Well, today they took me to Tatton Park, gave me a bag of peanuts and sat me down by a barbed wire fence. They showed me how to stick a peanut in the fence and wait for a bird to swoop down and eat it."

If it weren't so silly it would be sad. Me-dad's still very active and as strong as an ox and here he is literally being put out to pasture with a bag of peanuts. But Me-dad has other ideas about how he'll be spending his time. He keeps threatening to become a lollipop man and stand outside my school just to embarrass me. But he's offered several jobs, one of which is part time work with the company he's just retired from. He also keeps busy with his garden allotment, helping out at church bingo on Friday nights and, as usual, he's always busy helping somebody fix something.

As his final days at work draw near, we plan a big surprise celebration at a local pub. All Me-dad's siblings come, some even flying in from Ireland for the big "do." There's great excitement as we send him off to see a fictitious event at said pub. The brother is in charge of getting him out the door and just before they're about to leave, Me-dad says he's not going. He has no interest in going to a pub. More likely, he just doesn't want to go anywhere with his nightmare son.

Anyway, after much cajoling, off they go.

Everybody's waiting patiently at the venue. Me-dad walks in and there's a loud chorus of, "Surprise!"

He stops, turns around and heads back out, saying, "This is the wrong room. There's a wedding going on in there."

But then he sees familiar faces smiling at him, faces from far away and long ago. He laughs and cries, completely overwhelmed. It's a great night, filled with love and admiration and the party carries on to our house afterwards. Me-uncle Joe has his fiddle, Me-dad his tin whistle. I'm asked to dance a hard jig or hornpipe, which is not very impressive on a carpet. So, Me-dad goes out and lifts the garage door off its hinges, bringing it back in and laying it in the center of the living room. It's a great night of music, dancing, and, of course, the wonderful storytelling. There's also a lot of discussion of me going off to the "smoke," as Me-dad calls London. He's concerned, but his brothers reassure him: "Ah, the girl's got her head screwed on straight!"

And I hope I do.

14.

I'm more and more anxious as the time approaches to move to London. I'm sad to be leaving my home. I keep breaking down in tears, worrying how Me-mum will cope with me leaving. Somehow, I think Me-dad will be fine. But Me-mum, I'm convinced, will be devastated.

The day arrives and we load up my car. Sobbing uncontrollably, I hug her goodbye and she says:

"Come on, get a hold of yourself. I'm glad to see the back of you!"

That's a bit of a shock. Not so much as a tear. She's looking off at the bad weather. Meanwhile, I go to hug Me-dad and his shoulders start shaking. He falls to his knees, weeping! Me-mum hurries me out the door and the two of them stand in the driveway waving me off.

It's pouring rain and I'm crying the whole way, tears streaming down my face, rain pouring down the windshield, wipers swishing back and forth. And I know I better not stop because if rain gets into the distributor cap, I won't be able to start the car again.

The plan is to drive to North London and meet Mark, who's

visiting his sister. From there, he'll accompany me to my halls of residence in South London. It takes me four hours to reach North London from Manchester and another two to make it to South London. At one point, we board a ferry and I think we might be leaving England! What do I know? It was quicker to get to France that time I went with the girls. But at long last we arrive at my halls of residence in Battersea. I'm met by a fellow student who takes me to my room. He opens the door and says:

"Welcome to your home for the next year!"

My heart sinks.

It's a little featureless room with a bed, sink, desk, and a large window overlooking a dreary council estate. There's communal bathrooms and two phones on each of the six floors. There's a large common room and a huge cafeteria. All my meals are included in the tuition and I know this is going to be a problem— I'm a finicky eater.

So, I say goodbye to Mark and start to unpack. I'm already homesick and I've only been gone forty-eight hours. The halls are bustling with people excitedly introducing themselves with a strange confidence completely alien to my northern sensibilities. Where I come from, we don't go around offering our hands to complete strangers. No, we quietly suss up the situation, avoiding eye contact at all times, and only then decide whether to partake in conversation. When asked where we come from the typical response from us up north is something like: "Never you mind where I come from," or, "What do you want to know for?"

As for my accent, that'll be a big giveaway and open the door to the usual, "Aye up lad, put cloth cap on, there's trouble at the Mill," plus a boatload of typical northern jokes. If they find out I'm Irish too there could be a bloodbath.

But there's no turning back now. This is my cross to bear. And, just to make that cross a little heavier, I decide I don't *need* to make friends. I have a boyfriend not too far away who I'll be able to see on weekends. Plus, I am here to study, not to have fun.

First day of school is the usual getting familiar with the set up and new surroundings. The rest of the week, we meet all our tutors and then there is a visit from the dean. She strides in with her staff, clad in designer gear from head to toe, and immediately recognizes me.

"Ah," the dean exclaims in her super posh accent, "here's the girl I told you about! She has the most marvelous stories. I can't remember her work, but she's very entertaining!"

I'm not sure this is a good thing. But, seeing as how I'm in an Art and Design program and not a Drama School, I keep my head down and try not to draw attention to myself.

Our group of thirteen is a mixed bunch. A few men and a lot of girls, all from pretty posh backgrounds. It's as though the wealthy send their girls to art school not as a career decision but more like: "Cordelia is very good at art. She *does* enjoy it *so*. It will be fun for her to pursue it before she marries Lord Somebody-or-Other from the bank." There's even a girl in my group whose name is Barclay, as in daddy *owns* a bank! There are students who went to boarding school with royalty, girls whose parents buy them actual houses in London rather than let them reside in some dreary halls of residence. Trust Fund is a new phrase I hear a lot and become familiar with. People are always "popping off to the country for the weekend," or taking "a little jaunt to Paris for a break!"

Paris! As far as I'm concerned, you can't pay me to go back to that stinking place.

So, I watch and observe and cultivate the big northern chip on my shoulder. And I tremble underneath when I see the formidable talent I'm now surrounded by. When the dean mentions my less than noteworthy work, I know she's right.

What am I doing here? I struggle all over again, intimidated, afraid I can't compete with the rest of the class. Again, a tutor takes me aside and can't believe I've even been accepted to the school. So, I'm miserable, missing home and the comfort of being with my own people back up north. I begin thinking I've made a big mistake and should transfer back to Manchester. London's not the place for me after all; struggling with my work, humiliating critiques, and the burden of my chosen exile—my decision *not* to make friends!

At least I have Mark, I console myself. As everyone makes friends and enjoys the wonderful things London has to offer, I return to my little room and wait for the weekend so I can get together with him.

But things are changing there too. Mark's attitude to his new surroundings is markedly different from mine. He's making friends, going to parties, and loving this great adventure. And as Mark's demanding social calendar fills up, he's not able to spend as much time with me as I want.

This is all unbearable.

Finally, we're going to a party at Mark's sister's house, which is always fun. But Mark's acting distant and begins picking fights with me. When we're alone, I confront him about this and, without a second's thought, he holds up the corner of the duvet in front of my face and punches me.

My head's reeling and, as I'm coming to terms with what just happened—bam!—another fist to the face.

Even in my confusion, I know this is it. I'm not going to be anybody's punching bag. I'd seen Me-sister allow all this, seen the pain on Me-dad's face at the sight of her all bruised and battered. That's not going to be the misery I bring back to his doorstep. I have a choice right here and now not to be a victim. I'm choosing it. My heart's broken and my only happiness is gone. But I'm going to get on with my life without the crutch of a boyfriend.

I get myself back to the school.

I'm still toying with the idea of transferring back to Manchester but I finally decide to make an effort. I'm beginning to suspect my biggest problem is Me-myself. I'm insecure. And there's a way insecurity can be turned into a kind of snobbishness. Who do I think I am, anyway?

I try to get involved with my peers. This is not easy, as most of them are now comfortable with their own sets of friends and I'm an outsider even though I've been there all along. But I work at it. If I learn nothing else in these dark days, at least I learn this: If you do not have friends, you have nothing.

So, after this, my first semester in London, I head home with a heavy heart and to my usual routine working at Walls for the Christmas rush. Me-mum and Me-dad are sad Mark's no longer in the picture, but they don't ask too many questions. Which is good. I can't tell them what's happened. That's better left alone.

Christmas up north is a very festive time and, of course, the ladies at Walls host their Christmas party in the lady's toilets. I help a friend from my foundation year get a job for the holidays. His name is Pat and he's probably the most talented and creative person I've ever met. He's an accomplished artist as well as musician. Plus: he's crazy.

His job at Walls is putting the tops onto the long Grovesnor pies. All is going well until he becomes bored by the monotony of it all and decides, in his sweet and naive way, to decorate the pies with little messages of glad tidings. Nobody notices his handiwork until Quality Control stops by and sees all Pat's best wishes carved into hundreds of pounds worth of pies. He isn't fired, but he's moved to a job where he can't come into contact with Walls products directly.

In our house, Christmas Eve is quiet, just the three of us. And that's how we like it; except, of course, for Midnight Mass with all the local drunks stumbling around. That's the best part of it all in my books. Christmas Day is the usual people stopping by for a glass of sherry or a beer. Then there's a dinner of turkey, potatoes, Brussels sprouts, peas, carrots, and sage and onion stuffing before Me mums infamous Christmas cake.

Me-mum made this cake back in June. Then it was sealed in a metal tin and stored beneath the bed until a few days ago when it was taken out and smothered in half an inch of marzipan and hard icing.

Ugh! The thought of eating a piece of this concoction makes me shudder. But Me-mum and Me-dad relish it and will continue having it as *afters* well into February.

After all the coziness of being at home for the day, I go off to the Bailey's house where there's bound to be a lot of boozing and *knees up* going on. Lynne is visiting from Wales where she now lives with her husband, Phil, and their two daughters. It's deemed a great night when the party gets so raucous Mister Bailey, who recently had a leg amputated, forgets all about it, jumps up to join in the dancing, and goes crashing to the floor.

"You stupid git!" calls Missus B.

But Mister Bailey is beside himself with laughter and the party goes on. Phil is feeling no pain either and is throwing one of the kids in the air. (Why is it when men get drunk and there's a child present their first instinct is to throw the poor mite up at to the ceiling?) Sadly, for Phil, the child he's "chukking" thrashes wildly and kicks his front two teeth out. It's a sure sign of a great night when there are actual physical scars to show off proudly the next day.

Meanwhile, I get some alone-time with Lynne out back and confess I'm still seriously debating whether to return to Manchester and give up on London. I tell her all my woes: my lack of confidence, fear that I'm untalented, the pressure of making friends, all about Mark. And in no uncertain terms Lynne tells me to snap out of it.

"Knock it off and get back to London, you! You've been given a great opportunity and I'm counting on you to go out into the big wide world, do things, and come back to share all your great experiences with me!"

She then explains her lot. She loves her family and her girls are everything to her. But she's living in the middle of nowhere and sometimes doesn't see another adult for days on end. Phil is happy out in the country, that's his world, but she feels her life is passing her by.

"It's what I chose and it's where I'll stay. But it's not exciting. For that, I count on hearing from you. So, I need you to wake up and get on with it."

How can I not go back to London now? And I get on with.

15.

I return to Central School of Art and Design. With a newfound groveling attitude, I'm determined to make friends and stop being such a snob. Truth be told, the thirteen students in my class are varied and interesting and now I need to assimilate and become part of the team. I'm still intimidated, of course. Open critiques still make me break out in a cold sweat. I'm still taken aside and lambasted for my inferior work and, again, I decide I can overcome all this.

At some point I realize I've got to stop worrying about whether or not I'm talented and, instead, just work hard at the tasks I'm given. I begin to understand the school is not trying to nurture in us some mysterious and ephemeral essence called talent, but to impart practical creative skills. So, Little Miss Wythenshawe begins working in earnest and doesn't have *time* to let anyone intimidate her. She churns work out like a machine and receives great reviews from teachers and peers alike.

This also opens doors to some valuable friendships and I'm suddenly in a world I didn't know existed. I discover that when you're at table you put your cutlery down at intervals and do not thrust your knife and fork in the air while making a point. You especially don't point with your fork when there's a big chunk of pork chop attached to it. I learn to place a napkin on my lap, not to stir my Vodka and Tonic with my finger, and how to order a meal in a restaurant. I learn that if you spill tea into a saucer, you do not pour the overspill into your cup. And, definitely, do not slurp tea from the saucer to cool it down.

Before long, with my new friends and acquaintances, I'm going to Covent Garden for cocktails after class. I'm eating at fine restaurants like San Lorenzo's and Mr. Chow's. I'm visiting friend's country homes and even traveling to Paris for a weekend to see the incredible city, really, for the first time. I visit the Louvre, the Pompidou Centre, walk along the Seine, drink wine at outdoor cafes and fall in love with the beauty of it all. What a difference it makes when you're not sleeping in the train station!

By the end of my second year at Central, a British entrepreneur named Freddie Laker makes my dream of going to America a possibility by introducing affordable flights to New York. I've saved some money from working at Walls and I've received another modest scholarship to help with tuition. But, even so, I can't afford a trip to America. So, sadly, I sell my Mini for ten times what Me-dad paid for it.

I'll make this trip with a friend, David, from my Manchester days. There's no romantic interest here, but I think it best to travel with a male companion. Our plan is to fly to New York and travel cross-country by Greyhound to the west coast after a short detour down south to New Orleans in Louisiana because David is a fan of the blues.

We arrive in New York on a rainy August, take a shuttle to the subway, and head into Manhattan, not knowing where we're going to end up. 34th Street sounds familiar to me, so we get off and head upstairs to the street.

The first thing I see is Macy's!

I look up and can't believe my eyes. I never imagined the buildings would be so huge! The roads are like corridors lined with building after building. The rain stops briefly and people are rushing about their business. Suddenly, the skies open up again and it starts pouring. Within seconds, from out of nowhere, men appear with armloads of umbrellas for sale. Cars are honking, people are yelling, "Taxi! Taxi!" A man in a uniform outside a hotel is blowing his whistle. The road is filled with enormous bright yellow cars with checkerboard patterns decorating the sides. The air is hot and very heavy, which I can't understand as the sky is grey and no sun is shining.

We stand outside some other large building, our jaws open in amazement, stunned by the sheer magnitude of it all. Then we realize we're looking at Madison Square Garden, the actual Madison Square Garden where Muhammad Ali fought Joe Frazier! It's right there, right in front of our eyes! Macy's, Madison Square Garden, yellow cabs, the noise and—best of all—the American accents!

The two of us stand there for a few minutes just taking it all in. We look like two dopey hicks, prime targets for a mugging if ever there was one or two. Reality sets in and the first order of business is to find a bathroom as I'm dying to pee. We head downtown to the fine and—more importantly—cheap YMCA we've arranged to stay at. We're given rooms on different floors where we dump our belongings before setting off to explore the great city.

It's everything and much more than I ever dreamed of. I'm loving it but the sheer hugeness of it all is a little frightening. After a while, we grab something to eat from a vendor on the sidewalk and head back to the YMCA to make it an early night. We want to be well rested for the next day's adventure. David goes off to his dreary little room and I go off to mine.

I fall asleep immediately only to wake a couple of hours later in a cold sweat. My head is spinning and I know I'm going to throw up. I drag myself down the darkened corridor, staggering from side to side, and find the communal bathrooms. I reach the stall just in time to vomit for what seems like hours. Finally, I collapse on the dirty floor and pass out, coming back to life every so often when I need to vomit some more.

Eventually, I can stand and step weakly out of the stall. I lunge for a sink and splash cold water on my face. Two girls applying makeup a few sinks away glance over and pause:

"Junkie," one of them whispers knowingly to the other.

I literally crawl back to my room. I can't call David as I don't know what room he's in. I call reception but nobody picks up

This is not what's supposed to happen. This is not what America is supposed to be like. I'm terrified I'm going to have to go to a hospital and pay thousands of dollars for treatment and sell all my belongings—which, of course, won't be enough. I'll be like the people you read about who go to America for a holiday, get sick and have to sell their homes to pay their medical bills. I make up my mind then and there to go back to England the very next day, where I can be as sick as I like—for free!

Morning comes and, miraculously, I feel fine. Actually, I feel great.

Maybe I'll stick around America, after all.

As arranged, I meet David in the cafeteria for breakfast and tell him of my dreadful night. He lifts his bruised thumb and informs me he's spent the night crushing cockroaches and hasn't slept a wink. We check out of the YMCA and learn of a better place from, incredibly, another couple of German travelers! (Those Germans definitely know how to travel!) We get ourselves situated in our new hotel, centrally located in the heart of Times Square.

Now, this is 1978; long before the area is cleaned up and made a family-friendly tourist attraction, and though the place is reasonably priced, David mentions how friendly the women outside the hotel are, always inquiring:

"You need anything, sugar?"

We pay a proper visit it to the world's largest department store: Macy's. I don't have any money to buy anything but David, I discover, can't resist a bargain. On a sweltering, humid, ninety-degree day in August, David buys himself a sheepskin coat suitable for tending sheep in the cold, wet, winter highlands of England. And now he's got to drag this around the United States of America for the next five weeks.

We walk every street, visit every park, look at every bridge, and marvel at it all. As we're finally heading out of the city on the Greyhound bus to begin our cross-country adventure, I look back at the skyline and know this is where I want to live.

Heading south, we travel at night so we can save money and sleep on the bus. It'll take some days to reach New Orleans. There are many stops in cities along the way. People get on, people get off. By the time night falls on the third or fourth day, we're rolling through Alabama and we're the only white passengers. As we cruise quietly past the lush, swampy landscape on either side of the road, in the middle of the night, a woman starts to sing in a melodic soulful tone. Then someone else joins in. Before long, everyone's lost in sweet, heartbreaking song.

David, the blues fan, is transfixed. And it does feel like we've been allowed into something very special. It's a privilege to be there.

Eventually, we reach New Orleans and look for cheap digs. We study our little student accommodation reference book and decide on a house in the Garden District. We take a streetcar there and discover a massive Victorian house. A tall, pale young man with dark hair answers the door and invites us into the immaculate, almost museum-like, home.

I feel uneasy.

He tells us the house rules and that we're the only guests. Then he stops mid-sentence as a cough is heard in another room:

"Okay, Mother! I'll be right there."

That's it for me. I'm practically running down the street when David catches up and stops me, bewildered.

"What's going on!"

I can't believe he needs to ask me this.

"Have you not seen Psycho?"

"The Hitchcock movie?"

"I am not staying at that creepy fucking house," I state plainly and move on.

We find a place downtown.

The energy of the city is joyful and contagious, especially at night. David is mesmerized by the music bursting from every doorway. We splurge on a riverboat trip down the Mississippi. But after twenty minutes, I'm ready to throw myself overboard. Brown water, green embankment, brown water, green embankment, more brown water and more and more green embankment. The worst part is knowing we will eventually turn around and travel back through the same brown water and green embankment. I'm happy, finally, to disembark and get back to the nightlife of The Big Easy.

Then west. Texas, New Mexico, Arizona. Brown desert, brown desert, brown desert, those pumpy-things looking for oil, more brown desert, brown desert, more brown desert. After seeing nothing but desert for days and days, the signs announcing our approach to Los Vegas start popping up. We start seeing these neat little houses, then more neat little houses, then neat little houses with immaculate green lawns! It's a sight for sore eyes until I realize the gorgeous green lawns are fake! Emerald green plastic grass! It's everywhere. And I swear I even see sprinklers watering this plastic grass.

But now we head into Vegas itself and I cannot be more excited. It does not disappoint.

I think back to my childhood and recall how fascinating the Blackpool Illuminations were. But this, Los Vegas, is like the Illuminations on acid times a million. The world-famous Strip with huge marquees emblazoned with the names of such stars as Frank Sinatra, Dean Martin, Jerry Lewis, Englebert Humperdink and—my teenage idol—Tom Jones!

(A Digression: During my crazy obsession with Tom Jones as a young girl, I would take a bath, wash and blow-dry my hair just to watch his TV show. Me poor mum camped out all night with me to get tickets to his concerts. One time, we were camping outside the Odeon in Manchester, hoping to secure great seats, when these two young men joined the line; two young men amongst over two hundred women. I thought it a little strange, them with their long hair and hippy outfits, they seemed the most unlikely of "Tom's" fans. It was only the next morning when the box office opened that they realized their error. They thought they were queuing for Rolling Stones' tickets! Poor sods. That would be a hard one to live down...)

We get off the bus and, again, do what we do so well by now: find the cheapest place to stay, stow our bags, and wander off to look around. But this time, it's into another world called Las Vegas. Millions of light bulbs, even in the bright light of day, that throw off a weird kind of heat, neon signs, the constant din of ringing slot machines, and the clatter of coins spilling out of rows and rows of brightly colored one-armed bandits.

I'm in kitsch heaven.

When I get back to college, I have to begin work on a theme for my degree show. And here I'm feeling very inspired. I'm planning it out in my head already: *The Art of Las Vegas*.

Besides the spectacular visuals, there's another fantastic side to Vegas in the seventies: free food and drink if you know where to find the millions of vouchers hidden throughout the town. After living on a student's shoestring budget for much of our adventure thus far, we cannot believe our luck.

"All you can eat!"

"Free cocktails!"

"Buy one get two free!"

This is the greatest place I've ever been. And the best is yet to come. David discovers that if you give a dollar bill to a cashier, you're given two dollars back in change!

This cannot be true! But it is. We're going to have full bellies and actually *make money* on this jaunt!

Of course, we were not born exactly yesterday, so we realize we're expected to gamble and spend money too. But we think we can get away with not doing so before the casino owners are on to us. So we go from casino to casino, methodically doubling our money. As we drift from place to place, our pockets bulge with coins and our bags get heavier and heavier. After a few hours we've made around fifteen dollars in change, not worth the risk of getting caught.

But we eat well.

We wander around with no clue what time of day it is. There's no clocks or windows in any of the casinos, so we're eating breakfast in the wee hours of the morning and having the occasional vodka and tonic at 9:30 a.m.

Well fed, tipsy, and totally disoriented, we decide that, for the sake of our sanity, we should probably continue our journey westward.

Even though I'd watched the American television show *The Streets of San Francisco* religiously as a kid, I'm shocked at the actual streets of San Francisco. Riding a tramcar, climbing yet another massive hill, just before we reach the crest, all you can see is the bay up ahead and it feels like we're going to tumble off a cliff and end up in the water.

Thrilling and terrifying all at the same time.

We meet a lively Englishman who's filming a TV show. He's kind enough to show us around for a couple of days. He takes us to a diner and insists we try this amazing concoction called a BLT.

"What the fuck is that," I ask, squeamish.

"Well," he explains, "it is a sandwich which consists of toasted bread, mayonnaise, bacon, lettuce and tomato."

"Is this a joke," I continue. "That's not a sandwich. It's like a salad that's having a bad day. "Look," I lord it over my fellow countryman, "I've worked on the assembly line at Walls, so I know what fine food looks like. Who came up with this idea? This has to be a joke."

"No, no," our new friend assures us and orders it for David and I to try. I'm reluctant to taste it and insist David sample it first. He takes a bite and his eyes open wide.

"It's good," he assures me.

I pick up the sandwich and bring it to my mouth. But I put it down again a few times, saying "I can't, no, I just can't." But after a while, I do take my first bite and can't believe what I'm tasting. Bacon mixed with lettuce, tomato and mayonnaise on toast is genius! Who thought this up? They should be given a medal. Ah, America, land of promise!

Finally, we're on the bus to Los Angeles. It's only now David chooses to tell me he's run out of money and doesn't have enough cash for airfare back to England.

"Excuse me?"

David had been more than a little impressed with the beauty of Vegas and revisited the casinos when I was asleep. He blew all his money. Now he doesn't even have enough to pay for a place to stay when we reach LA. But he tells me not to worry as he has a plan.

David is an extremely talented artist and after graduation he is going to pursue a career in animation. He always carries a sketchpad with him and has a solid portfolio of characters he's designed. His plan is that on reaching LA he will contact some small animation studios and try to secure work for a few weeks. He has a few numbers to call and is confident it will work out just fine.

We reach LA and from the bus station David calls around to the various studios looking for work. Shockingly, he is invited to stop by for meetings at a couple of places. We navigate the public transit system of LA and make it to his appointments. At the first one, I wait outside as he's ushered into a cool, funky building. After about thirty minutes he comes out with a big smile on his face saying they loved his work and will happily give him a trial job once he has something called a green card.

After two more interviews we realize the green card is essential. A foreigner cannot work in the United States unless they have this thing called a green card.

Well, we're truly fucked now. I can't just leave David stranded in Los Angeles and head home to England on my own. And, after the third interview, we realize we have no idea where we are. We walk along the road and it becomes apparent we are the only pedestrians in the whole of LA. We stand out. People drive by and look at us like we're dangerous. Then a car pulls up alongside us and a young man yells: "Hey, you wanna ride?"

I swear at this point it could be Charles Manson offering us a lift and I'd take it.

"Yes, we do," I reply and push David into the passenger seat.

"Where you headin'," asks the young man, whose name is Dennis.

"We're looking for a cheap place to stay for a few days."

Dennis drives for a while, then suggests: "I have a couch you're welcome to if you want it."

Do we want this? Do I want this? David looks worried but grateful. That is to say desperate. Dennis, I decide, does not seem like a serial killer.

"Yes, please, we would love to."

So, off we go to Dennis' apartment directly behind Grauman's Chinese Theatre on Hollywood Boulevard. By the time we're there, I definitely get the feeling Dennis is a little too interested in me. So I take David aside.

"Listen, we're boyfriend and girlfriend and have been dating for two years. Got it?"

David gets it and immediately starts acting like my boyfriend, putting his arm around me and calling me *love* and all that. He knows it's driving me crazy and decides this is all great fun. He's getting progressively affectionate whenever we're with Dennis and I have to start acting like his prudish ladylike English rose.

We're given the living room which has two couches. Dennis says we could put them together to make one bed and David's all for it.

"That's a great idea, thanks!"

But I'm glaring at him and, for Dennis' benefit, pouting like I'm just freshly out of a convent.

"That's okay, Dennis, thank you, but we'll make do as is."

Dennis, though, turns out to be a good bloke and takes us

around to all the sights. We visit Muscle Beach in Venice and I'm confused because I think we're going to collect mussels from a beach. But, no, we watch big musclebound men exercising on monkey bars as I worry about David's money situation and my own scheduled flight back to London to start school.

"What are you going to do," I ask.

"I got a job at a carwash off Hollywood Boulevard."

"Without a green card?"

"They pay me in cash."

16.

Finally, it's decided I should head back home and contact David's family, let them know where he is, and ask them to wire money for airfare. Though worried, I do so. I say goodbye to David, thank Dennis, and head for the airport and my flight for London.

The first thing I do after landing is find a phonebooth and call Me-mum and Me-dad to let them know I'm back safe and sound. Me-mum answers the phone and, although she seems happy to hear from me, it's not the great reaction I expect. After all, I've never been away from her this long—or so far away.

I know something is very wrong.

Me-mum tells me, "We have a visitor."

"A visitor? What visitor?"

It turns out that once I left for America, the sister called saying her eldest son, now eighteen, is getting into a lot of trouble and has been kicked out of his father's house. She can't cope with him. So, she decides this troubled teenager should live with his elderly grandparents who he barely knows.

I'm standing there in the phonebooth at Heathrow, burning up.

This thug, raised by his criminal father with little supervision, at the height of his problems, is now supposed to move to Wythenshawe where he's bound to take up with a new crowd of delinquent cohorts. Me-mum explains he's already been caught breaking into houses, setting fire to a school, and shoplifting.

"Oh Moya, we don't know what to do. I'm scared to open the door as every time I do there is a policeman standing there."

"Don't worry. I'm coming home and we'll sort this mess out."

I get the tube to college, sign up for my classes and explain I have a family emergency.

"I've got to head home but I'll be back in a few days."

As I sit on the train heading back to Manchester, I think about the horrendous divorce my family endured after Me-sister finally found the courage to leave the Queer Fella. I think about the long-fought custody battle she went through. I think about the Queer Fella going to the house she was staying at and beating down the front door, then beating down the bathroom door she was hiding behind. I think about how he punched her and threw her down the stairs. How he snatched their two-year-old daughter. I think about how he kidnapped the boys from their school playground. I think about that now and that his eldest son has turned out to be a sly, lying, lazy, deceitful, criminal just like his father. And the father no longer wants him. So now Me-mum and Me-dad can have him.

Reaching the house, I go upstairs to the bedroom he's staying in and find his suitcase. I fill it with all his belongings. I place it by the front door and sit in the living room telling Me-mum and Me-dad about all my wonderful adventures in America. I hear the backdoor slam, then the door to the living room bursts open and the little shit is standing there. He's more than a little surprised to see me and says: "Aiya Moya, how was America?"

"Great," I reply, "but I need to have a chat with you."

We leave the room and go out into the hallway. I take a five-pound note from my pocket and hand it to him. He readily accepts this. But then I walk him over to the front door and grab the suitcase, tossing it out into the garden.

"Now fuck off back to your father."

I close the door, lock it, and go back to the living room to sit down.

"Where's he at," Me-mum asks.

"He's gone back to his dad's house."

"Oh," she replies, only momentarily mystified. "Do you want a cup of tea?"

"I would love one, Mum. And I have souvenirs I brought back for you and Me-dad."

Such gentle, trusting, and responsible people at the mercy of cowards and scoundrels. I'm almost afraid to ever leave home again.

But I must.

Loaded with fresh ideas from my trip to America, I can't wait to get back to college. I work at a feverish pace, using my Las Vegas ideas. I design items of clothing heavily influenced by the western movie styles I've encountered. I create pajamas consisting of slot machine tops and bottoms with coins cascading down the trouser legs. My wedding outfit is literally a "shotgun wedding" with guns in holsters printed on both the wedding dress and the groom's shirt.

The degree show, where we present our work, is with outside adjudicators giving the final grades. That's to say: professionals from the real world of commercial design will size up my work. It's nerve-racking but I'm tougher than I once was and I've learned a thing or two along the way. I'm awarded a first-class degree and wander around London for a day and half in disbelief.

I did it.

Then, immediately after the graduation ceremony, I go home for a few days and, before I can even take off my coat, I receive a telegram asking me to return to London to be interviewed for a show at the Royal College of Art showcasing the top ten textile graduates of Great Britain.

Nervously, I sit through the interview. The panel is made up of accomplished designers, busy and focused. No small talk here. I can't seduce them with my storytelling bluster. The work will have to shoulder the weight. But a couple of weeks later I receive news I'm selected along with nine other students to take part in the show which is to be presided over by Sir Terence Conran, renowned designer, restaurateur, retailer, and writer.

This, by now, I'm aware enough to understand is a great honor.

The opening night is fancy and full of design celebrities. The show itself is quite a shock.

There are around thirty professional textile artists showing their latest collections. I'm assigned a booth and promptly start displaying my work, putting my strongest pieces on the walls for all to see. The rest of my work I place in full view on a large table. But as I look around at the booths of the more established professionals, I notice a common denominator: there's not one single piece of work visible. Everything is hidden, covered, or secreted away in some trendy zippered portfolio.

First lesson after graduation: never let your competition see your goods.

Who knew there's no honor in the fashion world! I'd find this out again and again in the years to come. But right now, I've got my naiveté plastered up around me, sitting there hoping for my big break.

Meanwhile, a gregarious American man stands nearby chatting to a glamorous lady. I overhear him saying he's "doing Europe— next stop Milan, Paris, Rome, Florence. Looking for designs for my spring collection."

I nearly faint when he turns and asks me for my card. I eagerly give him one of the freshly printed business cards I've had made with money Me-dad gave me. But the friendly American pulls out a pen, crosses out my name and writes down the telephone number of this posh chick he's talking to.

Welcome to the real world!

The show lasts a few days and there's nothing in the way of a promising lead. But, then, who would want to buy my work when you can just look at it on display and use the ideas free of charge?

Nevertheless, I'm given a freelance position at a small design studio in North London from a little Japanese Lady. I'm grateful for the opportunity and I'm eager to start work. I show up promptly, raring to go. Apparently, she's raring to go too. On my third day she keeps coming up to me, touching my cheeks and saying: "You have lovely skin, oh so pink."

The only sensible reply I can think of is: "You have nice skin too, oh so very yellow."

It's a short-lived experience. But hopefully no one's feelings are hurt too badly. I get a job as a cashier at Sainsburys supermarket, ringing up groceries for a hundred customers an hour. I'm standing there totaling up a large order for a middle-aged couple. The husband starts chatting to me as his wife scrambles to bag the groceries.

"Do you like your job," he asks.

"Not really, it's a little tiring standing all day."

"Hm," he says. "Well, that's your own fault, isn't it? If you'd worked a bit harder at school, got yourself a couple of O levels, you might not be stuck here in this dead-end job, now, would you?"

I can't believe my ears.

"Excuse me, sir: I actually just graduated with a first-class honors degree from one of the world's top art schools and was chosen to present my work in a show at the Royal College of Art. Maybe you read about that? It was in the papers."

He looks very confused now and his face starts to go a deep purple. His wife is still frantically packing up their supplies and he hands me his Sainsburys shopping card with its pre-approved spending limit. As their order is only over the limit by a couple of pounds, I can accept it without a problem. But this little shite is not going to get away that easily.

I pause just enough to see the long line behind him get very long and I press the button which sets off the bell and a flashing light to signal I need assistance. As he stands there huffing and puffing, I shout to the waiting customers:

"Sorry for the delay. He's overspent on his card. I have to wait for my manager."

By now his wife is ready to run out the door. As my manager approaches, I say again at the top of my lungs:

"This gentleman has spent over his limit."

The manager clears the spending and the bastard takes off after his humiliated wife.

How bad do I feel about this? Do I regret it? No. This creep might've said this to somebody who *didn't* have a couple of O levels and really *did not* have other options for employment.

Prick.

I work at Sainsburys for a couple of weeks and land a job in my field. It's nothing glamorous, but it's the tiniest bit creative and I'm happy for the opportunity. I stick it out for a year, but realize I need to be earning more if I'm ever to emigrate to New York. America is always at the back of my mind.

And then I get a job working nights at a famous jazz club in Soho called Ronnie Scott's.

17.

Ronnie Scott's has been a premier hot spot in London's music scene for many years. Sadly, by the time I arrive in the early 1980s, it's seen better days. Jazz is no longer fashionable. The club itself is a dark cavernous space with red velvet curtains and tiered seating. Most of the artists are notable American jazz musicians completely unknown to me. My first night, the artist is Art Blakely and his band, The Jazz Messengers, featuring a very young Wynton Marsalis.

Mister Blakely plays—or rather massages—the drums as he sways and utters a low, groaning sound. Then he bursts into a crazy, frenetic crashing, pounding and tapping, only to retreat back into the quiet swaying and groaning. I've never seen or heard anything like this. I've never imagined anything like this. And I'm immediately a jazz fan!

There are two owners of Ronnie Scott's: Ronnie, the man himself, and Mister Pete King. Ronnie is a morose figure who shows up occasionally and disappears immediately into his office backstage. Moments later, he calls for a bottle of *Châteauneuf-du-Pape*. He drags himself onstage to deliver the same stale jokes he's been telling for twenty years before introducing the evening's entertainment. Then he returns to his hole and orders dinner. If you're chosen to serve him, he never looks at you or acknowledges your presence. Sometimes a gorgeous young woman shows up and joins him for dinner. I'm told it's his girlfriend.

"Shit, then," I think to myself, "why is he so fucking miserable?"

Mister Pete King is the opposite. He's at the club every night and is very present. Cockney through and through, he has a mop of curly blond hair and, when he speaks, he pushes his head way back and looks at you with his eyes half closed.

It's clear to me somehow—this new jazz fanatic—that Pete carries the weight of the world on his shoulders. The club is a massive drain on him financially and emotionally. It's bleeding money. People aren't into jazz anymore. There are few artists that guarantee sold out shows without fail, though I'm fortunate to see some of the greats: Dizzy Gillespie, Clifford Jordan, Buddy Rich, Art Blakely, Betty Carter, Stan Getz, Max Roach, Art Pepper, James Moody and—my favorite—Panama Francis and the Savoy Sultans.

Panama Francis and the Savoy Sultans turn out to be a big surprise

We all work on commission, so we're always hoping for a big turnout. When the Savoy Sultans show up, we all groan. The youngest member of the band is seventy years old. The oldest is eighty-six. Some of them require canes to walk. But when they take the stage that first night, to a half empty house, they blow it up! They're incredible and word soon gets out. TV crews show up to interview them and the club is sold out for the rest of the week.

The *maître d* is in control of who sits at your tables. So, if he likes you, he'll sit people at one of your tables who look like they might spend some serious money. If not, he puts cheap student types in your area. Unfortunately, he does not like me. So, imagine my shock one night when the Sultans are playing and I go to one of my tables and find Paul McCartney and his wife, Linda, sitting there.

They order cocktails and I when I'm back at the bar to fill that order I see the *maître d* and say, "Hey, thanks."

119

He gets this puzzled look on his face, looks around the room, and figures things out, only now realizing who he has just seated in my area. When I return with the drinks, he's literally pulling Paul McCartney by the shoulder, saying, "I have much better seats for you over here, sir."

There's a buzz from the staff that's worked at the club for many years about the next artist to appear—the great Dexter Gordon. Personally, I'm clueless. But everybody agrees he brings in a big crowd.

The first day Mister Gordon is scheduled to perform, his band arrives in the afternoon to set up. Their first set is at nine o'clock and the trio is on stage promptly.

But no Dexter.

The band is grooving along without him when Pete King comes up to me and says in his heavy East London accent, head back, eyes squinting:

"ere Moya, can I arsk you a question?"

"Of course."

"Do I av the word cunt tattooed on my forehead?"

Before I can answer he ambles away. The trio are happily playing along when Pete comes up to me again asking:

"Did I really book Dexter Gordon from Amsterdam? The biggest fucking drug capital in the world?"

Still, the band is playing. The phone rings and I discover the club chauffeur is at Heathrow meeting flights from Amsterdam and there is no sign of Mister Dexter Gordon.

Two hours into this fiasco, Pete's telling the chauffeur to come back to the club and he saunters over to me asking:

"Is this a fucking dream?"

While the weight of the world is crushing poor Pete, I look over his shoulder and see a large figure looming in the club's doorway.

"Pete, what does Mister Gordon look like?"

"He's a huge, tall black man wiv blue eyes."

"Like him?"

Pete turns around to see the man of the hour standing, swaying, in the doorway shouting: "I got ma horn and I got ma toothbrush and I lost ma moverfuckin' luggage! Where's the stage?"

Pete looks at me and says, "Tremendous, look at the fucking state of him! Shoot me now."

But Dexter gets on the stage, much to the delight of his exhausted band and the positively gleeful audience. First, he decides to stumble and pirouette for about ten minutes. All the while Pete is muttering something about wanting to "fucking vomit." Then Dexter decides to tell a couple of anecdotes. He begins:

"Billy Holiday... Billy Holiday..."

The audience is salivating, anticipating some wonderful story they're going to be told about the great Billy Holiday. He continues: "Billie Holiday was..."

What *was* Billie Holiday? Please tell us. This goes on for fifteen minutes. Finally, he puts us out of our misery:

"Billie Holiday was... a singer."

And just in case we miss the point, he repeats: "Billie Holiday was a singer!"

But then the master picks up his saxophone and plays like no one's ever heard before, certainly not this recent jazz convert. Even not knowing what the hell is going on, musically, I know I'm in the presence of true genius.

And he plays and plays and plays. The club closes at 2 a.m. and he's was still playing. At 3:30, him and his mates are still at it with all the lights turned up and the staff counting our tips.

Part of our duties as waitstaff is to take care of the visiting musicians, make sure their dressing room is clean and that they have fresh water and all that. Because of last night's fiasco, nobody wants to be in charge of Mister Dexter Gordon's needs.

"What's the problem," I think. "I'll take that job."

I walk into his dressing room where the great man himself is "hanging with the cats." I've got a tray, water jar, several glasses and a bar cloth over my arm. Introducing myself, I explain I'll be taking care of him this week. He looks up at me and I notice a lot of white powder on the dressing table.

"Oh, let me clean this mess up for you," I say, all concerned and diligent, as I wipe the powder up off the table with my damp bar cloth.

Gordon jumps to his feet, shaking with rage.

"No! I'm gonna kick your moverfuckin ass!"

Terrified, I run out of the room and find Pete standing there just outside the door.

"He obviously has a problem with women, Pete. Honestly."

"Ere darling, you just wiped-out Dexter's cocaine supply for the week!"

I don't know what he's talking about. But my coworker, Shelia, does.

"What'd you do?"

"I just wiped up all that talcum powder with my bar cloth."

She grabs the bar cloth and starts sucking on it.

Pete walks away muttering, "Fuck, fuck, fuck." He stops and turns back: "You need to keep out of Dexter's way. Where's the chauffeur?"

So, I guess the chauffeur is sent out into the night to replace Dexter's cocaine and I walk back up front expecting this is my final night at Ronnie Scott's. But nothing happens. By showtime, Gordon's high as a kite and blissfully playing his sax. Everyone's happy. Packed house.

Still, after a few more months, I'm getting the feeling I'll have to be waitressing for years to make enough to get to America. I'm saving all I can, but it's not much. Finally, Pete comes up and says he wants to buy me a coffee. And I suppose I'm about to be fired. Which surprises me because I'm actually getting pretty good at waitressing. I definitely never mistake cocaine for talcum powder anymore.

We go around the corner to a little place on Old Compton Street. Pete sips his coffee, sets it down and leans back:

"What va fuck are you doing here?"

And I just gush. I tell him everything: my dreams of working in the fashion industry, of moving to New York, I describe in elaborate detail my slot machine pajama designs.

He takes it all in, then: "Why don't you just go, darlin?"

"Well, I got enough put aside for the airfare," I explain. "But I need something to live on while I get myself set up."

"How much do you need?"

"Probably around seven hundred pound, I think."

Pete shakes his head, looking off at the street, figuring. Then he stands up. "Back to work," he says.

That very night, when I was cashing in my receipts and waiting for my commission, Pete hands me an envelope with seven hundred pound in it.

"Don't waste your time here, darlin'."

This crazy, tough, cockney man has just opened the door for me to fly and I'm going.

It's getting more and more difficult to visit the States for any length of time. They're cracking down on illegal immigrants. My friend, Shiela, from back at Ronnie Scott's, is an Australian physiology student working her way around the globe before settling down in her homeland. She asks me to drive her out to Heathrow for her flight to New York, the next stage of her world tour. I'm happy to do so and tell her to stay in touch because I won't be far behind. Less than twenty-four hours later she rings me up in tears. The heavy Australian accent combined with the sobbing is hard to make sense of:

"Moya, I've got pleurisy!"

"Pleurisy," I ask, bewildered. "How the fuck you get that!"

"No," she tries again, controlling herself, in something a little closer to the Queen's own English. "I got deported."

"Deported," I repeat. I'm already afraid.

"I didn't even make it out of the airport at JFK!"

It turns out Shiela was stopped at immigration upon arrival and, when they searched her belongings, they found a postcard she'd written on the plane to her mum. In it she says she's on her way to

America and hoping to find work.

Done. That's all the US Customs people needed to see. A day trip to JFK in New York is the extent of my friend's American Dream. She's back waitressing at Ronnie Scott's and sleeping on someone's couch.

I begin to sense my own American Dream crumbling. And my young self is becoming dimly aware of how much—in my own head—I *already* live in America. And now it comes home to me. What if I never make it there? What if I never work in New York's famous Garment Center? What if I never go shopping and carry my groceries home in brown paper bags, twisting the key in the lock of my apartment door with one hand and holding it open with my foot like they do in the movies? Will I ever hail a taxi with one subtle flick of the wrist like all true New Yorkers? Can I live without being told to have a nice day every time I buy something? (I love that. And it never happens in rainy old England.) I've got to make the big, hard world understand I have plans. It's all worked out in my head. I've got to work in the Garment Center, marry the man of my dreams, and have children with cool American accents! I'm supposed to put those children on a big yellow school bus and wave, yelling to them without feeling embarrassed, "I love you guys!"

More to the point: what if I'm stuck in England for the rest of my life knowing I belong elsewhere? And when am I going to tell Me-mum and Me-dad I aim to make America my home? And am I just kidding myself?

It's a traumatic few days.

Narrowly escaping a complete meltdown, I organize myself and decide not to meet the same fate as my Australian friend. I go to the US embassy and secure a six-month visitor's visa. That's all I need for now. I buy a roundtrip ticket to New York and, in my crazy paranoid state, I give myself a little backstory. Being a freelance textile designer is a bit too much of a red flag. They'll know I'm coming to look for work and don't have any real ties to England as far as employment goes.

So, I decide I'm a talent scout for jazz musicians!

Brilliant, I think to myself. I know something now about jazz. Fuck, I've rubbed elbows with the greats. I've brought Dizzy Gillespie a vodka tonic and thrown out Dexter Gordon's cocaine. Also, it's not a very common occupation. It won't seem like I'm trying to steal some honest American worker's livelihood. And, anyway, who knows anything about jazz these days? If someone starts asking me about myself, I can drop a few names and record titles and fake my way through it.

Finally, the day arrives. I dress conservatively in a two-piece suit, tame my ridiculously wild hair into a neat *doo* and make my way to Heathrow. I have a friend visiting New York long term, so there's a place for me to stay for a few nights, hopefully more. With a grand total of three hundred and fifty pound to my name, I'm on my way.

On the plane I notice a very attractive man eying me up. When I get up to go to the loo, he follows me and we start chatting. He's from Paris, traveling to New York on business.

"Oh, me too," I say.

"What is it you do for a living," he then asks.

"I'm a talent scout for a jazz club in London."

"Really," he replies, amazed. "So am I!"

I go blank.

He rushes to qualify, "Well, not for a club in London, of course. I work for a jazz record label in Paris."

I can't believe this.

"What a coincidence," he adds.

"Yeah," I agree, vaguely, trying to think how to change the subject. In fact, I'm thinking this is too *much* of a coincidence. That's how paranoid I am. Maybe this handsome Frenchman works for the US Immigration Service and is just pretending to be French. Maybe they've been surveilling me (studying my daydreams!) and know all about my jazz talent scout ruse and my real aim to cheat some hardworking American out of a job!

Somehow, I get back to my seat. But all through the flight he keeps coming up to me, crouching in the aisle to have these little chats about jazz. He brings me a magazine with an interesting article about someone named Roy Eldridge who was a big influence, apparently, on Gillespie. Finally, I explain I had a very late night at the club back in London and need to sleep.

Once landed in New York, I spend over an hour trying to avoid this guy while we're on line to get cleared through customs. But he's waiting for me at the baggage carousel. But I'm almost there, I just need to get through those doors with my luggage and into the arrival hall. My friend, Anne, from back in London, said she'd meet me. So, as I drag my bags out into the huge, crowded, and noisy hall, I'm scanning the faces of all these strangers, looking for someone I know, my heart pounding. Then a man in a uniform is approaching me and I go cold.

Busted.

I stand back and he takes my luggage and walks off calmly.

Only then do I see Anne waving ecstatically from the far edge of the crowd. She reaches me and we follow the man, the chauffer, out to a limousine!

"Everybody coming to New York should be met with a stretch limo!" she insists.

My big cloud of paranoia dissipates and we head into the city. Cruising along Fifth Avenue, I stick my head up out of the sun roof and yell: "I LOVE NEW YORK!"

18.

New York City in 1982 is dirty, noisy, smelly, and scary. And I love it all. Knowing that I have limited funds and not much time to find some kind of employment without the necessary legal papers, it's not going to be easy. Honestly, waitressing at Ronnie Scott's turns out not to be such great prep for waitressing in New York. In England, as regards food, you get what you're given—no changing or substituting, no questions, and definitely no specials.

"What? I don't know how it's made. It's made in the kitchen by a chef."

The one great thing I have going for me, though, and which I never imagined could be an advantage, is that I'm Irish! For the first time in my life, I'm special because I'm Irish!

"Yep, Irish that's me," I'd find myself saying to some admiring Americans from Ohio. "Top of the freakin' morning to you, too."

But that all comes later. First, I have to find work.

I'm blessed Anne has great contacts in the Irish community and, through a few calls she makes, I land a job at a very nice restaurant in the heart of Manhattan. I'm not a very good waitress but no one seems to notice because on my very first day, the owner, who has several restaurants in the city, fires the entire staff of his place down near Wall Street. Me and a couple of other girls are rushed into a town car and driven off to take over the bustling lunch trade in the financial district. There's a very brief introduction to the rules and setup of the restaurant and off we go, thrown in at the deep end and expected to swim. There's food on this menu I've never even heard of. What's a London broil? Surf and Turf? Salisbury steak? Pot Pie? I have lots of questions. And my compatriots, my lovely Irish Colleens, are no help at all. It's bad enough to be Irish in England. But to be Irish with an English accent in New York with a crowd of bitchy Irish girls is even worse!

The customers are all investment bankers and traders and so on, pretty much what you would expect for Wall Street. They order martinis, gin and tonics, knocking them back one after another. It seems food is the last thing on their minds. I'm serving a group of men who are paying very little attention to me as I carefully read the soup of the day and the specials. The one thing on the menu I'm familiar with is the soup of the day:

"Tomato soup with herbs," I announce with confidence.

This somehow manages to pierce the alcoholic lunchtime fog of one gentleman. He cups his ear and hushes the others:

"Wait a minute. The soup of the day. Can you repeat that?"

"Tomato soup with herbs," I repeat, dutifully.

Now they're all looking at one another, intrigued. As if challenging the others, the ringleader decides:

"I'll have that."

"One tomato soup with herbs," I say as I'm writing it down in my pad. Then they all jump onboard and it's four tomato soups with herbs. Fine. Off I go to the kitchen, returning five minutes later with four steaming bowls of soup. But now they look at it, and at each other, concerned, hesitant. They taste it and are disappointed.

"Hey," one of them says, "this is tomato soup."

"Tomato soup with herbs," I correct him.

They send it all back and order another round of martinis.

At last, the lunch rush is over and the place is deserted. We tally our tips, clean up, and head home. The problem for me, though, is that I have no real idea where I am. We were driven there in a car and now it's getting dark and I have no clear idea of where East Eighty-First Street is in relation to Wall Street. I ask the girls if they can show me to the correct subway station.

"Where ye stayin," one of them asks, lighting a cigarette, looking me up and down and trying to decide if I'm worth helping. But I have this memorized:

"East Eighty-First Street between Madison and Fifth Avenue."

You'd think I was telling them I'm staying at the White House with the president and his family. Their mouths fall open.

"Well, lardy fucking da," one of them declares.

"Not bad for somebody what's new in town, is it then, huh?"

They take off laughing.

A tough bunch.

I'm on my own. I find the nearest subway station and, studying the map on the wall, I do figure out what direction I need to be going in. I jump on the first train that comes and sit nervously, watching the street numbers of each station we enter. They're going up, so that's good. The twenties, the thirties. The stops are regular and frequent and it all seems to be working out. But then I notice we haven't stopped in a little while. In fact, we're flying through a whole series of stops. Finally, the train starts to slow down and I see a sign with two words well-known enough to send chills down the spine of even a kid from Manchester, England: The Bronx!!

"Holy shit," I exclaim to no one, since I'm alone on the train at this point. "I'm in the *Bronx*!"

The Bronx in 1982 is the most famously scary place on earth. This place makes Wythenshawe look like Disneyland. Even back home, the news always has stories about outrageous murders and horrible crimes all perpetrated in The Bronx.

Terrified, torturously undecided, I get off the train and find my way to the opposite platform. Of course, I could just stay on the train and wait to see where it takes me.

Maybe someplace safer?

Or not?

The station is deserted and I'm wondering if that's a good thing or a bad thing. Then I hear a commotion and look down the platform to discover two huge black transvestites heading toward me, one saying to the other, "Hmmm, looky what have we here, girlfriend."

I can see they're probably harmless, just stoned and mischievous. They just want to have a bit of fun with me. But I am not in a playful mood. So, I start rocking back and forth and talking to myself, spitting onto the tracks like an angry psychopath desperate for her medication.

They stop immediately and frown, turn sharply around on their extravagant high heels, muttering, "We don't do crazy, honey. Don't do crazy."

Finally, I make it back to the apartment. I'm completely exhausted. But it's true, I realize only now: I'm staying in a very exclusive part of the city. Anne is the daughter of a famous English actor of Irish lineage. She came to New York to study and her folks set her up nicely. Eighty-First between Madison and Fifth Avenue is ritzy. The Metropolitan Museum of Art is around the corner. But to my horror, the famous Frank Campbell Funeral Home is also right across the street, organizing final arrangements for the super-privileged and well-known citizens of New York and elsewhere. I'm freaked out to see deliveries of caskets on a regular basis. On particularly warm days, when the window is open, there's a distinct aroma of formaldehyde.

Anyway, as I'm sitting there reflecting on my day's adventures on Wall Street, in the Bronx, lost on the train, fending off troublesome transvestites, Anne's demanding we hit the town.

"It's not even midnight yet," she exclaims.

And suddenly I'm thrust into the very glamorous social scene of Manhattan's elite. It's almost surreal. Night after night, I'm going to rooftop parties thrown at the homes of European royalty, invited to soirées on Park Avenue, dining at fancy restaurants, being rushed through hordes of people trying to be admitted to the trendiest nightclubs. I never have to pay to go to any of the top places: Area, The Palladium, The Mud Club, The World, Limelight, Danceteria, The Tunnel, Save the Robots and, of course, Studio 54. It's fabulous and crazy and a long, long way from Wythenshawe. But it can't last long. Anne is accepted to an Ivy League college in New England and I'm working every day at an Irish restaurant on Fifty-Seventh Street. I have to find a place of my own.

19.

At the restaurant, there's a crowd of men that stop in at the bar after work. They're ironworkers, longshoremen, teamsters. Some of them literally clock in at work in the morning and come straight to a bar for the rest of the day. But generally, they show up at around three in the afternoon. If I finish my lunch shift and don't have a dinner shift afterwards, I join them for a couple of drinks. Everybody's name seems to end in Y: Davey, Billy, Franky, Mickey, Whitey, Jimmy, Johnny. They're all from the neighborhood known as Hell's Kitchen. Everyone knows I'm looking for an apartment and they spread the word. One little frail bald individual in his seventies—a regular too—hears of my dilemma and says he has an apartment I can have. The rent is in my price range and so I'm eager to see it. Conveniently, it's right next door to the restaurant and I go check it out after my shift. It's a large studio on the sixteenth floor of a prewar building.

"When can I move in?"

"Right away," he says.

"Great," I reply. "Done."

As we're leaving, I ask him where he lives.

"Right here," he says.

I stop and turn.

"Excuse me, hold on a minute. This is your apartment?"

"Yes."

In my desperation to find a place to live without the immigration authorities finding out, I'm willing for a moment to entertain the prospect of sharing an apartment with an old man.

"Okay," I ask, calming myself, trying to be open minded, "so where will you sleep?"

"Right there," he says pointing to the large double bed dominating the one room. Myself, I'm looking around trying to figure where another bed might be placed.

"And where will I sleep?"

"We can share this bed. It's big enough."

When I tell the guys in the bar, they're all laughing hysterically. Then, finally, Davey tells me Franky found a place for me in *his* building.

"Okay, is this another situation where I have to share a bed with some old geezer?"

"No, no. This is legit."

It's a tiny studio apartment one block from my job. The super is a nervous little woman with a deep, gravelly voice as a result of smoking two packs of cigarettes a day since she was eight. She says things like "bada bing bada boop, like that. Understand?" Like the guys in the bar, she's Hell's Kitchen born and bred. There are no questions asked about immigration status and all that since I'm in with my friends from the hood. Payment under the table. Bada bing bada boop, like that. Understand?

It's quite a change moving from the elegant Upper East Side to the raucous Hell's Kitchen. And it's a tired and dreary little apartment, true. But nothing I can't fix up with a little fresh paint and some imagination. I'm settled into a steady routine of work and a nice social scene. I know I won't be able to work as a designer without the proper papers. And that's a massive hurdle I can't figure out how to overcome.

Every day I arrive at the restaurant an hour before lunch to stack glasses and prep. One morning is like any other. I'm standing at the end of the bar polishing glasses and putting them on the shelf. Two gentlemen saunter in and come up to me.

"Is the owner around?"

"I'm terribly sorry, I am afraid he's not here at the moment. Shall I get the manager for you?"

One of the men reaches into his pocket and pulls out a badge.

"Immigration," he says. "We're here to have a look around."

I immediately drop the glass I'm holding. And in my strongest just-off-the-boat British accent call out weakly: "Martin, these two gentlemen are from Immigration."

Without missing a beat, Martin walks over and offers his hand. "Nice to meet you," he asks in his massively strong brogue, "What can I do for ye?"

They tell him they're here to check out the place and see who's working in the kitchen.

"No problem at all, absolutely. Come with me."

The second they've turned towards the kitchen Martin gestures for me to get the hell out. I don't have to be told twice. I'm ready to run, but I've been told that when Immigration raids an establishment, they often have people waiting outside, ready to catch anyone fleeing. So, I just casually stroll out of the bar, walk to the corner, and look around to make sure nobody's on my heels. Then I take off for the only place I can think of: the nearest Catholic Church!

I've seen those Jimmy Cagney films where a church is a safe haven and nobody can touch you in the house of God. I push in through the massive doors of The Church of Saint Paul the Apostle on West 59th, kneel down in a pew with my head in my hands, and start praying. Within a minute, the doors open behind me and in comes Shamus the bartender. Then again, a moment after that, it's the waitresses, Marion, Bridget, and Maggie. Finally, the chef, Colm.

I guess they're all Jimmy Cagney fans too.

We're all whiter than our freshly laundered waitstaff shirts.

"Holy mother of God," Shamus sighs loudly, which I think is

the start of a prayer until he continues, "I nearly shit me fucking pants!"

"Shamus, watch yer mouth," one of the girls says. "Look where you are and have some respect, for God's sake!"

Nobody seems to know what to do next. But I know I'm not going back to the restaurant until I know the coast is clear. My heart's pounding and my head's ablaze with how close I'd just come to having all my hopes and dreams just tossed aside.

Finally, I leave and walk the length and breadth of the city, wondering what the next move should be. After a few hours I call work only to be told the only people the Immigration men questioned were the Greek chef and a Mexican bus boy, both of whom had all their papers and were legal.

Part Three

20.

Slowly but surely, I'm able to furnish my apartment. I even buy a black sofa bed on sale at Sir Terence Conran's worldwide furniture retail empire: Conran's! I tile the floor with black and white squares, paint the walls white with black trim, put up black window shades and—the *pièce de résistance*—I paint the entire kitchen in zebra stripes!

It looks pretty amazing until one day when I wake up and see my brilliant zebra patterned shoes next to the bed and seriously think I'm losing my ability to see color at all. Not a good thing for a budding textile artist.

Meanwhile, the girls at work still don't like me. For most of my life I've been ridiculed for being Irish. Now, I'm not Irish enough. Then, there's the bartender from Northern Ireland who hates England with a passion. He refuses to serve the Irish whiskey, Bushmills, which is produced in the North. If a customer requests Bushmills, he won't pour it and another bartender has to do the honors. He shows such disdain for me that one day I get right up in his face:

"My name is Moya Hession. You don't get more Irish than that."

There's one particular and adorable young man working with us, though, who's charming and who has a crush on me. As lovely as this is, I'm not in the market for dating anyone all of a sudden because I get a kidney infection and have to stay home and recuperate for a week. One of my recent purchases, however, is a smart little sound system and that's all the company I need while bedridden.

So, I'm lying there in bed, listening to music and admiring the zebra striped kitchen when my buzzer rings. There's a delivery, I'm told. I'm not expecting anything. Then, moments later, I'm amazed to discover the sweet guy from work has bought me a TV!

A color TV!

A Sony Trinitron TV!

I'm shocked. I've never received such a generous gift in my life.

Well now my little apartment has everything I need and I'm not even feeling sick anymore. I set up my drawing table to keep my hand ready in case one day I get an opportunity to practice my craft professionally. And though I'm feeling much better, I'm not anxious to go back to work. I decide to stay in for a few more days before heading back to the unlovely company of the Colleens and bartender.

Then my charming friend stops by and suggests we take a drive around the city.

"Just to get out for a while," he says. "It'll be good for you."

"Great idea," I say.

We drive down the West Side Highway, see the gorgeous Statue of Liberty shining brightly in the harbor, the massive World Trade Center, we drive down around the bottom of Manhattan, under the beautiful Brooklyn Bridge, then head up Riverside Drive, along the dark swirly waters of the East River, back over to the West Side and, finally, back down the West Side Highway, making a left onto Fifty-Sixth Street and back to my apartment.

What a beautiful and spectacular city New York is, I think. I'm blessed to be living here. And how worried I am that I'll be kicked out and sent back to England. But this drive—the grandeur of this place—encourages me to do everything I can to get that green card.

Back at my place, my friend insists on walking me up to my apartment. When we reach the door, it's ajar. He knocks before entering. Getting no response, he steps carefully inside

What a mess.

In the short time we've been out, I've been robbed. Actually, I've been cleaned out: the TV, the stereo, all my money. But this person has also filled my suitcases with everything they could carry and hauled it all away: sheets, towels, the clock on the wall, clothes, cutlery, everything from my medicine cabinet—aspirin, perfume, even the tampons!

All I really want to do is call home and talk to Me-mum and Me-dad. But if I do and tell them what I'm going through, they'll be out of their minds with worry. So, I learn to do what I still do to this day: get on with it. I haven't come all this way for nothing. And there's no way I'm going back—at least without a fight.

Back at work, I'm not expecting sympathy from the lovely Irish Roses. But what knocks me sideways is when one of them says, "Well, ye must have been making good tips to afford a new stereo and TV! Indeed, a Sony TV and all!"

"You know," I reply, "I thought you were just a miserably unhappy cow. But you really are a *fucking* bitch!"

Then the manager gives me a hundred dollars to see me through.

"Thanks," I say, "I'll pay it back as soon as I can.

"No worries," he says, "I'll just dock it from your wages at the end of the week."

Ouch.

Tough love?

The American way?

The Irish-American way?

Still, I'm undeterred. I want to be an American worse than anything.

21.

I've been doing occasional freelance work for a couple of textile designers, helping out with little chores around the studio when they're swamped. It pays hardly nothing but I love being in their Fifth Avenue studio! They ask me to apartment-sit for them as they make a trip to the West Coast to sell their work. No one has answering machines yet. So, they want me to be in the apartment and take messages from clients. I'm delighted to do this. I get to the apartment after my lunch shift one Friday afternoon just as the phone is ringing. I answer and a woman asks to speak to one of the designers.

"I'm sorry, but they're on the West Coast and will be back in a week."

The woman becomes a little panicky. "Oh, my," she frets. "But I need them to do a job and, and..."

"I'll pass along the message when they call in."

"But there's no time. We bought a specific design from them and nobody here at my own studio can figure out how to reproduce the work!" Then, out of the blue, she asks: "Are you a designer?"

"Well, ah, yes," I stammer, not really sure if I'm lying or not. But what can I say? Apart from watering the plants, feeding the cat and answering the phone I really am a trained textile designer. "Yeah," I add, a little more confidently, "I mean, yes, I am a designer."

She needs me to come *immediately* to her office in the garment center and pick up the job. She needs four colorways of a small design—that is, four variations of a textile pattern on a selection of fabrics. When I arrive, the original design is in a large envelope on her desk.

"I need it by eight-thirty Monday morning," she says.

I'm a little nervous because it's a very specific technique I have to replicate. But I've seen my employers at work on it and I think I know how it's done. I set to work immediately and within thirty minutes I think I've mastered the technique. I have the first colorway done. I continue with the rest of the job and it's accomplished in a couple of hours.

Now the doubt sets in.

What am I doing! I've taken it upon myself to represent my designer friends professionally without even asking permission!

I set aside the original work and decide it's not good enough. I start all over again, convinced I can improve on the first set of colorways. I work myself into a frenzy throughout the weekend, not satisfied with anything I do. I'm a mad woman. I revise and revise again—five, six, seven times. By Sunday night, I decide the original four designs are the best after all. I set the alarm for six-thirty Monday morning, then toss and turn all night, worrying myself sick. I get up and shower, do my hair and makeup, iron my clothes. I reach the garment center and ride the elevator to the twenty-sixth floor.

"Hi, I'm Moya Hession. I'm here to deliver some work to Miss D'Amore."

"She's not in yet," the receptionist announces, smiling. "But you can just leave it here on the desk."

"No," I decide. "I'll wait. She needs it urgently and I want to make sure she receives it."

"She'll receive it, I promise," the young woman assures me, her smile fading. "There's no need for you to hang around."

I'm confused. Part of me is disappointed because I want to see if Miss D'Amore likes what I've done. But another part of me is relieved that I don't have to be humiliated if she thinks otherwise.

"What is this, this... rubbish!" I imagine her screaming.

I go back to the apartment and get ready for my lunch shift at the restaurant. Miss D'Amore's studio doesn't call, so I automatically assume my efforts have been wasted and the whole thing is a disaster.

Eventually, my friends return from their trip and, sheepishly, I explain I did a job for them, expecting to be lambasted for being so presumptuous. But I'm relieved when they say it's fine. So, emboldened, I also mention, indignantly, that the company hasn't called since the work was delivered.

"Not hearing from somebody in the fashion business is a good thing, Moya," one of them says. The other adds, "You only hear from a client if there's a problem."

Weird.

But they say they'll follow up and see what happened.

Later that day, my friends call to say I have done, apparently, a brilliant job and that D'Amore wants to know if I'm looking for work and, if so, do I want a job working on Jane Fonda's new line of exercise wear.

Hello!

Do I want a job?

Like a job as a textile designer in the garment center?

Like a job in the greatest city in the world?

Yes, I say. Yes, I want a job. I want a job right now. I want a job very much. I want to walk into the restaurant, in fact, and tell that coven of witches that I'm not working alongside their sour and ill-tempered mugs anymore! I want to buy a shot of Bushmills from that grumpy bartender and watch as he makes the Mexican busboy pour it for him. Then I'll hand it off to one of the regulars who actually drinks the stuff!

Yes, I want a job.

And a green card.

And that will be the next order of business.

I'm told that as a matter of protocol I have to have an interview and show my work. I have a small portfolio, so that's no problem. I arrive for the interview dressed in my usual highly fashion-forward outfit, which is literally five articles of clothing of varying plaids. As I wait to be interviewed, I sit looking out the twenty-sixth-floor window. I can see Times Square and the roof of that shady hotel I stayed in with David on my first visit to the States. But, also, up Broadway, Midtown, the trees in Central Park. It's like a dream.

A long way from Wythenshawe.

Miss D'Amore enters the room and I nervously show my work, some of which are small paintings.

"How much do you want for these," she asks.

"What, are you interested in buying them?"

"They'll look great in my house in the Hamptons."

"Oh, well, I guess, four hundred dollars each?" I venture.

Without a blink of an eye she says, "Great, I'll take all three."

Great I'll take all three. They will look great in my house in the Hamptons.

Now I'm starting to think: this is crazy. Unreal. Something bad is going to happen. But—

"When can you start," D'Amore continues.

"Right away," I respond.

"We can only offer you a low starting salary of $400 a week, but there will be opportunities to increase that as time goes on."

This, of course, is not bad in 1982. That low salary will pay my bills and leave me with plenty. But I now know I have to shoulder my way forward into the main issue:

"Miss D'Amore, I'm not a citizen of the United States. I don't have a green card. But I've been doing some research and I've learned that if I get a company to sponsor me on account of my, forgive me, "irreplaceable skills," I can qualify for an H-1 visa and work here legally."

She's pulling together the three new artworks she's just acquired and seems hardly to have heard. But then, pausing on her way out the door, studying the little paintings, she turns and says,

"Not a problem. We've done it before. Tell Jessica who works with me what you need and when you need it and we'll make it happen."

Pinch me now. I have a job. Sponsorship for my working papers. And a check for twelve hundred dollars in my pocket.

God bless America!

And Miss D'Amore.

And God bless Jane Fonda! I loved you in *On Golden Pond*!

I'm very excited for my new job as a textile artist and a little nervous as I have very little work experience. Attending an art school channels your creative side and encourages expression, but the real practicality of learning a trade begins when you are actually practicing your craft and making a living. I doubt that Welsh Pete has much call for shoving a toothbrush up his arse in whatever his chosen profession became.

My first day I ride the subway with the work force of NYC, get off at my stop and fight my way along the bustling sidewalk of the garment district. I enter the building and stand with a group waiting for the elevator in the marble foyer. The doors open and I join the crush of people holding their Styrofoam cups filled with their morning coffee. Twenty-six floors later the doors open and the receptionist buzzes me into the next chapter of my life. I'm taken into the studio, a long wing of the building with large windows on either side. There are empty rows of drafting tables and swivel chairs alongside taborets filled with bottles of ink and tubes of gouache. I look around at the library of art and reference books and shelves of multi colored papers.

I'm in textile design heaven.

My boss shows me to my drawing table and tells me where the kitchen is. "You can help yourself to coffee in there. On Fridays there's complimentary bagels and breakfast pastries. Lunch is one hour which you can take whenever you wish. If you chose to work through lunch the company will pay for whatever food you have delivered." This all seems very civilized to me. One by one my colleagues arrive. They're a mixed bunch; predominately women and a couple of young men. One woman, Melinda, introduces herself, then:

"I'm going to call the *Brush Man*. He'll come and outfit you with your own set of sable brushes."

This is beyond belief. There's a specialist who supplies me with brushes?

My first job is to create a color story for a floral design. This seems simple enough and off I go.

The studio has an informal air, people chatting, music on the radio, all the while it's a beehive of activity. I begin to hear words like *taupe* and *perry* when referring to colors. I have no clue what these are and I don't want to show my ignorance by asking any questions. I take my trusty scalpel and begin sharpening my pencils, just as I've been taught on my first day of art school.

There are a couple of puzzled glances in my direction and I think nothing of it until Melinda says: "Honey, you're in America now and we have something called electricity. We even have pencil sharpeners that *use* electricity to make pencils nice and sharp."

I feel myself blushing but I'm not about to explain that using an electric sharpener wastes about fifty percent of the pencil because I'm getting the message loud and clear: Time is Money.

All in all, I adapt pretty easily to the studio and enjoy what I'm doing enormously. Some days I'm working on pretty generic stuff, then the next, it's designs for swim wear. One of the first jobs I'm working on is swim wear for the US team to wear at the Los Angeles Olympics. But I still can't figure out the two mystery words *taupe* and *perry*. So, one day as I'm working on a design and Melinda asks what color I'll be adding to the piece, I say:

"Well, I was thinking maybe taupe."

"But you've already got taupe right here," she tells me, pointing her paint brush at a beige background.

Beige.

Taupe is beige.

Remember that.

"Ah, of course!" I exclaim. "What was I thinking? I meant to say violet."

"Oh, that will work nicely," Melinda agrees as she walks off.

Now I just have do is find out what the fuck *perry* is. And an opportunity presents itself the very next day:

"Does anybody like this perry next to this mauve?" one of my coworkers asks aloud, holding up her example.

Perry, I now learn, is blue; kind of a periwinkle blue.

Remember that.

It doesn't take long before I'm given more responsibilities, including putting designs into repeat for production. I'm happy for the change of pace and the more challenging work, even though it's very labor intensive.

Deep down, I'm chomping at the bit to show that I can produce original ideas. But there's no call for it as most of the designs we use are bought from studios around the world. Several times a year there is an onslaught of textile design studios converging on New York City. They go to the hundreds of manufacturers hoping to sell their ideas. These studios show up in reception after making an appointment with our stylist. They're shown into a conference room, place their stack of up to three hundred designs on a table, and the stylist plows through them with great speed, pulling out ones that are immediately appealing. Next, the ones selected are laid out and a final decision is made about which ones to purchase. Literally months and months of creative blood, sweat, and tears perused in about ten minutes and then on to the next appointment. Sometimes I'm allowed to join the stylist as she looks at work and, eventually, I'm even allowed to pick work alongside her.

About a year into my job, we get a new stylist named Carol. She's English and her approach to things is a little different. One of the first things she does is to ask everyone in the studio to come up with some original ideas.

"What," I say to myself, "this is exactly what I'm talking about!"

Delighted, I take off with this challenge. Most of my colleagues, oppressed, are groaning about being simply colorists and not designers. But I crank out ten simple ideas in a couple of hours and pin them all up on the wall. Carol's very impressed and four of them are put into production. I still do repeat work. But my main focus, now that I'm appreciated as a design resource, is producing original ideas. I acquire an ability to work fast and execute efficiently because it's not unusual for Carol to come rushing into the studio asking me to whip up something for a customer who's sitting out there in the conference room. One day she barges in saying they just received a call from *Women's Wear Daily*. They're doing a piece on this year's trends based on Egyptian art and she needs a design in two hours in order to make the deadline.

No problem.

Egyptian Designs R Us.

I get down to work. I love it. I always work through lunch, anyway.

After work, I usually stop in at the bar on my way home to see Davey and the gang and have a couple of drinks before calling it an early night. Weekends I look forward to walking around the city and meeting up with friends for dinner and the occasional club night. I often browse in the Strand bookstore down on lower Broadway, looking for inspiration since I've decided to start working on my own collection.

22.

Besides allowing me to work and pay taxes, the other great thing about being in America legally is I can fly home to see my family. My first trip back to Wythenshawe, Me-mum and Me-dad are sitting in the kitchen, hanging on my every word about life in New York. They want to know everything. Especially, what church I go to.

As much I resented going to church when I lived at home, since I went off to London, I've never missed Mass on Sunday. It's the same in New York. It's not so much religious devotion, I suppose, as something that links me to my parents. And it gives me an hour to collect my thoughts and have a little peace.

On this trip home, I suggest that Me-mum and Me-dad come to New York and visit. I expect a little resistance, of course. The cost! The extravagance! Who'd take care of the... And so on. A long list of reasons why it's impossible to leave Wythenshawe. So, I'm totally unprepared when they say they've been thinking about coming to see me over there too.

"I always wanted to visit New York City on Saint Patrick's Day," says Me-mum.

"Well," I reply as soon as I get over the shock, "if that's what you want, then I'll make it happen."

But now, of course, I have to figure out *how* to make this happen. And how to make it the best time they'll ever have. Me-dad tells me he has a childhood friend he believes is now living somewhere in the States. So, once I get back to New York, I track him down to the Jersey shore where he lives in retirement with his wife. That will be a nice jaunt for them, I think to myself, to go visit old friends at the seaside. I use all my Irish contacts to get seats on the reviewing stand on Fifth Avenue for the Saint Patrick's Day parade. And we'll follow that up with a Chieftains concert at Carnegie Hall. I book and pay for a room at a hotel on Central Park West for their first few nights. After that, we'll just have to make do at my little apartment.

I'm so excited as the day of their arrival gets closer. I can't imagine what they'll make of America. And their very first time on a plane! Me-dad will be excited and curious about everything he encounters. But Me-mum will be a little shy.

The guys at the bar are almost as excited as I am. They call in some favors around town and help me book a stretch limo because I told them Anne's opinion: "Everybody should be met by a limo when they come to America!"

I stop in before heading out to JFK and Old Man Anger (the Irish bartender) surprises me with a bottle of Dom Perignon in an ice bucket to serve my parents on the drive back from the airport.

"Jesus Christ, are you smiling?"

"No, it's just the light in here. Take it and go. The limo's out there waiting."

And off I go, rattling around in the back of this cavernous dance hall of a vehicle with thousands of twinkling little lights in the ceiling. Out at the airport, I wait anxiously in Arrivals for my parents to appear. And after about forty minutes, there they are.

I don't know why it should seem so. After all, I've been arranging all this for months. But all of a sudden, it's surreal to see Me-mum and Me-dad walking towards me three thousand miles from home. I've never even seen these two on holiday. And here they are walking towards me in their brand-new holiday outfits, carrying their scuffed and scarred old suitcases.

151

Me-dad's attached a huge bright yellow piece of yarn to the suitcases so he can spot their luggage easily. But I think it serves another purpose, really. It's a deterrent to theft. Nobody, not even a thief, would be caught dead carrying this crappy old luggage.

But their eyes light up when they see me and immediately Me-dad is telling me all about their first time on an airplane as though he's just discovered something that nobody, nowhere, has ever experienced before. They ate things they never ate before and the air hostess offered them drinks they felt obliged to accept so as not to hurt her feelings. So, the pair of them had a whiskey *before* dinner and wine with dinner!

Delighted, I ask: "Did you like it?"

"Well, a whiskey after dinner, that's fair enough. But two glasses of red wine before dessert, that's a bit grand, don't you think?"

As the chauffeur is nice enough to carry the luggage a few paces ahead of us, we exit the terminal and make for the parking area, all the while Me-dad describing each detail of the journey, from arriving at the airport in London to check-in, boarding to seat belt fastening, takeoff, drinks coming around, food, even the pilot speaking over the intercom.

"Tell her what happened when we took off," Me-mum sighs, relieved.

"I sat next to the window because your Mum didn't want to see how high we were off the ground," Me-dad starts, giggling a little. "It was an overcast day when we took off. Then we went through the clouds and when I looked out the window, I saw this massive wing. I told your Mum, 'blimey there's somebody passing us on the left here and they're very close.' Your Mum didn't like the sound of that and got out her rosary beads. She prayed all the way here. Kept asking me if the other plane was still next to us! Ha!"

Finally, we're standing beside the limo as the chauffeur places their luggage in the boot like it was made out of porcelain.

Me-mum is impressed: "Oh, they do have very nice taxis over here, don't they?"

But Me-dad is laughing and nervously rubbing his hands together.

"This is for us?"

"That's right," I say.

"You sure?"

"And there's a very nice bottle of champagne too," I add as we all climb in. "Fancy some?"

"I'll have a cup of tea, instead," says Me-mum. "I'm parched."

"A cup of tea!" I'm practically speechless. "A cup of tea? Mum, this is a car. There's no kitchen, no kettle, no stove!"

"It is bigger than our house, though," Me-dad thinks to add as he studies every little gadget he comes across. He pushes each button he finds. The privacy screen goes up and down. The radio changes volume. The twinkling little ceiling lights dim and then glow brightly again. And, of course, there's his running commentary on the ingeniousness of all these features. Part of me is hoping he doesn't discover the button that makes the roof open up, what's called the moon roof. But he does find it and it's hysterical to watch him pointing out the size of every building we drive past once we're out of the Midtown Tunnel and firmly in Manhattan.

"Look at the size of that one! That's a whopper. Look at that. Blimey, you wouldn't get many of them in a pound."

He's over excited like a little kid. But they've had a long day of it already and Me-mum is starting to fade. After a light dinner at the hotel, I settle them into their room and return to my place a few blocks away.

The next morning, I head back to their hotel to see Me-dad sitting on a wall watching traffic. When he sees me he jumps down and approaches: "Aiya, I've just counted one hundred and eleven taxis! Look there's another three. One hundred and fourteen."

And so it begins, Me-mum and Me-dad's big adventure.

Like at the airport, it's strange to see them in Manhattan. It's a bit like the first time you see your teacher out of school and it's as though she's an alien. And God forbid she's with a spouse or a boyfriend. And, also, you've got to suddenly get used to the fact that she has legs, since you haven't noticed them before as she is always sitting behind a desk. It was a little like that with my parents in Manhattan. Look! Me-mum standing on the sidewalk outside Rockefeller Center! How'd that happen?

I take some time off work and arrange guided tours for them. We go to the bar to meet all the guys and are given a rousing welcome. Me Mum can't figure out how to get up on to a bar stool and Me Dad can't stop talking. I swear I think I even hear his Irish accent coming in and out. Davey gives him a present of an electric razor and Me-dad is overwhelmed. I don't have the heart to tell him it's probably off the back of a lorry somewhere and will most likely be useless back in England because of the voltage difference. Doesn't matter one bit to him, though. He's proud as punch of this, his latest technological acquisition. I take them to restaurants and every time I leave a tip on the table Me-dad says:

"Why are you leaving so much?"

"That's how it's done here."

"Some funny ways they have."

"Dad, I've been a waitress and it's not the easiest job. They deserve a good tip."

Wherever we eat, they're both shocked at the massive portions of food delivered to the table. They're served a sandwich at The Stage Deli on Seventh Avenue and nearly faint at the size of it. Me-mum insists we take a picture of it and makes Me-dad put his big fist next to the plate so people back home can get a clear idea of the thing.

But Me-dad's primary photographic subject is taxi cabs; mainly, how many can he see at one time. I pity the poor souls of Wythenshawe who will be subjected to these precious holiday snaps; basically Me-dad's clenched fist alongside a variety of sandwiches and endless views of New York City yellow cabs.

When they leave the hotel we all manage to fit into my apartment. After a long day of sightseeing, Me-mum is happy to relax with a cup of tea and put her feet up. Not Me-dad. He wants to explore and look around the neighborhood, insisting he's fine walking around on his own when I express worry. This is, after all, Hell's Kitchen in the early 1980s.

154

"I'll be fine, Moya."

"At least, don't wander over towards the river."

"It's rough, is it, along the river?"

"That's what I'm told. I never go near it."

"Can you lend me a few of the American quarters so I can buy myself a mineral?"

"They call it soda over here, Dad."

And off he goes. Though I admire his curiosity and fearlessness, I am worried. Nevertheless, he returns a couple of hours later, no worse for wear, saying he met some nice colored lads washing windscreens down the road.

"We don't say colored here, Dad."

"No?" He's sincerely interested in this. "I worked with a colored fella at the factory and he said negro was not the thing to say these days."

"No, definitely not negro," I agreed. "You can say black."

"Really? And there's no offence given?"

Anyway, my suspicions that he'd allowed himself to wander towards the river are confirmed the next day when one of the guys from the bar tells me:

"Moya, I coulda' sworn I seen your pa hanging out with a bunch of squeegee guys down near the piers yesterday."

Mercifully, I don't have to worry about him wandering too far anymore because he's discovered a massive crane being assembled on Fifty-Sixth Street and Eighth Avenue in preparation for the construction of an enormous high rise. It's going up directly opposite a McDonalds he likes as well. So, whenever Me-mum needs a rest or we two want to go do a bit of shopping together, Me-dad happily sits for hours with a bag of French Fries and a Coke, watching "me crane," as he now calls it. So along with the fist-sized sandwiches and the taxi cabs, he now has dozens of photographs of an enormous crane being assembled piece by piece.

As I have to go into work some days during this adventure, I schedule a whole day of sightseeing for them with a well-known and trusted bus group tour. This should keep them out of trouble and I'll meet them in the evening. I give them my phone number at work just in case.

Three thirty in the afternoon the phone's ringing in the studio and I hear someone call: "Moya, it's for you!"

"Hello?" I ask, tentatively, taking the receiver.

"Aiya love."

"Aiya Mum. Is everything alright?"

"We're lost."

I need to sit down. I do. I remember to breath.

"Where are you?"

"Hold on a minute," Me-mum says, then turns away and calls, "Charlie, ask the man where we are."

Muffled sounds. Then:

"We are in Staten Island."

"What! Where's the rest of your group?"

"I don't know. We were on this big boat and Me and your dad got off when it docked. When we turned around the boat had left and took the group with it."

My colleagues sense my agitation.

"Moya," someone calls, "everything okay?"

I make a gesture pretending everything is okay. Then:

"Okay Mum, I want you get on the next big boat that comes in. But make sure it is going back to Manhattan. When you get to Manhattan and get off the boat, call me again. Okay?"

I go back to my table and rush through the work I still have to do, waiting for the phone to ring. Finally, at about quarter to five in the evening:

"Moya, it's your mom."

Now, the whole studio is involved. A crowd follows me to the phone.

"Aiya Moya, it's your mum."

"Aiya Mum, where are you now?"

"I don't know. But your da…"

"Can you ask someone?"

"He is. Your dad…" Then, as she turns away again, I hear her calling, "Charlie, ask that man. Well, ask him. Try that fella." She returns to the receiver: "Hold on Moya, your dad's trying to ask somebody but everyone's in such a hurry here. Such a crowd and..." But now Me-dad seems to have gotten some information. I hear him calling to Me-mum and she relays the intel to me: "Alright, Moya," she announces with some relief, "so, we are in Manhattan."

That's not what I needed to know, exactly. I sit.

"Mum, *where* in Manhattan?"

"Your Dad's talking to a man in a uniform. Hold on."

More muffled sounds. I hear something that must be a foghorn in the background. Then an intercom announcement. Me-mum fumbles the receiver and it bangs against the edge of the booth sending a spike of pain through my ear. I fall back, wait, then:

"Moya?" It's Me-dad.

"Dad?"

"Blimey, Moya, everybody's in a right rush around here!"

"It's rush hour, Dad. That's why they... Forget it. Where are you?"

"We're at the Staten Island Ferry Terminal."

Okay, that's a help. Nevertheless...

"And where is that, Dad?"

"In Manhattan."

We're going around in circles. I've never been to Staten Island or taken the ferry so I have no idea. Finally, I just press the receiver to my shoulder and look to my colleagues: "Where is the Staten Island Ferry Terminal?"

What I learn is not terrifying. But there are complications. The Ferry Terminal is at the very bottom of Manhattan. Getting there from the Garment District at the height of rush hour, when over a million people are making their way home from work, is not easy.

My parents have mastered American payphones. Now, they'll have to hail a cab. But hailing a cab in New York City at five o'clock in the evening, when the day shift drivers go off duty and before the night shift drivers come on, is nearly impossible. Still, I'm not crazy about them huddled on a bench like refugees in this mysterious thing, the Staten Island Ferry Terminal.

Me-mum's back on the line.

"Mum, this is what I want you to do: You've seen me get a taxi, right?"

"Oh, yes we have."

"Well, I want you and Me-dad to do the same thing. When you see a taxi, make sure the light on its roof is on, then just wave and it will come to you."

"Wave how?"

"You know, just any old way! Hold your arm out and wave!"

"Oh, I think I'll let your dad do all that."

I tell them that once they get a cab, they're to tell the driver to take them to the Fifth Avenue entrance of the Empire State Building.

"When you get there, pay him the fare and give him a dollar extra for a tip. I'll be there waiting for you."

I scramble to get out of the door and run the seven blocks to Thirty-Fourth Street. I pace nervously, watching every cab that stops. Ten minutes, twenty minutes. Still no sign of them. I'm beginning to get very concerned when, at last, a taxi pulls up and out hops Me-dad, looking a little agitated. Me-mum follows, doubled over with laughter. When Me-dad turns back to look, she straightens herself up and stifles the hilarity. Later, she tells me, laughing again: "You should've seen your dad trying to stop a taxi!"

I take a last few days off from work and rent a car to drive them down to the Jersey shore for a visit to Me-dad's childhood friend, Barney. It's a treat to see these two old men walking along the beach, deep in conversation, piecing together memories from forty years ago, with Me-dad telling stories and cracking Barney up.

The big day arrives and it is time to celebrate the great man himself, Saint Patrick. I don't want to burst Me-mum's bubble about the reality of this day in New York City, as it's been a life-long dream of hers to witness this, the world's biggest celebration of the Irish. So, I carefully plan the day so we're not amongst the throngs of wearing-of-the-green lunatics drinking their green beer and puking up green vomit all over the city.

Saint Patrick's Day in New York is truly a mad time. Thousands and thousands of people coming from all over the world, streams of revelers pouring out from every subway, teenagers already partying on the busses and trains in from the suburbs. Every Irish bar you pass have crowds waiting outside, desperate to gain admission, to fight for the bartender's attention, to consume as much alcohol as possible.

The day I plan is far more genteel. We have a good breakfast before heading out to the parade. I've wrangled the best seats available on the reviewing stand along Fifth Avenue, elbow to elbow with the dignitaries and celebrities. As usual, Me-dad's a bundle of nervous energy, swiveling around in the back of the cab, pointing in every direction at the hordes descending upon midtown Manhattan. Since coming to New York, it's like sixty years of meekly suppressing his heritage comes suddenly to a stop and he transforms into a very cocky Irishman! He's pointing to a black man wearing a green nose or a Chinese fella with an enormous green hat and saying, "Now, he's not Irish. He don't look Irish at all." It's comical and a little sad. For the first time outside his homeland, he can demonstrate the pride he feels. But it's been hidden too long somehow. It seems clumsy and out of proportion now.

We find our places on the reviewing stand. It's a beautiful, sunny, clear day and Me-mum and Me-dad watch every flag-waving politician, firefighter, cop, union, every Aran-sweater-wearing, kilted bagpipe blowing, Tam o' shanter sporting, drum beating, whistle-whistling, banner-carrying marcher with eyes wide open. It's like this has all been put on for them. They're like two children watching the greatest show on earth. From out of nowhere, I start weeping. I'm so blessed to have them in my life.

After the parade we go home to prepare for the concert later, I can't bear the thought of going to an Irish restaurant and being served corned beef and cabbage, which incidentally I had never even heard of until I came to America and I'm pretty sure Me-Mum and Me-Dad are oblivious to as well. All dressed up, we head over to Carnegie Hall for something I'm particularly excited to see: the great Irish band, The Chieftains.

All three of us wander into Carnegie Hall, gazing about us at all the magnificence: the plush red velvet chairs, the white and gold balconies. We take our seats four rows from the front. Just perfect. The music is brilliant. Plus, the added bonus of having two great Irish dancers, Michael Flatley and Jean Butler (long before Riverdance), who take the stage periodically. After the show ends, I tell me parents we're going backstage to a little reception to meet the band. Me-Mum's first reaction is:

"Oh no, that's alright. I wouldn't know what to say to anybody."

"You don't have to say anything if you don't want to, Mum. But it is a great privilege to be invited backstage at Carnegie Hall."

Of course, Me-dad is raring to go. I can't get over his newfound sense of adventure. We head for the stage door, give our names, and we're admitted. There is a lounge area and the band are mingling with the rather elegant crowd. I turn to get myself a stiff drink and Me-mum an orange juice. I'm about to ask Me-dad what he wants only to see him right in the middle of the posh group, talking to the band.

Who is this man, I think to myself—Me-dad?

The next thing I know, he's walking over to Me-mum and me with Matt Malloy, the band's world-renowned flautist.

"Moya, here's Matt Malloy. He's from Ballaghdareen. He knows your Uncle Pat. When Matt's dad retired as a Ganga man, Uncle Pat took over his job."

"I do, indeed," Matt said, shaking Me-mum's hand and nodding to me. "I know all your father's family. I remember your grandfather who was the town cobbler."

This is surreal. I've never met any of my grandparents and here I am backstage at Carnegie Hall hearing stories about my father's family back home. I know that when he was younger Me-dad played the flute. But I only realize now that the town he comes from is renowned for producing great Irish flautists, of which Matt is arguably the world's greatest. He stays and chats with us for quite a while and before he steps away, he makes sure to introduce Me-mum to the rest of the band.

The two weeks fly by and it's time for them to head back home to Wythenshawe. I'm sad to see them go but thrilled to have shared such a wonderful adventure with them.

23.

And then it's back to my steady routine: nine to five in the Garment District and stopping in for drinks at the bar on my way home—hanging out with the guys. There's a whole community of friends and neighbors I meet there, one acquaintance leading to another. There's one character who comes in frequently. He's probably in his fifties, with a bald head and a strong Northern Irish accent. He drives a Rolls Royce. Back when I was working as a waitress, he took me aside and, knowing my illegal status, advised me to make sure to always pay my taxes. Looking back, I see this was, indeed, sound advice. He introduced me to a young man named Jackie. Jackie and his wife were accountants and helped me with my tax filing. And then there was Jackie's Mom! She often came in for dinner with her partner, Angelo. An adorable, gentle couple in their sixties, when Angelo had a couple of Martini's in him, he'd serenade his lady with a ballad or two in a high falsetto voice.

Sometimes another group of younger guys come into the bar and Davey and his group don't stick around. They try to explain that I shouldn't stick around either. I do as they suggest but it's all lost on me. All I gather is that these young men are part of some gang.

But now, as a professional textile designer, I still use Jackie and his wife to prepare my taxes. But I haven't seen Jackie for a while and I'm very sad to hear he's gravely ill in Roosevelt Hospital, just around the corner from the bar. People stop by with updates after visiting him. It's always very secretive as to what malady he's suffering from. One day he improves, the next he was failing badly. Everyone's on edge. There's this deadly strange sickness going around. No one knows how you get it. No one knows how you stay safe. Since a lot of gay men get it, its commonly assumed it has something to with that—gay sex. But that can't be right. Jackie's not gay.

Even though it's expected, it's a shock when I hear Jackie's died. I'm told of the arrangements: a two-day wake at the local funeral home and a requiem mass at The Sacred Heart church on Forty Second Street.

I definitely want to attend the funeral and pay my respects to the family, but I'm not sure about the wake. Given my desperate aversion to coffins and the dead bodies inside those coffins, it's not likely I'll be able to stand beside an open coffin with the dead body laid out for me to contemplate compassionately—and not faint. But it's got to be done. I like all these people. They've been good and helpful to me. I make my way to Barrett's funeral home. There's lots of people dressed in black milling around outside the front door. I join the line leading into a large formal room. The air is filled with the aroma of lilies and various sweet-smelling blooms emanating from massive wreaths lining the walls, just like those huge elaborate floral displays from the *Godfather* movies. I follow along with the rest of the mourners, shuffling solemnly into the main room. I stop briefly to sign the book of condolences and leave my name and address.

Then I see it: The huge dark, wooden coffin, sitting on its pedestal. Oh no! And it's wide open! And there lies poor Jackie for the whole world to see! I watch as everyone approaches and kneels at the *prie-dieu* in front of the coffin. They bow their heads in prayer, some even reaching into the coffin and touching the corpse! Oh no! I'm freaking out. That woman just kissed his forehead! Shit, I have to get out of here. But I can't. How would it look?

I approach nervously. I look at Jackie lying there in a dark suit and blue tie, his hands folded, rosary beads intertwined in his fingers, one of which is wearing a *Claddagh* ring. His face is powdered heavily in an effort to cover the obvious lesions. And I'm oddly calmed as my mind, distracted, considers the bigger picture. Jackie is the first of many more people I'll see perish from this nightmare disease that's creeping into the world. All across town, all kinds of people are dying from this mysterious sickness which I only recently heard someone call AIDS.

And everyone's terrified.

I look at the quilted interior of the casket lid, covered with photographs, notes, an Irish cross, a Rangers hat, and a teddy bear. I nod my head and quickly rush through the prayer for the dearly departed then rise and offer my condolences to his mother, his wife, and Angelo.

All this accomplished, grateful I haven't fainted yet, I take a seat with the rest of the mourners and wonder what happens next. The funeral director then announces that, with the exception of Jackie's mother, wife, and Angelo, everybody has to leave. The place clears out and there's a flurry of activity with beefy plain clothes detectives hustling a blond young man into the viewing room. There's the sound of chains jostling and everyone's eyes are fixed on the floor. I go back to the bar and mention I'm just back from the wake and somebody says they heard Jackie's brother was there.

"I hear they brought him in shackles to say goodbye to Jackie."

"Oh," I say, "so, that's who the blond guy was?"

"Yeah, that would be Jimmy."

And then I'm treated to an afternoon of stories that shed a whole new light on my own little neighborhood. The blond young man surrounded by all those burly men in suits is Jimmy Coonan, currently on trial for murder and racketeering. Jimmy's head of the notorious Westies, a terrifying band of organized crime operating out of Hell's Kitchen. I'm sitting there shivering on my barstool as the guys detail the particular and brutal traits the Westies incorporate into their crime repertoire. One of these, for instance, is to cut off the hands of a murder victim so when they commit other crimes, they can use the dead man's hand to leave fingerprints and fool the investigators.

Holy mother of God! These were the hoodlums Davey had warned me about and with whom I'd sometimes chat after work! But it seemed unreal, too: how could the ferocious Jimmy Coonan have been raised by Jackie's lovely Mom and the angelic sounding Angelo?

A week after the wake and the funeral I receive a thank you card from the family. Of course, my address is written in the condolence book at the funeral home. Shit, I think to myself, does this mean I'm on a watch list with the FBI now?

Not long after that, the lovely older man from Derry with the Rolls Royce who introduced me to Jackie in the first place, has a terrible accident. He was, it's said, injured in an explosion when repairing his Rolls. Now, this seems mighty strange even to me. He never struck me as the kind of guy who got his hands dirty with manual labor.

"He survived the explosion," someone says, grinning, "but died in the hospital after being given the wrong medication."

"How unlucky can you get," someone else down the bar adds, ironically.

"Those who live by the sword—and so on," Davey concludes to no one in particular.

Now I'm well and truly confused. So, even this kindly, paternal, soft-spoken gentleman was a killer of some sort? Who else in this bar is a Westie? Jesus, I think, Wythenshawe was rough but this is a whole other league.

24.

As much as I love my job, I know I need more creative freedom. Thankfully, Carol is aware of this and eager to have me come up with original designs. I'm even told that I can hire another artist to assist me with the increased workload. I place an ad in *Women's Wear Daily,* the trade newspaper, and, after being inundated with applications, I set up interviews for a number of the most promising candidates.

My heart breaks every time I'm summoned to reception to meet another young graduate looking for their first job in the fashion world. I remember the sheer panic I felt when I walked through the huge glass doors for my own interview. I remember the anxiety, nausea, sweating, and the fear of being rejected.

But as accommodating as I'm prepared to be, my excitement at seeing fresh talent soon turns to dismay. The standard of work by most applicants is very sad. Though, as I meet each one, dressed in their best and putting forth a confident demeanor, my hopes are raised. But then I chug through their portfolio and I'm appalled at the badly executed and poorly presented work—the general lack of skill. It seems like only a few weeks ago I was being browbeat by Katy back in London for doing the same half-assed work. Just because your family thinks your work is great and the neighbors all refer to you as the talented one does not mean you are! I know Me-mum thought I was a creative genius when she saw my badly drawn sketches of a flower or a cup and saucer. But really, my work had been average—at best. So, at this stage, I can vouch for it personally: a little potential with some encouragement and hard work can go a long way. With this in mind, I continue in my quest for my very own assistant.

It seems endless, but it is varied and sometimes even amusing. I have to keep from laughing one day when an applicant proudly displays his work and there, right before me, are four of my very own designs!

"These are interesting," I say, intrigued. "What was your thought process in coming up with these designs?"

He replies with some convoluted art school answer, something about simplicity of design, symmetry, color balance, blah, blah, blah.

I'm not impressed.

Another candidate incorporates some photography along with a collection of his textile designs. As I thumb through the photographs, I come across a beautiful shot of the earth taken from outer space.

"Nice," I say, and mean it. It's a good idea to have that photograph from outer space right there amongst his textile designs.

"That's my best one," he adds, proudly.

"These are all your photographs?"

"Of course."

"Are you an astronaut?"

He's only a little caught off guard. He blushes and explains that, though he did not actually take the photo, merely printed a copy, he nevertheless considers its inclusion in the portfolio a creative choice made by him alone and therefore his work.

"Like, not actually painting the Mona Lisa," I joke, "but visiting it in the *Louvre* and calling it your own."

He doesn't like this. I doubt he'll take the job now even if I offer to him. Instead, I hire the young man with my own work in his portfolio, since what he lacks in talent he makes up for with good taste!

I'm approached by a couple of studios to do freelance work too. Four nights a week now, after I finish my day job, I get the subway to the East Side, walk through Bloomingdales, and continue on a few blocks more to my evening job. There, I work until about ten and usually get a cab home. Working all these hours is fine by me as I enjoy the work and feel privileged to be getting paid for something I love doing. The more freelance work I do, though, the more I realize it's time to design my own collection.

I start spending all my free time locked up in my studio apartment, feverishly creating a collection of textile designs. I show it to the studio I'm working with and they eagerly ask to incorporate it into their collection and show it for me. I agree and anxiously wait for the response when my designs are shown for the first time. It's very successful and I sell fifteen designs on the first day, which amounts to almost six thousand dollars!

Not bad for a few day's work!

The only drawback is I'm obliged to give up forty percent of my earnings to the studio. Still, it's confirmation that I'm capable of coming up with fresh ideas and that I'm an able design source for the fashion industry.

I continue working freelance with every opportunity that comes my way and, with the exception of a few social events, I'm happy to be locked away in my little apartment designing to my heart's content. I'm able to save money, which means I can visit home more regularly.

And I venture out to my first baseball game at Yankee stadium. I'm invited by a guy who is Bronx-born-and-bred and a lifelong Yankees fan ever since his father took him to a game when he was five. Of course, I've always been a fan of sport. It was inevitable growing up in a small house with one television and a father who watched any sporting event he could find. This meant enduring those interminable five-day test cricket matches that droned on and on and on. Inevitably Me-dad would doze off. The second I got up to change the channel he'd wake and say, "I'm watching that. Leave it on."

Me-dad's devotion to cricket and soccer was equal to his dedication to rugby, tennis, snooker, ping pong, car and motor bike racing, not to mention darts—where massively overweight men consumed numerous pints of beer while throwing sharp projectiles at a small round chunk of hard cork. Then, of course, one of the defining aspects of lively competition for certain types of rural folk in Great Britain: sheep dog trials. Hour upon hour of farmers and their trusty dogs trying to guide a flock of dopey sheep into a little corral. Gripping television by anybody's standards.

All I know about baseball, though, is the great looking uniforms the players wear and the baseball caps that mean *America* all over the world. And nothing compares with the excitement of going to Yankee Stadium for the first time.

We get the subway from Columbus Circle and head uptown on the number 6 to the Bronx. At each stop more and more people enter the train and, slowly but surely, we're surrounded by fans wearing the famous blue and white logo of the Yankees. The excitement grows and grows until we reach the 161st Street stop, just outside the famous stadium, "the house that Babe built." And I'm wondering, "who's Babe?" We go through the turnstile and meet the yells of vendors out-yelling each other:

"Programs! Programs! Get your programs ere!"

"Suvineeers! Get 'em now!"

"Pretzels! Pretzels!"

We're swept along with the crowd and carried up through the many levels of the stadium. Once we reach the level that our seats are located on, we enter a short corridor which thrusts us into the arena.

The sheer size, coupled with the bright lights, the emerald green field, and the roar of the crowd takes my breath away. I could not have imagined a more thrilling scene. My head's buzzing from the excitement and all I keep repeating to myself is, "you're in America. This is America. I love America."

Stalking carefully down the impossibly steep steps to our seats is a little frightening. One misstep, I'm sure, and I'd be hurled head first down three or four stories and out onto the field. But I manage it and we're seated at last. Then a cacophony of passing vendors rises up all around us, offering infinite choice:

"Peanuts! Ice cold beer! Hotdogs, crackerjack, ice cream! Who wants ice cream! Pretzels! Hotdogs! Git yo hotdogs ere! Soda, soda, soda, ice cold water! Who wants water! I got knishes! Knishes!"

My head's spinning with each shouted offer and the man next to me calls, "Peanuts!"

A bag of peanuts comes whizzing past my face and smacks neatly into the man's open hand. Then a box of something called Crackerjack is sailing over my head. Somebody sitting down the aisle wants a beer and I'm thinking, shit, I hope they don't throw that too! Someone reaches over and is handing me cash to pass on to the vendor who then gives me change to send back along the seats.

All this action and the game hasn't even started yet.

Meanwhile, my date is trying to cram the basics of the game into my already awestruck head. He tells me the team the Yankees are playing are the California Angels and that the former Yankee, Reggie Jackson, known as "Mr. October," one of the greatest players ever to play the game, is now on the Angels.

So, there's drama too, I think. Heartbreak, betrayal, mixed emotions, divided loyalties! Who knows, maybe even forgiveness and redemption! This is better than the sheep dog trials any day of the week. Wow, I decide. I really do love America.

Then the roar of the crowd rises to a deafening pitch. Everyone is standing which, given the height and the steep angle of the seats, is terrifying. Their beloved Yankees are introduced one by one to the crowd and, as each player trots out onto the field, they chant his name.

"Goose! Goose! Goose!" everyone starts screaming. This, my date explains, is the pitcher.

"His name is Goose?"

"Gossage."

"Gossage."

"Goose Gossage."

I'm still pondering this unfortunate name when the opposing team is introduced and Mister October himself shuffles out onto the field. The crowd goes crazy, screaming affectionately, "Reggie! Reggie! Reggie!"

"Oh, that's nice," I say to my date. "No hard feelings and all. Just lovely."

Then the announcer asks that we all stand for the national anthem. A hush falls over the crowd. Everyone removes their caps, sets aside their beer, and, with hand on heart, sort of sway side to side a little, waiting patiently, while someone semi-famous down on the field belts out "The Star-Spangled Banner". I'm already feeling like I've I had a whole evening's entertainment by the time the game gets underway.

Every time a player comes up to bat, music is blasted over the PA system. It dies down as he steps into the batter's box and the pitcher pauses to decide what he'll throw. Even the vendors shut up and wait. Then there's the pitch, followed by oohs and ahhhs throughout the stadium.

I have no idea what's going on.

"Did he throw a strike?"

"No, a ball," my date explains, patiently.

I'm thinking: how dumb does he think I am?

"I *know* it's a ball he threw. But was it a strike?"

"Well, that's for the umpire to decide."

Now I'm totally baffled. But I'm enjoying myself too much to worry about it. Food, alcohol, music, and baseball is a winning combination. Also, inning after inning, the crowd chants, shouts advice, or yells out insults and it's totally entertaining. We're surrounded by comedians. One guy off to our left, dismayed by a decision the umpire has made, calls down to the field:

"I thought only horses slept standing up, asshole!"

And then another smart aleck, after the Yanks just barely make it through an inning after giving up three runs, calls down to

Mister Goose:

"Nice route, Magellan!"

Now Mister October, himself, gets up to bat and the crowd goes nuts again. The pitcher throws the ball, the great man swings, something like the crack of a stick of celery is heard and everyone's on their feet. Trying to look through the standing crowd, I catch a glimpse of Mister October running from base to base. But mostly I'm just trying to stay out of the way as everyone around me scrambles, lurches, and dives towards a certain spot five or six bleachers above us. It looks like a fight, so I sit firmly in my seat. I cast a quick glance back at the ruckus of tangled bodies above me and notice a baseball bouncing down the steps in my direction. I pick it up and, to the sheer horror of my date, I say innocently:

"Shall I throw it back?"

He's white as a sheet.

"No, no, no!" he manages to reply, grabbing my wrist to make sure I don't do anything so thoughtless.

Now everybody is around us, congratulating me and asking to see the ball that the great Reggie Jackson has just sent careening into my own personal orbit. I oblige, happily, while my date shakes his head.

"Twenty-five years I've been coming to Yankee Stadium and I've never caught a ball—from anybody. You come here once and catch one from Reggie Jackson!"

I offer him the ball, which he refuses on principal. It's me that caught it and me that should keep it, he insists. Later, he even buys me a little plastic case to put my souvenir in. He instructs me to write the name of the batter on the ticket stub, too, and keep it in the case alongside the ball to make the memory complete and official.

"What was his name again," I ask, pen raised, just to be a smartass, "Mister December?"

From this day forward, though, I'm an avid baseball fan.

25.

After four years of working at my fulltime job, I'm ready to go it alone and create my own studio. I've saved enough money to get me through a few months in case I'm not immediately successful. The big problem, though, is how to continue working legally, as my work visa entitles me to work only for the company employing me. I consult a lawyer who informs me I'm not eligible for a green card and will lose my work privileges unless I'm sponsored by another company.

Disheartened though I am at first, I'm starting to see a pattern: 1) problem situation leads to, 2) disheartening funk, which leads to, 3) twenty minutes to think things over. Finally, one arrives at, 4) a solution so obvious only a lawyer could miss it.

Though people are suggesting the quickest and easiest solution is to get married, I'm having none of it. I call the lawyer and make another appointment.

"What if I create my own company and sponsor myself?"

Mister Big Shot Lawyer, Esquire, is intrigued. He thinks about it. You would have to incorporate," he says gravely, "and come up with a business plan, have letters of intent from potential clients and so on."

"I can make that happen."

He looks up from his paperwork, raises an eyebrow, and assesses me like he's only just noticed I'm there.

"Can you?"

So, I throw myself into the tedious and fairly expensive task at hand. But I learn a lot about business, law, finance, and taxes. A few months later, I'm the president of my own company. I successfully sponsor myself and receive a work visa.

I do feel bad about leaving my job, though. I'm eternally grateful for the opportunity I've been given in the first place and for all the challenges and experience, the responsibilities they've trusted me with. But I'm ready to move on. I hand in my two-week notice and they offer me more money to stay. But I can't be swayed. Later that same day, I'm summoned to the business managers office.

"Moya, you'll have to pack up your belongings and leave with an escort immediately."

"Why," I almost can't manage to ask, on the verge of tears.

"This is standard protocol for workers all through the fashion industry. Nothing personal. It's to prevent any stealing of ideas or, possibly, stealing of materials."

Now I feel like I've been slapped in the face and I'm too stunned to even curse her out properly. I'm escorted from the building.

The sting of that rude dismissal dissipates gradually as I enter this next uncertain chapter of my young life. Sequestered in my apartment, I work night and day, taking a break in the evening to walk to my favorite Chinese restaurant on Columbus Avenue at 72nd Street for the same dish, every evening, of chicken and broccoli. I'm so consumed by my work I can't be bothered to even read the menu and try something else.

My goal is to have around one hundred and fifty designs for my first collection. I achieve that in a matter of a few weeks and, finally, I feel I'm ready to show my work. I start making phone calls to all the manufacturers I know are potential clients. This is the most difficult part for me. But I'm surprised and encouraged by the response I get and soon my calendar is filled with appointments. I crop, clean, number, and mount my designs on fresh, crisp sheets of white paper. I know from viewing countless collections that presentation is crucial. The worst thing is to present work on ratty, scuffed, marked-up paper.

The time comes and I feel fully prepared. I've bought a few new outfits, a fancy new portfolio case to carry my treasured efforts around in, and I've had a good night's sleep. My first appointment is with the current doyenne of the garment center. She likes to be the first to see a collection and, since I'm lucky enough to have been granted this royal audience in the first place, I'm not about to haggle. In the conference room I'm led to, I undo the portfolio and carefully lay out my precious cargo.

Fortunately, I've witnessed the showing of a collection many times, so I know the routine. The stylist goes through the work with great speed, as though thumbing through a phone book. Then, if anything catches his or her eye, it is set aside. Next, the selected works are laid out and perused again. It is then that the decision to purchase or not is made. Sometimes a stylist will ask to take the designs away to show other departments. I know enough to agree to this only if I can accompany my work. You can't let it out of your sight as there are unscrupulous bastards who will photograph, xerox or have another artist replicate it on the spot rather than purchase it.

So, all is going well as the grand dame of Seventh Avenue is gliding through my ideas. I notice she has the hideously unhygienic habit of putting her thumb to her mouth every time she flips along to another page. But I think no more about it. In the end, she thanks me graciously for showing my work but says there's nothing in it she's looking for at this time. She leaves. And as I'm organizing my drawings, I'm horrified to see there has been an ulterior motive to her thumb-licking habit. Every time she brought her hand to her mouth, she made sure to graze her lips so that when she touched the lovely clean mounts, she'd deposit a smear of lipstick on each page—ensuring that any appointments I had afterward would know she'd been the first to see these designs.

I had a short break between appointments, just enough time to rush home and remount the entire collection before getting back on track. I'm furious the whole time. But I do learn a lesson: always do the page-turning myself.

Anyway, my first collection is a great success and I sell over half of it in my first series of appointments. I'm thrilled, of course. But I'm relieved, too. As easy as it is for me to push myself and work hard, I'm still half convinced I'm untalented. So, this little success is doing more than just paying the rent, it's giving me confidence.

26.

Flush with cash, I decide to treat myself to a holiday. I fly to Europe and seek inspiration for my next collection. Paris, Milan, Florence, London, then finally head back to Manchester, meet up with Me-mum and Me-dad, and make a trip to Ireland for a much-needed family getaway.

I arrive in Manchester exhausted after a whistle stop tour in Europe, catching eleven flights in eight days. As usual, I'm met at the airport by two little grey-haired figures excitedly waiting in their two-door brown hatchback Datsun.

Back in Wythenshawe, the only thing to see is the obvious and rapid decline of the neighborhood. There's new neighbors moved in who take great pleasure tormenting Me-dad by stealing his lovely hanging baskets and parking their car so it's impossible for him to get in and out of his own driveway. I'm ready to walk over there and read these miscreants the riot act, but Me-mum and Me-dad are eager to get going.

We fly from Manchester to Dublin. The plan is to rent a car there, travel around the country, and end up in Connemara where we'll stay with some friends. All seems straightforward enough until we're at the luggage carousel in Dublin Airport. Me-mum and Me-dad's luggage comes tumbling into view with the usual massive yellow yarn intact. But distressingly, there is no sign of my own bags.

I find the airline's help desk:

"No need to worry," I'm told. "It'll most likely be on the next flight.

We're given vouchers for lunch at the airport restaurant.

But the next flight arrives and—no luggage. Then the flight after that arrives and—no luggage.

I return to the help desk.

"Well, dearie," the kindly but helpless help desk attendant confesses, "since the address on the ID tag on your luggage was an address in New York..."

Wow. I gather my belongings are winging their way back across the Atlantic Ocean. I'm assured my bags will be retrieved and sent back this way by overnight courier and taken wherever I am staying. This sounds perfectly reasonable but for the fact that we do not know where we are going to be staying, at least for a couple of days. Our intention is to find bed-and-breakfasts wherever we decide to lay our heads.

Me-dad has a solution, though: why don't we first go visit his oldest sister, Mary, as she runs a post office and that will be an easy address to locate for anybody bringing my luggage.

Now, the term *Post Office* might be a little deceptive. Bekan Post Office is actually the living room of Me-auntie Mary's house. Basically, there is a counter by the front door where people suddenly appear just as you're engrossed in a TV show or a family get together. It's not unusual to hear a timid little cough and look up to see a farmer standing in the living room, money in hand, requesting a first-class stamp.

"For a letter I'm now going to be writing and sending to our Bridget who herself is now living in a community in America called Brooklyn that I hear is a grand place and not far from a place called New York that is also in America and which is where Me-uncle Shamus emigrated to after which he got a job digging a tunnel for a train that was under the earth if you could ever imagine such a thing and we all thought it would be the death of him which it was God have mercy on his soul because he was buried alive after the tunnel collapsed and nobody knew he was buried there for a fortnight when the wife couldn't find him and thought he had gone off on one of his long drinking binges as we all knew he had a problem with the drink which we thought would be the death of him also but we was wrong there and who would have ever imagined a train could run under the streets of a city? What will they think of next?"

And so on.

But that's where we go, showing up on Me-auntie Mary's doorstep unannounced and given a *great welcome altogether* (pronounced as one word). And me in my aggressively fashion-forward get-up! Red leather fringed jacket, narrow leg denim jeans, and my prized pink leather pointed ankle boots (a recent acquisition from my visit to Florence) plus, of course, my wild blond hair teased and tied into a pony tail with my trademark black velvet ribbon. What a sight this early-eighties fashion victim must be traipsing across the courtyard of Me-auntie Mary's house, tooth brush in hand, looking for the outdoor toilet!

"Now Maya," Me-auntie Mary inquires, puzzled (all my Irish relatives, including Me-dad, say my name like this): "Now Maya, let me ask you a question. Are you a cowboy in America?

"No, Auntie Mary," I explain, "I work in the fashion business and my clothes are in fashion right now. Really."

"Are they, now?" she replies, amazed. "Now, would ye ever had thought that? I believed I had seen it all, but this is a great enlightenment to me altogether now."

Of course, it's wonderful to see Me-dad reunited with his family and he's treated like royalty. Unfortunately, being a little lower on the regal scale, I'm given a blanket and told I'm sleeping on the couch in the living room. I'm shown where the stamps and the cash tin are in case Missus Malloy comes in early with letters to send.

Sure enough, Missus Malloy is bright and early:

"I am intending to write a letter to me son who is now living in England in a place called London I believe which I hear is such a grand place that the Queen herself lives there not that I have any interest in the Almighty Queen of frickin' England for she has done nothing to help the dear people of Ireland but prolong the misery and sadness which caused me uncle Malachy such torment that he was driven to the drink and chronic headaches that some people said was a direct result of the booze but I know he was such a sensitive soul that the thought of the injustices that were heaped upon our forebears was altogether too much for him to bear."

And so it begins, our little family jaunt becomes a lesson in the absurd and I've never laughed so hard in my life. Still waiting for news of my luggage, I decide to take matters into my own hands and called Élan overnight couriers. I'm informed a courier came to the address, found no one home, and so drove back to Dublin with my bag!

Clearly, this is a lie as I've been sitting there in the *post office* all day. Then I'm assured my stuff will be overnighted and arrive first thing in the morning. Which it is not. By now I'm wearing Me-mum's bloomers, which literally came up to my armpits, and my patience is wearing thin. To cool my worsening disposition, Me-dad suggests a visit to his youngest brother, Uncle Pat, who I haven't seen for years.

Uncle Pat is a quiet, gentle, beanpole of a man who is always puffing on his pipe. He shows us his lovely garden and his abundant crop of vegetables. When he hears the story of my lost luggage, he puffs on his pipe, pauses, then:

"Now Maya, I wouldn't have known ye yesterday," puff-puff, "but I will know ye tomorrow," puff-puff, "as ye will still be wearing the same clothes then."

We say our goodbyes and head back to Me-auntie Mary's house. We stop at regular intervals along way.

"Let's stop here and look at the view and have a bit of fresh air," Aunty Mary says.

This means she wants to have a cigarette.

I think I'm doing a grand job chauffeuring everybody through these narrow and twisting lanes of County Mayo until Me-auntie asks:

"Now Maya, do ye ever have problem driving on the wrong side of the road in America?"

"No, it isn't a problem for me, Aunty Mary."

"Well," she informs me, "Ye be having a big problem now as ye are on the wrong side of this Irish road!"

Three days wearing Me-mum's clothes and no bag in sight.

But it's a blessing in disguise, really, as it gives Me-dad time to show us all his childhood haunts; all the places we'd heard about for years and years. We visit the one room schoolhouse where he and his brothers and sisters made up almost a third of the students. This was the school he'd walk to barefoot to save wear the and tear on his precious shoes, only putting them on when he reached the school's gates. This was the school whose annual photograph one year showed Me-auntie Mary sitting proudly with the rest of the school kids, even though she was a married woman with her own children. But her presence built up the numbers and secured more funding. This was the school to which Me-dad would bring a couple of bricks of turf to put into the fireplace and heat the classroom.

His stories are endless and his blue eyes twinkle more than ever as he roams his beloved Ireland.

We visit the crumbling, tiny, one-room house he was raised in with ten others, crammed into a space no bigger than my studio apartment back in New York.

"Ye will never recognize the road now Charlie," says Auntie Mary, "it is a great feat of engineering. It is tarmacked all the way!"

Well, maybe. Maybe it was tarmacked all the way twenty or thirty years ago. Today it's a thin, winding, bumpy road with pot hots every three feet.

Me-dad's delighted to hear some of his childhood friends are still living in the area and Auntie Mary insists we should stop in and say hello.

"You're sure to be given a great welcome altogether!"

First stop is Finbar Lavin. She's heard he's been under the weather lately but is sure a visit from Me-dad will cheer him up enormously.

We pull up at a traditional thatched cottage that's seen better times. An older lady, Finbar's wife, opens the top half of the kitchen door. She and Me-auntie Mary exchanges pleasantries.

"Me brother, Charlie, is visiting from England and has come to visit Finbar."

We're asked to use another door as, "our good milking cow is giving birth in the kitchen and it's best that we not disturb her."

That sounds reasonable to me. If I was giving birth to a massive calf on the kitchen floor, I would not want to be disturbed either. So we go around the corner of the house and enter through another door into what might be a living room. It's difficult to tell due to the amount of squalor and chaos filling every corner. On a tattered armchair sits the great man himself, Finbar.

To say the sight of him is shocking would be an understatement. In the dark, gloomy room sits a gaunt, almost skeleton creature with a bandage wrapped around his face, exactly like the image of Van Gogh after he cut off his ear. This bandage is bloody and filthy and, apparently, covers the lesions from the cancer that is devouring him. I think I'm going to pass out and Me-mum turns a shade of green I've never seen before. But Me-dad carries on as if nothing was the slightest bit unusual. We're offered tea, which I decline before Finbar's wife can even get the question out of her mouth. After all, I think of saying, we wouldn't want to interrupt the enormous groaning cow in the kitchen.

Anxious to get out of this stench and gloom, I say I'll be outside looking at the lovely scenery. Me-mum jumps up and joins me in a flash.

"Lovely idea, Moya!"

"I wouldn't mind a bit of fresh air, myself," adds Auntie Mary, fumbling for her cigarettes.

The three of us stand out by the road, gazing bleary-eyed at the far mountains, trying to catch our breath. Eventually, out comes Me-dad, waving his goodbyes, seemingly unaware of the horror and sadness we've all just witnessed. Back in the car, it's suggested we stop in and see the famous Mary Gallagher.

Me-mum's a little antsy at this. She leans close and whispers:

"This is your father's old girlfriend."

I can see she's uncomfortable and yet a different shade of green—the jealous shade!

What a relief it is to pull up to a new, immaculate, modern bungalow. There will be no cow birthing a calf in this house, I assume. We walk up the path to the front door, ring the bell, and are met by a woman in her forties, and in the usual Irish way she says:

"Hello, who are ye? I don't know ye!"

Me-dad explains he's an old friend of her mother's and is visiting the area with his family.

"Me name is Charlie Hession."

We're asked to wait while she turns in and yells out:

"Mammy, you have a visitor! Charlie Hession!"

"Charlie Hession!" we hear. "Charlie Hession, the greatest man in the county! Where are ye?"

We enter the living room and I can't believe my eyes. There she is, the famous Mary Gallagher, her enormous soft body squeezed into an armchair, her legs spread wide, around her ankles the remnants of pantyhose that have long given up trying to support her massively swollen legs. Her toothless mouth is wide open to reveal a tongue that flickers in and out like a turtle looking for insects. And the crowning glory is her beard!

I look at Me-mum who mouths to me, in a smug yet uncertain way: "That could have been your mother."

Mary Gallagher's excitement fills the room, though. When Me-dad bends down to kiss her forehead, she grabs him and holds him in something like a headlock. Finally, she lets go as her daughter pulls in a dining room chair for Me-dad to sit on right up alongside his old flame. Taking advantage of his nearness, Mary Gallagher puts her arm around his shoulder and doesn't let go for a second the whole time we're there, all the while repeating, "Charlie Hession, the greatest man in the County!"

We're served tea in nice clean China cups with soda bread. The conversation is one-sided, to say the least, but it's great to see Me-dad visiting old memories.

Day four with no bag is a Sunday, so there will be no reunion with my luggage today. Off to church we go, me looking like a bigger pratt than ever, sauntering up the aisle for communion in my pink Italian ankle boots, my red fringe leather jacket swishing with every step I take. After mass, I find me uncle Pat standing outside puffing on his pipe. He looks me over and shakes his head, not surprised. I tell him of our previous day's excitement and how we visited Mary Gallagher.

"Tell me something, Maya," puff-puff, "did she shave yet?"

Looking for something to do, Me-dad wants to drive around the old familiar roads and stop by again to see poor old Finbar. But me and Me-mum are screaming our heads of:

"Noooooooooooo!!!!"

So, we compromise and stop into see Mary Gallagher again. This, we can handle. We go through the motions again. "Charlie Hession, the greatest man in the county!" Vicelike grip. Me-mum quietly seething and me just fascinated by the facial hair. Truly astonishing.

"Now, tell me, Charlie Hession," Mary Gallagher, asks, "when was the last time I saw ye?"

Checking his wristwatch, Me-dad answers affectionately:

"It was twenty-four hours ago, Mary."

Mary Gallagher throws her head back and sighs:

"Twenty-four years ago! Be Jesus, it seems like just yesterday!"

Back at Auntie Mary's I decide to take drastic measures and call Élan overnight couriers again. Me-mum sits by listening as I start in on the poor soul who has the misfortune to be on the receiving end of my wrath:

"Can you tell me what your definition of overnight is? Because where I come from the definition is that when I go bed at night, the next morning I wake up to find my lost luggage on the doorstep! I have been very patient with you but I need my bag as I have a very serious kidney disease and I have just used the last of my medication, the rest of which is in the bag that is now in your possession. So if I do not receive my medication within the next twenty-hour hours I will be forced to have a dialysis treatment which is so very expensive and as I have no insurance you will be responsible for all the costs that I incur due to your negligence!"

I slam the phone down and look at Me-mum who's now on her knees, praying.

"Moya, you should never lie about something so terrible! I am ashamed of you!"

Ashamed or not, she's relieved to see my battered but intact luggage waiting for me on the doorstep early Monday morning.

There's a sadness leaving Mayo after seeing Me-dad in his natural element, so to speak. But we're excited to travel to the beautiful county of Connemara and the picturesque town of Cliftden.

I spent some wonderful times in Cliftden during college with my friends and met some great people. On the first night there with my parents, visiting a local pub, I run into one of them, a lovely girl named Erin. Catching up with Erin, I learn she now lives in Galway city in a great flat she shares with a very nice young man. I ask how she likes having a roommate and she explains:

"Ah, it is grand altogether! But I must admit I felt awful sorry for him yesterday. He was in a terrible state. He works for a courier service and yesterday he had some maniac Englishwoman on the phone saying she needed her pills for a very serious medical problem and if she didn't get her pills immediately, she'd be on dialysis and he'd be responsible for the cost of the treatment!"

I'm incredulous. Erin sips her drink and shakes her head:
"Have ye ever heard such a terrible thing?"

I confess, "Erin, that was me!"

Wide-eyed, crushed with sympathy, Erin grabs my arm: "Ah, no Maya, I never knew you had such an illness! I am very sorry to hear that! I will keep ye in my prayers!"

"Erin, I don't—" But how do I explain this? "I'm fine."

Like every little girl, I've always thought Me-dad was the greatest, strongest, handsomest man in the world. Nevertheless, I'm surprised by the attention he's getting from some of the local ladies of Connemara! Charlie—who only looks in the mirror when he's shaving and walks out the door sometimes with a clothes hanger still inside his jacket—Charlie is proving irresistible to women of a certain age. This is not going unnoticed by Me-mum, even though Me-dad is completely oblivious of the stir he's causing. Before long, a woman starts to flirt with him. He's his usual gentle self, smiling innocently. But Me-mum sits straight up and glares at this pushy floozy who just turns to Charlie and asks:

"Do ya know what I would like to do to you?" Puzzled, Charlie just sits there innocently. So, she continues: "I'd like to take ye to the river, role ye down the embankment and pick the thorns from your arse afterwards."

Holy Mother of God! Are my ears deceiving me? Still, Me-dad just sits there, smiling amiably. I don't think he's even heard what this gal has said. But Me-mum has. And she's either going to burst out crying or faint. I gently take the lunatic by the arm, move down the bar, offer to buy her a drink, which she eagerly accepts, and whisper into her ear: "If you come anywhere near my parents again, I will take you to the river, roll you down the embankment, and put the thorns *in* your arse afterwards."

~

Cliftden is a typical small Irish village in that it has a pub about every fifty yards. The last call to order drinks is ten thirty and no more alcohol is supposed to be served after that. The landlords just draw the pub's curtains and everything continues as is—out of sight out of mind, even with the sound of clinking glasses and boozy revelry which you can hear perfectly well from half way up the road. Though the Garda, or police, occasionally do make the rounds after last call and raid the pubs.

On the last day of our holiday, I make sure Me-mum and Me-dad are safely in their beds and go out to make a night of it with my friends. We start in one pub, then onto the next. Three pubs later, we're into after hour service and all is going well until the phone rings and we're informed the Garda are making the rounds. They're one pub behind us. Everybody scurries out the back door and I follow blindly. The crowd of us stumble down the backyard, climb over a neighbor's wall, and enter the back door of the Riley's house.

Missus Riley is sitting by the fire, a gentle lady of late middle age, sipping her tea, as we all march through the kitchen and into the living room towards her front door.

"The Garda raiding tonight, are they?" she says, mildly.

"Evening, Missus Riley," says a young man just ahead of me, removing his cap respectfully.

"Thomas Murtuogh, say hello to ye mother," Missus Riley replies. "And Bridey," she calls, spotting a teenage girl, "tell ye mother I will see her at benediction tomorrow, ye welcome."

She's perfectly unperturbed by this steady stream of fifty or so drunks marching through her home.

We all spill out into another street around the corner. The Garda has, meanwhile, been and gone at the pub and are now on to the next one. So, we all parade back to where we started and pick up where we left off.

27.

Back in the States, rested and refreshed, I crank out another collection of designs. I fall back into my routine, locking myself away in my apartment and doing what I love doing most: designing. I've built up a steady group of clients now and secured commissioned pieces as well. So, I'm busy. And I now decide I will try selling my work on the West Coast too. I've been having some success in the swimwear market.

In, Los Angeles, there's a totally different way of working. In New York, for instance, all the manufacturers are in the garment center, a single crowded neighborhood in the center of the city, so you navigate your way around on foot. Los Angeles is a city that sprawls. It's impossible to get from client to client unless you have a car and are familiar with the relentless LA traffic. This means hiring an agent who makes all the appointments in advance, is my personal chauffeur, and who takes forty percent of all sales made. I'm responsible for airfare, car rental, and hotel accommodation. I interview a few candidates and settle on a lively and energetic woman named Marcy to be my West Coast representative.

It's quite a change from dragging my massive portfolio around on a cart down the bustling sidewalks of Manhattan, then trying to squeeze into a crowded elevator, hoping not to piss off too many people as I awkwardly maneuverer the portfolio and trap them into its corners. Then I have to drag the monster out every time somebody needs to get off at a different floor.

Not so in laidback LA.

I stay at the Shangri La Hotel in Santa Monica with a beautiful view of the Pacific. I wake up and make myself a nice breakfast, peruse the newspaper I find sitting outside my door, and await the arrival of my "agent." Downstairs, I'm greeted by Marcy, itinerary in hand, and her spanking new Mercedes, ready to whisk me off to as many appointments as the LA traffic will permit.

It's a much more civilized way to conduct business and there is nobody trying to smear lipstick on my work or trying to kidnap my designs. And even if that does happen, I have Marcy taking care of me.

At the end of my first LA trip, I've sold about forty designs, which is pretty good. But after the agent's commission and expenses, it's nowhere near as profitable as selling on my own. Still, I think, it's great to get away to sunny California every once in a while.

I'm fortunate to meet some friends of friends one evening at a dinner party and I'm introduced to a couple named Richard and Claude. To this day, they remain my dearest friends. Richard is a respected Oscar nominated film director and Claude is this tiny French woman whose previous occupation was—lion tamer! Yes, a fucking lion tamer.

"You mean real lions?"

"*Oui*."

"Like lions that can tear you to pieces? Those kinds of lions?"

"*Exactement*!"

Later, Claude asks if I want to spend a day up in the mountains at Big Bear Lake. I have no idea where that is, but I agree immediately because I somehow know this fascinating couple are going to be my friends for life. Claude says she'll pick me up Saturday morning.

Saturday arrives and so does Claude, alone.

"Where's Richard," I ask.

"Oh, he's at the airport waiting for us."

"Airport?"

"Yes, he's getting the plane ready for our trip!"

"Plane as in like you have your own plane?"

"But, of course! Moya, here, get in!"

And off we go to the Santa Monica airport to find Richard waiting for us, seated in the cockpit of his twelve-seat Cessna. I'm not put off by the array of good luck charms around the door. But I am a little nervous. This aircraft looks to be about the size of a small school bus. Smaller maybe. But before I know it, we're up in the air and Richard is piloting with ease and confidence. In any case, I learn Claude is also a pilot. So, if Richard should have another heart attack mid-flight…

ANOTHER!!!

But all goes well.

This is to be the first of many trips I take with this dynamic duo. Sometimes we fly to San Francisco for lunch. We go skiing in Aspen. But my favorite is a jaunt to Las Vegas, especially the flight back over the desert, watching shooting stars in the black night sky. Definitely different than my first time in Vegas!

Claude insists I stay in their guest house whenever I come to LA on business. They live in Bel Air, the fanciest neighborhood in LA, basically mansion after mansion, most of which are hidden behind massive hedges and enormous gates.

The first time I stay with them, it occurs to me to take a little stroll and check out the neighborhood. I walk down the driveway and press the button that opens the large metal gates. As I pass on out to the road, the gates automatically close behind me. And now I discover something about wealthy communities: they don't have sidewalks! Plus, they love winding curvy roads. So, every time you walk outside your property, you're basically taking your life in your hands. Wealthy people like fast cars too, cars that aren't very noisy either. So, you don't even hear them coming. This turns your lovely little stroll into a big game of *Split the Kipper*.

It's then I realize I have no identification on me. I decide to turn back and get it since if I get run down and killed on the roads of Bel Air who the hell is going to know who I am? I walk along the road with my back up against the hedges like I'm inching my way along a twelve-inch ledge ten stories above the street. Finally, I reach the wrought iron gates of Richard and Claude's compound, ring the bell, and wait.

Nothing. They don't glide open majestically. There's no polite and curious voice coming to me through the shiny little intercom. I stand there in the brilliant California sunshine in my usual New York top-to-toe black ensemble feeling not a little out of place. Then I come to my senses and ask myself:

"What would a girl from Wythenshawe do?"

Only one thing to do: climb over the gate and hope I don't get shot, electrocuted, or arrested. My major concern, however, is that I'd scuff my fabulous Russell and Bromley black crepe-soled rockabilly shoes. But desperate times require desperate measures. And so here goes.

It's not quite as easy as I thought. These gates, it occurs to me, were definitely designed to keep people out. No fooling around. They're not here for show. Job well done, whoever you are. After climbing slowly up the outside, carefully finding purchase for each delicate toe of my well-loved shoes, I'm now straddling the dangerously pointed spikes at the top of the gate, riding the thing like a rodeo cowgirl on the back of a bucking bronco, standing in her stirrups. A car passes by occasionally, fast and quietly, probably not even noticing me. Relieved when they don't stop and yell at me, I'm about to swing my other leg over and jump from the top when here comes another big problem. A very huge problem by the name of Leroy.

Leroy, the seven-foot-tall Great Dane, who was ever so friendly as I was petting him by the pool earlier. But Leroy is definitely not so friendly now. He's barking and woofing like a maniac. Fuck, fuck, fuck. Maybe I can charm this dog, calm him down with an old Irish lullaby. I start singing and Leroy goes ballistic, beside himself with doggish outrage. I consider going back out and taking my chances on the formula one racing circuit of Bel

Air. But just as I'm about the swing my leg back out over the gate, I feel an unfamiliar yet not totally unpleasant sensation throughout my entire body. The gate is moving, humming with calm electric efficiency, opening.

It is the pool man outside in the road. He has a remote for opening the gate. He's sitting behind the wheel of his truck with a puzzled look on his face.

"Hi, I am staying with Richard and Claude and my name is…"

But he just drives inside and lets the gates close again with me still perched up top. Just as I think he's going to leave me there he goes over and calms Leroy down. This gives me time to make my descent and try to claim some semblance of self-worth.

Back in New York, working alone in my apartment for days on end, I feel the need to visit the bar to check in with my friends a couple of times a week. I have a busy social life with people my own age but, as always, I enjoy the company of the guys I know from when I was waitressing. I know they *have my back*. Especially Davey. He's the sweetest man. An ironworker. His job entails assembling the structural iron beams for the massive skyscrapers of the city, balancing hundreds of feet in the air. Fearless. I also know teamsters, longshoremen, detectives. Plus, as the bar is located on West Fifty-Seventh Street, I meet numerous people working in the television stations located nearby: CBS, ABC, Channel Thirteen. And the one that interests me the most—MTV.

Like most young people in America in the eighties, I love my MTV. The music, fashion, the great videos, the whole look and feel of the network is fresh and exciting. So, I'm very happy to meet the head of human resources one evening. Davey or one of the other guys points out I'm a designer. And I express my enthusiasm for MTV. So, the next time the man comes in he asks if I have a current portfolio.

Do I ever! My portfolio is so current I'm working on tomorrow's ideas yesterday. He says if I give him some samples of my work, he'd show it to the creative director when he got a chance. I select a bunch of work I think might be suitable for a graphic design position at a TV network, even though I really don't have a clue what that is. I give it to him, but I don't expect too much to come of it. So, it's quite a shock when, a few days later, I receive a call saying the creative director is impressed and would love to meet me.

As usual, I'm excited and nervous; anxious to try but afraid I won't be good enough. But the brat from Wythenshawe deep within badgers me: "You got nothing to lose! Get on with it!"

So, I get on with it.

A meeting is arranged with Nan Cadorin, the creative director.

Incredibly, I discover the MTV studios are directly across the street from my apartment. I'm taken into a large, dark, smoky, windowless room where the only light emanates from the four TV monitors glowing along one wall. Nan is very welcoming and friendly, we chat and she explains the basic tasks her department is responsible for creating: logos, show openings, news graphics, special events, etcetera. I listen intently, not knowing what she's talking about but trying to seem like I do.

"Have you had much experience with computer graphics," she asks.

"Computer graphics," I repeat, dazed, winded. I'm still sharpening my pencils with a freaking surgeon's scalpel! "Actually," I continue bravely, "I've never really worked on a computer. In fact, I'm not sure I've ever even been close to one."

Undeterred, Nan shows me the system they use, something called a Quantel Paintbox. I'm immediately intimidated. I pretend to understand what she's talking about as she demonstrates for me on the large glassy drawing surface in front of one of the monitors.

"You use the pen tool to draw here on this surface and what you're doing shows up there on the monitor."

Nothing too unnatural about that, is there, I think, still skeptical. Drawing and looking up at a TV screen. Kind of like looking at the reflection in the mirror from another mirror and trying to fasten a button on the back of your dress.

Impossible! I'm overwhelmed by all the machinery: cameras hooked up to monitors, massive cabling, blinking lights, scary sci-fi looking waveform monitors, complicated potentiometers, artists sitting in front of screens, rapidly swiping the pen tool to the right before dragging it back in a downward motion to bring up menus and palettes, palettes and colors appearing in an instant. Back down in the garment district, or alone in my apartment, I'm used to spending as much as two hours painstakingly matching colors from tiny swatches of fabric, trying to match some precious swatch of silk that changes color as the light fades or brightens; trusting my instinct, knowing the material, hands on. Not here in magical MTV land where a mere tap on a surface of the touch screen and—*voila!*—the desired color is literally staring you right in the face.

Nan then opens a door and shows me the inner workings of the Paintbox, a room the size of my apartment filled to the gills with more lights, buttons, switches, wires, plugs, monitors and the ever-steady hum of MTV's visual splendor cranking away. I'm informed this machine cost half a million dollars and that the only place to train on it is at Quantel headquarters in Connecticut, and that costs five thousand dollars for a weekend course and, even then, there is no "hands on" with the valuable equipment.

Well, thanks for the tour, Nan, I'm about to say, but I have four swatches to match back in my apartment and so I will be busy for the rest of the week. But, not noticing my dismay, she asks me to write down my information in case something comes up that I might be useful for. I write these down and hand her my details. When she reads them, she says: "Great handwriting. We need somebody that can write like this for on-air titles and lower thirds." Again, I pretend to understand this lingo and nod appreciatively. But then Nan has another idea. She offers me the opportunity to learn Paintbox by coming to the studio and observing the other artists at work. "Then, when there's downtime," she adds, "you can come in and practice using the equipment when nobody else needs it."

So, it begins. I'm still able to work on my textile designs and can pop into the studio whenever I have a break. On the weekends, and especially on Sunday after Mass, I spend hours trying to figure out how to operate this alien creature, Mister Quantel Paintbox. It definitely does not come easily to my untechnical brain and antiquated system of working. But I'm determined to be open to the new technology, even though deep down I think it's a bit of a fad. I like being in the studio, though. The graphics department is sequestered away in a cave on the second floor. It's easy to recognize the graphic artists as they have the pallor of a video screen tan and when they leave the building they stand outside blinking, shielding their eyes as they rummage through their belongings, desperately trying to find their sunglasses.

Initially, I'm nervous at being entrusted with such a valuable piece of equipment. But eventually I relax and focus on trying to learn the basics of this brave new world. I begin my steady routine of observing. And, after all, it is fun going over to the studio and peeking into the soundstage on the ground floor. It looks like just a bunch of teenagers having fun most of the time. But big things are happening, apparently. I enjoy seeing the daily parade of musicians and movie stars coming and going. It's cool passing celebrities in the hallway, being herded by their *people*, on their way to another interview on the neon-colored sets.

All is going along smoothly until I decide to stop by the graphics department one Monday afternoon. As I enter, I sense there is something very wrong since the overhead lights are on in a room I didn't even realize had overhead lights. Nan and a couple of her colleagues look distressed.

"Moya, did you use the Paintbox over the weekend?"

"Yes, I was in on Sunday," I reply, already assuming the worst.

"Did you notice any problems?

"No."

"Did you do anything different with it?"

"No, just practicing with the drawing tool and saving my work."

Meanwhile the house technicians are unplugging things and frowning, flicking switches and plugging things back in, typing on keyboards, all the while, casting dark looks at me.

"Now, when were you here again," Nan asks, truly worried, "Sunday?"

"Yes, after Mass."

"Did you bring anyone in with you?"

"No."

"And everything seemed okay?"

"Yeah. Nothing out of the ordinary. But, of course, how would I know?"

Nan nods. She sighs.

"The whole system is down and we're waiting for the engineers from Quantel to get here and figure out what happened."

Horrified, I go over in my mind what I might have done. Since it seems like I must have done it. But as far as I can recall, nothing was amiss when I left on Sunday evening. Now I am being told the entire library of MTV graphics has been wiped out; every logo, title, show opening, photograph, animation, background, basically every image that has ever appeared on all the network's programming is now gone forever and I was the last person to use the equipment that created it.

Fuck, fuck, fuck, nooooooo! This is horrible. Worse than horrible. Worse than anything I have ever experienced. Worse than Sister Sheila! That kind of bad. Not to mention it's hugely embarrassing.

I excuse myself and return to my apartment. I really want to go to the bar and have a drink but I'm far too humiliated to explain that I've personally destroyed several years of MTV's graphics and it's gone forever. So, I sit in my little apartment and squirm, fretting about the havoc I've caused. Then the phone rings and it's Nan. Oh no! What now? Are they going to press charges? Deport me back to England?

"Listen," Nan begins, "the Quantel engineers are here and they think they've figured out what the problem is."

"I didn't touch anything I don't usually touch," I rush to explain. "Just trying out the color palette and filters with the drawing tool and... and..."

"Moya, relax."

Apparently, sometime after I'd left the building on Sunday, during a brief but intense downpour which I just narrowly escaped, the MTV studios were struck by lightning. That jolt had blown out the Paintbox.

"In fact," Nan continues, "it's lucky you weren't using it when it happened as you could have been severely injured."

I cannot believe my ears. If this natural disaster had occurred in my presence, and assuming I was not myself blown to smithereens, I probably would have covered the Quantel Paintbox with newspapers, skulked home, packed a suitcase, and left the country. So, what a relief—for me.

Unfortunately, however, there is no backup of any of the graphics. This is a huge setback for the network. But the bright shiny side of this coin—again, for me—is that, as I can draw without the aid of a computer, I'm desperately needed to assist in the long process of drawing logos, outlines, title cards, etcetera, all of which will then be photographed, scanned, and stored into the computer all over again and brought back to their funky neon-infused glory.

So begins my fulltime employment at MTV.

And, yes, I do *want* my MTV.

Part Four

28.

I like my new job even though the technological learning curve is steep. Though, as far as ideas and design styles go, I'm completely at home. I just have to learn as I go.

And it seems everyone wants to work for MTV. Nan is regularly deluged with requests for meetings and interviews, anything just to get to see the revered graphics department. As usual, she is receptive and generous with her time. I admire her for this and doubt I could ever be so tolerant. One letter has her grinning in disbelief:

"Oh, my, Moya, listen to this: 'Hi, my name is Edie Moss. Remember that name because I am going to work for you and will probably end up running the creative department.'"

The letter goes on to list the young lady's credentials, which include degrees from a pretty solid American college and the Sorbonne in Paris. These notwithstanding, my first instinct is to say she sounds like a fucking nightmare. But Nan says let's give her a shot.

Well, Miss Edie shows up and does not disappoint. She's very cute and clad head to toe in Jean Paul Gautier, with a Hermes bag thrown in for good measure. Gulp. So far, her confidence is clearly backed up by a tremendous sense of style. Nan, ever magnanimous, says she'll happily give the fabulous Edie a trial.

Edie seems to know her way around a computer and her massive cockiness encourages Nan to let her attempt some simple on-air graphics for the news stories. The first time she's left alone to illustrate a story about some band's tour, she designs a page with a clenched fist and it goes on-air right away. Next morning, I see the work and I'm impressed; that is until the phones start ringing with irate people looking for Nan. They want to know who approved the use of this copyrighted Amnesty International logo for a story about a band's roadie getting into a bar fight.

Edie doesn't stick around for very long. She quickly grows tired of the mundane realities associated with trying to take over Nan's job. But Nan is gracious and polite and wishes the cute young climber all the best.

But, otherwise, the great thing about MTV is the pool of young talent it nurtures. There are many young producers being given their first professional opportunities, madly enthusiastic about their work, and learning from everything all the time. So many shows we work on week after week, month after month! Entertainments with such titles as: *120 Minutes*, *Headbanger's Ball*, *Remote Control*, *Post Modern*, *Yo! MTV Raps*, *The Big Picture*, *Fast Forward*, *Half Hour Comedy Hour*. And many specials featuring new releases and movies. All of this coupled with the constant buzz about Madonna, Michael Jackson (who always has to be referred to as "The King of Pop"), Bon Jovi...

If I have to do one more graphic with Bon Jovi's *New Jersey* album cover which, along with Guns N' Roses' new album, is the daily staple in our department, I'm going to go mad and start a campaign to bring back Perry Como or Tom Jones. And it's not just me. In a kind of rebellion, the TV in our department is always tuned to some soap opera or other, as after a while a little MTV goes a very long way.

Seeing as we're tucked away in the studio a few of blocks from the main office, we're quite isolated from most of the people who are producing the shows. And it's always nice to get visits from colleagues when they show up to explain what visuals they have in mind for their projects. Sometimes, they're arrogant and brash. But the majority are bright and grateful for any input and ideas we might have.

There's one young producer whose show is *The Half Hour Comedy Hour*. His name is Bill Aiken and he's the sweetest, kindest, the most thoughtful of all the producers. I personally don't have any dealings with him as he always just meets with Nan who then delegates the work to whomever is available. Always, after he leaves, Nan comments on how delightful Bill is to work with.

One segment of Bill's show features various new comedians in a piece called *Ones to Watch*. I'm often delegated that particular job. Apparently, Bill spends many hours visiting all the comedy clubs in New York looking for upcoming talent which might then be given air time. So, I'm working on installments of *Ones to Watch* featuring Adam Sandler, Damon Wayans, David Spade, Steven Wright, Denis Leary, Louis CK, and many others who will go on to become household names.

One evening, late, I'm working away in the studio with another artist preparing news graphics for the following day's broadcast when the phone rings. I pick it up to hear somebody introduce himself as a reporter looking for a story on the raging fire that is currently consuming MTV.

"Excuse me," I ask, bewildered.

"The building is on fire," he insists. "Do you have any comments?"

"No. Goodbye!" and I hang up.

"What's up," my colleague asks, concerned.

"Come on! We've got to get out of here!"

We rush out of the building and stand on the opposite sidewalk on West 57th at 10th Avenue. It's two in the morning and there is nothing to even remotely suggest there is a fire happening.

"Just someone having fun with us," my colleague suggests.

"Maybe."

Back inside, we return to our work. Only then does it occur to me the package we're waiting for, a package that arrives daily from the main office over on Broadway containing the day's graphics to reproduce for the news, has still not arrived.

And it still doesn't hit me.

The phones are now ringing again with journalists asking about the blazing fire tearing through MTV.

"Clearly a hoax," I say, hanging up again. But now I'm not so sure. I call over to the main office. There's no answer. We turn on the TV and watch in amazement, our jaws hung open, as a report ensues about the blazing fire ravaging the main headquarters of MTV at 1775 Broadway.

By the next afternoon, the New York City Fire Department estimates that twenty-five percent of the 10th floor corporate offices of MTV are completely gutted. The cause of the fire is determined to have been an overloaded extension cord. Luckily, a lot of the graphics and programming data are still over with us at the 10th Avenue studio, so the network doesn't need to shut down. We go right on with the show.

Not yet sure, though, about what has and what has not been destroyed, Nan keeps us busy repurposing old graphics and speedily creating new filler to tide us over for a few days. We're all told to convene in the stage for a strategy meeting. The atmosphere is solemn, but we're reassured right away that we will recover and move forward. Somebody has gained access to the burnt-out offices and shows us videotape of the carnage: fallen ceilings, melted monitors and computers, mounds of video tape reduced to big, steaming, molten blobs, blackened desks and filing cabinets. The camera pans around in an eerie silence and comes to Bill Aiken's office door.

Bill, who is notoriously fastidious and organized, is presently on vacation and left his office in immaculate condition. Crazily, while his office itself is now obliterated, the only thing unscathed is a sign he taped to the door, reading: "If you use this office, please leave it in the condition you found it in. Thanks, Bill."

At that, all of us burst out laughing. A moment of much needed levity.

I become friends with an actor named Brian Murray whose brother, it turns out, is the hugely famous actor and comedian, Bill Murray. I get together with Brian every so often and we sometimes go to an Irish bar on 14th Street which, every Friday evening, hosts a night of traditional music, dance, and storytelling called a *caelli*. One night, his brother joins us and a naive young friend of mine visiting from Ireland asks him what he does for a living. The famous Bill Murray answers simply and humbly that he's an actor, which greatly excites my friend.

"Well, be Jesus! Would you ever believe that I am an actor also! Now tell me something: have you ever been in a filum?"

Bill just shrugs, "a couple." And he leaves it at that.

A little later, I get up to participate in the dance, "The Siege of Ennis", which requires a little know-how. There's a tap on my shoulder and when I turn around there's Bill Murray asking me to teach him the steps.

Some weeks later, before heading back to England for Christmas, I meet up with Brian to attend a small party for the people working at the stage. As it happens, the party is quite a nonevent as most everybody is still burnt out from the massive annual Christmas party MTV hosted the night before, featuring some huge rock band. I'm talking to a couple of my colleagues when Brian arrives. He steps away to get us some drinks as Bill Aiken comes over and mentions he's a big fan of Brian's.

"Would you mind introducing me?"

"No, not at all."

Brian seems happy to meet Bill and we chat for a while. It's the first time I've really spoken to Bill and, as Brian and I are leaving, I mention I'm heading to England later that night. "But when I get back, we should grab a drink sometime," I add, pretty innocently.

Bill thinks that's a great idea.

29.

That night, as I head to JFK to catch my Pan Am flight to London, the limo driver informs me there's been a plane crash at JFK and it seems very bad. I expect to see some kind of pandemonium as I reach the airport but there's nothing. I probably misunderstood the driver. It's only when I enter the terminal that I discover what happened. The date is December 21st 1988 and Pan Am flight 103 has crashed over Lockerbie, Scotland, en route to Detroit, killing 270 innocents, including eleven people on the ground.

After a solemn flight across the Atlantic, I land at Heathrow and immediately call Me-mum and Me-dad to let them know I'm safe and will be boarding the flight to Manchester shortly.

Coming into land at Manchester, I look out over the green fields and then to the crammed warren of Wythenshawe. From above it looks like any other green belt housing estate. But I know better. It's the place I try to avoid admitting I'm from, where I was raised, the place people ridicule and give names like "debtors retreat," the place that still causes me so much embarrassment.

But it's also the place where the two most important people in my world live. I stand outside the terminal and wait for the little two door Datsun hatchback to appear, carrying two figures whose hair is, now, white and who, like everything else at home, seem a little smaller than I remember. I also know that the moment Me-dad sets eyes on me he'll begin to cry and, as he drives us the two miles to the house, he'll be fidgeting and sliding his hands on the steering wheel, barely able to contain his excitement at having me home.

Christmas is the same as usual. Just like Me-mum tells everybody. "Quiet. You know, just the three of us. Oh, yes, Moya is home from New York for a month."

Quiet is fine with me. Being with them is perfect. I make them laugh with tales of New York and they hang on my every word. I meet up with friends for drinks, but every time Me-mum hears me making arrangements for a night out she can't hide her disappointment that I'll be out of their sight for a couple of hours. I dread telling her I'm going to Wales to visit Lynne, Phil, and their little girls and will be gone for a whole weekend. But she knows Lynne is my greatest friend and I'd never set foot in the UK without a journey to North Wales.

Lynne's life has turned out to be nothing either of us could ever have imagined. She's content, though a little lonely at times. Her house is on a remote section of the coast road, directly across from a farm and within a mile of the Irish Sea; nothing like the desolate grey streets of Wythenshawe. She loves living in the country and is happy to bring the girls up far from the smoky atmosphere of the city. Phil is still the avid outdoorsman with a garage full of stinky game aging in preparation for dinner. The freezer is crammed with trout and skinned rabbits, all of which I still find revolting. But at least they eat what he kills. The girls are a treat to be with and Lynne is a proud and dutiful mother.

The Holidays pass quickly and I head back to New York and my steady routine. My first day back at work, just as I'm approaching the front door of the studios, out walks Bill Aiken.

"Hi, Moya! How was your trip? When did you get back?"

"I just got back last night," I reply. "It was nice, saw the family and friends, and…"

What else to say?

"We should have that drink sometime," I suggest.

"Sure. Love to."

"I often stop by the bar there on 57th Street. I have some friends there. Used to work there, actually."

And with that we say our goodbyes. And I think no more about it. Or do I? He's not bad looking, I have to say. And he is ever so polite and considerate. Is he taking a shine to me? No, no. He's just being nice. Anyway, the following Friday night I stop into the bar to catch up with my friends and after about fifteen minutes, in walks Bill Aiken. It's nice to see him but I'm all of a sudden bashful about seeing him outside the work environment. (Yeah, me, bashful! Imagine that!)

He buys me a drink and we chat for an hour straight. Then:

"You want to grab some dinner?"

"I am hungry. Sure."

We walk a few blocks to the Broadway Diner.

Over dinner we talk nonstop for what seems like only an hour but turns out to be closer to three. We discover we have much in common: both practicing Catholics, both with an Irish heritage (Bill's grandmother was born five miles from where my father grew up), we're both the youngest in our families, both adore our parents, and so on.

Bill's so easy to talk to and he's a wonderful listener, an unusual trait for a young man who is pretty obviously brilliant and accomplished.

We leave the restaurant and walk the few blocks west to Ninth Avenue. He offers to walk me to my door, but I assure him it's not necessary. We say goodnight and, as Bill walks away, I watch him go and tell myself I am going to marry him if he turns around and looks back at me before he reaches Fifty-Fourth Street. And just before he reaches the corner, he turns and glances back at me, a shy smile on his face.

"Okay," I sigh. "I am going to marry Bill Aiken."

However, I do not hear from my future husband after this. He hadn't asked for my phone number. But, then, of course, he knows where to reach me. Maybe I'm wrong and he didn't enjoy our time together on Friday.

A few days later, I'm sitting at the drawing board in the corner of the graphics department when Bill appears. I'm momentarily flustered but it seems he doesn't even see me. He crosses to Nan and discusses some work he needs done. As he turns to leave, he finally sees me and just gives me a stiff little "hello," before walking back out the door.

I'm very quietly, but hugely, devastated. I guess the wedding is off.

Then, as I'm sitting there, unable to concentrate, seething, I notice a figure pacing back and forth outside the frosted glass wall separating the graphics department from the corridor. It's Bill. I watch as he pauses, turns back, and makes for the door. But then he stops again, turns, and starts away. Finally, he spins right back around and approaches the door to the graphics department. This time, he walks right in and comes straight over to me.

"Hi, Moya," he begins, faltering, just as if we hadn't spent a lovely four or five hours chatting one another up over dinner less than a week ago. "I was wondering if you would like to go out one night."

Phew! What a relief. The wedding is back on!

Of course, I say yes and my life is never to be the same again.

On our first date Bill takes me to his favorite restaurant, The Cottonwood Cafe, in the West Village, then to a blues concert which it turns out is his great passion. I discover he studied communications at North Western University, which is where he was determined to go ever since he was eight-years-old and watching his idol, Johnny Carson, say that he wanted to attend North Western but was not accepted. Bill has worked at MTV from the very beginning in 1981. After graduating college, he went door-to-door selling something called cable TV. Then he saw an ad for a job in the trade papers for a position working as a tape operator at a new network called MTV. The principal requirement was to operate a specific machine. He could not operate this machine. He had never even heard of it. But he lied and said he did. Fortunately, his father worked as an executive for General Electric and it just so happened he had access to this particular piece of equipment. Bill went to his fathers' place of work and studied the machine as best he could. After all, he thought, if he got the job he could study and learn more from his colleagues. Nervously, he bluffed his way into the job only to discover on the first day that he knew more about the machine and his position than anybody else in the room. He was promoted instantly to manager.

He was now in charge of the NOC, or the Network Operations Center, which is the physical location from which a network broadcasts its shows. MTV's NOC was in Long Island and it was here that Bill became the one to physically put on air the network's very first offering, "Video Killed the Radio Star".

As time went on and the network prospered, Bill did very well in his position. But he knew he wanted to work producing on-air material. So, he applied for a job as an associate producer at the network instead. This meant a drastic cut in pay. But he was determined to follow his dreams and now, as I meet him, he's doing just that with his very own comedy show. Every standup comedian in New York is desperate to get his attention.

It's all very impressive but not as impressive as the way Bill conducts himself. I've learned he is nicknamed, *The Nicest Man in Television*.

We have a lovely evening on our first date, January 27th 1989, a day to remember. Monday morning after our date I discover an envelope on my desk. I open it to discover a card thanking me for a great time and saying that when he looked in the mirror that night, he noticed the laugh lines on his face were more prominent.

As much as I know he's the one, I'm still cautious. I was never the girl who dreamed of being married, having a big wedding, and walking down the aisle in a beautiful gown. That is not me. I've always joked that my ideal would be to get married on my lunch hour and not tell anybody. To me, a wedding is a deeply private thing and not a spectator event. Bill is very handsome and in great shape. He also looks very young. His boyish looks shock my friends when they met him for the first time. He's not my usual type, they say. I'm told he looks like a choir boy.

I also discover that all these apparently happenstance meetings with Bill, like running into him on my first day back to work after my Christmas vacation, were not coincidences at all! He sat in the lobby at the stage for three hours waiting for me to show up. He waited across the street from the bar, too, watching to see me enter so that he might just happen to bump into me.

I know, too, that if we go for a late-night coffee at the Empire Diner on Tenth Avenue we'll still be talking and laughing hysterically at four in the morning, not knowing where the time has gone. I also know that when Bill says he'll call me at seven-thirty—guess what? The phone rings at seven-thirty!

This is how it is supposed to be: no stupid games.

30.

Bill's parents, his sister, and her husband are coming to visit him at his apartment in Hoboken, just over the Hudson River from lower Manhattan. He wants me to meet them. I suggest I can cook lunch and Bill bravely accepts.

The only thing I'm particularly good at preparing is shepherd's pie, though, which, being Irish, seems like a safe bet—meat and potatoes. I arrive at Bill's immaculate apartment early Sunday morning and we drive to the supermarket in his vintage, pale blue, VW bug—as perfect and cute as any young couple in town.

Once lunch is prepared, we wait for the big arrival. The doorbell rings, Bill answers, Missus Aiken enters and, not seeing her son, takes one look at me and says:

"Oh, excuse me, I thought this was my son's apartment." And she turns to leave but then sees Bill standing aside behind the open door.

"Mom, this is Moya."

She looks back over at me and I can tell from her face I'm definitely not the little Irish Colleen she's been expecting. Even though I've toned it down a little, it's still the eighties, after all. I'm all Thompson Twins chic: crazy teased blonde hair, head-to-toe black spandex, bright red jacket to match my bright red lipstick, outrageously cool ankle boots.

Once she gets past this strange looking creature dating her Brooks Brothers, buttoned down, wallaby, duffel coat wearing son, she'll probably get with it. And she does. Twenty minutes later, Rita Aiken is laughing at my stories and enjoying her lunch, convinced her son is in no danger from this wisecracking fashion-plate from Wythenshawe, of all places.

Bill's dad is pleasant enough. His sister, Maryann, and her husband, Mark, are great. I hear about the time Mr. Aiken spent in England during WWII, plus the vacation they had in Ireland. They're a lovely family. How can they not be if they've raised such a wonderful son?

After everyone leaves, Bill and I decide to head back into the city and attend Mass at St. Patrick's Cathedral. As we enter the beautiful neo-Gothic creation, an older gentleman approaches Bill and asks if he'd help out collecting the offering during Mass.

Well, if that doesn't say it all! To be asked to collect the cash in St. Patrick's is proof positive Bill is not only a special young man but that this is evident to everyone around him—even strangers! I have to stifle a laugh as he walks down the aisle with the collection basket, mutely demonstrating, for my benefit, a reverent and solemn attitude for his task.

He tells me he's always felt he's from another time, a different time.

"Not in a weird way. But, like, a more genteel time. Like a *Leave it to Beaver* time."

It's probably just me being crazy in love but my boyfriend does sometimes appear magical. Lights often go out as he passes by. Or burnt-out bulbs stutter and spark back into life. Everywhere. Streetlights. Fluorescent tubes above the produce section at the grocery store. He doesn't seem to notice. But I do. This guy is special, I think. And, pretty much, after meeting Bill's family we're inseparable. Even though we don't mention it all the time, we both know this is becoming serious very fast.

And around this time, we're talking of going to visit Me-mum and Me-dad in England. That would be a test: visiting Wythenshawe at its grim finest! It would certainly be quite an honest contrast to our recent visit to the Aiken's large, four-bedroom house on a couple of acres in upstate New York alongside a golf course in a leafy suburb where the neighbors *do not* shove lit newspapers through the letterbox or make fun of you when you're off to Sunday Mass. No, no, this would be an eye opener for the gentle young Mister Aiken.

Bill and I are very happy. His family is happy. Our friends and colleagues are happy for us. The only person who isn't happy about our blossoming relationship is Bill's best friend, Lou.

Lou also works at MTV and seems to be a pretty popular guy. Bill loves him. Within seconds of a call from Lou, Bill is howling with laughter. But I never get a warm and fuzzy feeling from Lou. In fact, I get the opposite: cold and hard. He seems clearly suspicious of me and his resentment is palpable. I can't tell if Bill notices any of this and I'm afraid of bringing it up.

Still, it's sudden. And though I've been thinking it will happen sooner or later, I'm still a little breathless: we're discussing getting married.

Bill thinks we should get engaged when we visit England in June. I know it's right but it's a massive step and—forever. We go to visit friends in Virginia and I'm feeling dreadful. We have to leave Mass one day as I think I'm about to pass out. I seem to have a hangover for days and can't understand what's going on. I mention it to Nan, who says:

"Maybe you're pregnant."

"No! That's not possible," I insist. "I know we're Catholic, but not *that* Catholic! We're careful!"

But not *that* careful, I suppose.

After work, I go over to where Bill is editing his show. When he's done, we walk along East Fifty-Fourth Street and I mention what Nan thinks. His face lights up and he gets on his knees right there on the sidewalk:

"Moya Hession, will you marry me?"

Well, the rush is on. We decide to have a small ceremony in New York and then another affair in England when we get there.

Obviously, this means a Catholic ceremony either at Bill's church in Hoboken or my parish Church in Manhattan. We're both adults and practicing Catholics, so we anticipate no problem getting a priest to marry us. We decide to go to Bill's church, St. Ann's, to get the ball rolling.

It's a cold, rainy night when we knock on the rectory door asking to speak to the parish priest. He comes to the door and we stand there in the foyer explaining we want to be married. He gives us a lecture on what the church requires. We'll have to go through a series of interviews and participate in what the Catholic church calls a Pre-Cana (or marriage preparation) course for six months. Bill tries to explain we just want a small service and as quick as possible at that. This seems to send up red flags for the priest. He might have glanced at my belly. Anyway, he ushers us out, telling us our request is out of the question.

So, like two soaking street urchins begging at the church door, we're turned away. But I'm confident my own church, Saint Paul's, being in the city, will probably be a little more liberal and facilitate our request.

Wrong!

I'm thinking this is unbelievable! Two adults raised in the church who have maintained their faith while living and working in the—let's face it—not so saintly contemporary world, cannot be married in the sanctity of Holy Church without a six-month indoctrination into matrimony and child-rearing by an old man who is, hypothetically, still a virgin.

Meanwhile, besides ourselves with frustration, we have our first prenatal visit to a doctor Bill has found, a highly regarded gynecologist on Park Avenue.

"Congratulations, you're having a baby," the venerable old man announces.

"Well, thank God for that," I sigh, relieved. "If I'd been feeling this rotten for nothing I'd explode!"

I can't understand why it's called morning sickness. I have morning, afternoon, evening, night time, and middle-of-the-night sickness. I feel rotten all the time. Oddly, the only thing the doctor tells me—besides the obvious reminder that there's no drinking or smoking—is that I should also avoid horseback riding.

Horseback riding?

Like there's an outside chance I'll be galloping along Fifty-Seventh Street on my way back to work at MTV later this afternoon! Then I remember we're on upper Park Avenue. Who knows what kind of dames this doctor attends to regularly? Ladies driven in limousines up to Westchester to ride their cherished mares for an hour before returning to the Carleton Hotel for tea?

Bill and I decide to keep the good news to ourselves as we navigate the next stage. The only person Bill informs of the pregnancy is Lou.

"Are you sure it's yours?" his friend asks. "She probably just wants a green card."

Bill is devastated and that's the end of their friendship.

31.

We decide to take a vacation and fly to Los Angeles for a few days. I'm anxious for Bill to meet Richard and Claude, whose guesthouse next to the pool we stay in. While Bill swims and accompanies Richard on short trips around LA in his plane, I stay close to home and the nearest bathroom. I talk to Claude about our dilemma with the church. She suggests we fly to Las Vegas and get married there. And I really do consider this except I'm made even sicker just imagining flying in that little aircraft. Though, I do go shopping on Melrose Avenue and find a perfect outfit for the wedding. I just hope it still fits when we get everything sorted out.

Feeling a little better, I'm up for a visit to Richard and Claude's good friend, Noel Marshall. Noel is another eccentric character with a ranch who was once married to the actress Tippi Hedron. He's also a successful movie producer whose biggest credit is *The Exorcist*. Noel, along with Tippi, run an animal sanctuary outside LA where they tend to a massive variety of big cats—lions, tigers, leopards, tigons, ligers—as well as elephants, ostriches, and a crowd of exotic animals rescued from circuses and zoos.

It's exciting to be up close to these magnificent creatures—and terrifying too. We visit two enormous elephants and Noel asks if

I'd like to ride one. I say yes without hesitating. Bill is slightly more cautious. But if I'm going, he's going too. He's helped to his mount and, a moment later, just as I'm about to throw my leg over the huge neck of the elephant, I remember the Park Avenue doctor:

"No horseback riding."

Does that mean no elephant-back riding too?

Probably.

I decide I better not ride an elephant. So, I back down and try to get to the ground again. But Noel, thinking I just need a bit more encouragement, pushes me back up.

"No, I really shouldn't!"

"Nonsense, girl! There's nothing to be afraid of!"

So, I'm trying to dismount gracefully and this man has his fist up my crotch trying to be helpful. Bill's off busy with his own ordeal, realizing riding an elephant is not as easy as it looks in the movies. Meanwhile, Noel is still pushing and shoving:

"Don't be worried! You can do it!"

"No, I can't," I shoot back in my fiercest Wythenshawe, adding: "And I am an engaged woman, so get your fucking hand out of my crotch!"

Thankfully, Richard steps in:

"Noel, she's pregnant. Let her down."

Thank God.

So, we just walk along beside Bill on his elephant, looking more unsure of himself and out of place than I've ever seen him.

"I know where we'll get married."

Back in New York, Bill's venturing out to different comedy clubs looking for new and interesting talent for his show. Sometimes I go with him. But mostly I stay home, worried about our Catholic marriage prospects. One night he comes to my place and is very excited.

As he was making his way back uptown from a club way down in the South Street Seaport, he strode through Little Italy and came across a large old church. He walked around the walled exterior and asked the friends who were with him if they knew what it was. He learned it was the original Saint Patrick's Cathedral.

"What," I said, confused.

"Yeah, right? Who knew?"

"I thought there was only one Saint Patrick's in Manhattan."

"This is the old one. I'm talking to the Monsignor tomorrow."

The next day Bill shows up in the graphics department and tells me the Monsignor at the old Saint Patrick's will marry us tomorrow if we want, as long as we meet with him first.

"Whoa! That's a bit *too* soon," I say. "I need time to… time to…"

I haven't told hardly anyone about our decision to marry or that I'm pregnant.

So, we arrange to meet with the priest after Mass the following Sunday. Then I think I better tell Me-mum and Me-dad. I've been so preoccupied with all these arrangements, doctor's appointments, and meetings with priests, it has not even occurred to me that my parents will be terribly disappointed not to be at my wedding! Not to mention I'm marrying somebody they haven't even met. And there's another wrinkle in the fabric of my happiness:

Being a single woman in New York, my friends and I always lie about our age. We're always two years younger than we actually are. It's never a problem, really, as most of the men we come across are a little older anyway and what do they care if we're thirty or twenty-eight?

But I did lie to Bill when we first met.

So, now, here we are attending Mass before we meet with Monsignor Vinci of Saint Patrick's to plan our nuptials. This means we'll have to show documents and fill out forms declaring personal information; personal information including—a minor detail—my age!

Mass ends and we sit waiting for the congregation to file out. It's now or never.

"Bill, I have to tell you something"

"What, sweetie."

"I lied about my age."

"What do you mean?"

"I mean that I am not the age I told you I was. I am older than you."

Bill smirks, amused. He looks me up and down, just plain curious:

"You're... *how* much older?"

I brace myself, pause, and face the music:

"I am fifteen months older than you."

Bill pretends to look very hurt, falls back in the pew, and hangs his head:

"I can't believe you lied to me."

"Well..." I stutter, "I'm sorry, but I lie to everyone about this. It's what girls do. And I just never thought, when we first met, that I'd be marrying you and so it would never be an issue and a problem and..."

Bill recovers, takes my hand, kisses it, and chucks his chin at the priest approaching from up the aisle. Nevertheless, I feel a massive purple blob land on my not-so-shiny soul.

Monsignor Vinci is an energetic, modern, and witty little Italian man. He asks us all the required questions and doesn't even bother with the crazy Pre-Cana program.

"So, when do you want to do it," he asks, frankly.

"How about next Tuesday," Bill replies and glances at me.

"It's fine with me" I say, "But what about your family?"

"It won't be an issue," he assures me, leaning down to pencil in May 23rd at noon.

When we get home, Bill calls him mom, excitedly, and tells her the big news.

"Oh, that's wonderful Bill," she says. "But Dad and I can't make it as we'll be in Las Vegas."

What! Las Vegas? Are you kidding me?

Bill's face drops and, dazed, in his infinitely understanding way, reassures Missus Aiken: "Oh, that's too bad, Mom. Well, ah... Anyway, I'm sure you'll have a great trip. We'll be thinking of you..."

Afterwards, he puts the phone down and just sits there, terribly disappointed. This whole wedding thing is turning into one nightmare after another.

"Call your parents back," I suggest. "Find out when they'll be returning and we'll work it around their availability." It's bad enough my parents won't be attending. But not even Bill's parents! We'll be like two sad little orphans again. I know I don't want a big wedding, but this is ridiculous. Bill gets back on the phone and his mom is delighted we'll wait for them to return from the gambling Mecca of the Universe. We reschedule with Monsignor Vinci and are good to go for noon, May 27.

Now I call Me-mum and Me-dad and, after dropping the bombshell of my impending marriage to an unknown American, I assure them we'll celebrate again when we come to England later in the year. They're encouraging and supportive and happy and sad and confused and excited all at once. And I don't know what to think. I call the sister right after. (She's just married a lovely man named Jerry.)

"Have you talked to them?"

"Just now, on the phone."

"Do you think they're disappointed?"

"Honestly, Moya, they're devastated."

I fall face down on the bed and hate myself.

Bill, meanwhile, does some calculations at the kitchen table and decides we can swing the cost of the airfare. I call my parents back immediately. Me-mum is over the moon and Me-dad is heard crying in the background. We book their flights, the sister takes them shopping for outfits, and they're scheduled to land at JFK the night before our wedding. That means the first time they meet Bill will be a few hours before we're wed. But that doesn't bother me one bit as I know they'll love him. Just like Claude said when I asked her what she thought of him. She'd sighed nonchalantly, pouted, and waved her hand in the air:

"Hey, what's not to like?"

32.

Typically—as it's raining—New York City traffic is a nightmare and me and my parents arrive at St. Patrick's twenty minutes late. Bill is inside, pacing nervously, as Me-mum, Me-dad, a few close friends, and I all bluster into the cavernous church. With only Bill and his immediately family waiting up near the alter, the cathedral looks ten times as huge. But Bill looks relieved now—as does Monsignor Vinci. I'll learn later that a parishioner died suddenly and he'd had to do a last-minute funeral at ten that morning. So, he's glad the bride hasn't arrived in time to see a hearse parked outside the church.

Our ceremony is simple and earnest. Bill is struggling to keep himself together, his voice wavering. As with me, waves of unexpected emotion are rolling over him. I'm relieved to be declared man and wife and shuffle back down the aisle before the two of us burst into tears.

Bill and my parents met yesterday when we collected them at JFK. They got along famously and now a lovely collision of two worlds is happening as they get to know Mister and Missus Aiken, Bill's sister, and his brothers. We leave St. Patrick's and head up town to the Saint Moritz Hotel for a small reception.

Wow, I'm married!

Bill and I take a few days off work and, along with my parents, head upstate for a couple of days to stay with the Aikens. Of course, Me-dad is wide-eyed as we cruise north up the New York throughway, marveling at the wonderful roads cut through the rich landscape. The trees, so many of them! The cars, all nice and new looking. And, of course, the massive *juggernauts*.

He's referring to the tractor trailers.

I look over at Bill behind the wheel, glowing with happiness and casting glances at the thin platinum wedding band on his finger. He catches me watching.

"Marriage really suits you," I say.

He just grins and drives on.

"I know."

Of course, pulling into the Aiken's long driveway you'd think we were going into Buckingham Palace to have tea with the Queen. Me-dad can't wait to inspect the garden. He's never seen such a massive spread. Missus Aiken's embarrassed to admit they aren't much into gardening and Me-dad says it's a shame because it's such nice rich soil. To say that both sets of parents get along well would be an understatement; they're immediately a close family. Missus Aiken is an incredible cook, too, and there's nothing you could want for when you're visiting her home. I'm comfortable leaving my parents there for the better part of a week as Bill and I return to work.

"How was your break, Moya? What'd you do?"

"Oh, I got married."

People in the graphics department know I've been seeing Bill, but nobody at the main office does.

"Moya from graphics?"

"Get outta here!"

"We didn't even know you were dating!"

And so on.

The phone lines in graphics are lighting up like a Christmas tree, best wishes flowing in from all over the network. But soon my parent's honeymoon with the Aiken's is over and it's time to go pick them up. They're clearly disappointed to be heading home but understand this is the start of a good, long friendship. In the car on the way back, Me-dad keeps saying:

"Rita Aiken's a marvel. She cooks, she drives, she arranges everything. I don't think there is anything that lady cannot do."

Saying goodbye to them at JFK is not so difficult as Bill and I are planning to visit them in just a few weeks and have our own honeymoon afterwards. Besides, we've got a few practical hurdles to clear first.

Most importantly, we need to find a place to call home. Obviously, my tiny studio apartment, even though it's a great location for work, is totally unsuitable for raising a child. Bill's one bedroom apartment in Hoboken is no better. So, still keeping our pregnancy quiet, we start looking for a suitable *starter home*.

I'm disappointed not to be able to find that home in New York City. But reality sinks in quickly and we look further afield. Bill persuades me to consider Weehawken, New Jersey. I'm reluctant at first. Even the name sounds ridiculous. But we find an old sheet metal factory that's been converted into loft style apartments overlooking New York City directly across the Hudson River, lined up perfectly with the Empire State building.

The apartment is huge: sixteen-foot-high ceilings; great big windows; three bedrooms, two baths, everything brand new as we'd be the first occupants. We can afford the rent with the option to buy after one year. The building even has an indoor pool, a parking garage, elevators, doormen. Plus, there's the added revelation that it's a much better view of Manhattan from this side of the river!

Now: the honeymoon.

We land in Manchester and head to Wythenshawe. Bill isn't obviously put off by the increasing bleakness as we approach my hometown. He's always putting a good face on things. But I'm appalled. Driving down the street our old house is on, we slow to a crawl and look. He does his best, but he can't disguise his shock.

"Wow, this is where you grew up?"

I can't belief it myself. I always knew it was rough and, even though the sun is shining, seeing it through his eyes brings back the harshness of those early years—when I was too young to really know how harsh they really were.

"Come on, let's go," I say, suddenly feeling a crushing tenderness for Me-mum and Me-dad.

Once we're home, luggage carried in, seated, and the tea is on the boil, every three minutes people are popping in to meet Moya's American chap. Bill's a great sport with all the giggles and curiosity about his accent. He has a bit of trouble adjusting to our own North of England dialect, but I'm happy to act as his translator.

And, sorry: I have to brag a little here.

Everybody is in awe of his good looks. "Fuckin' ell Moya, he looks like one of them movie stars in the magazines!" His gentle disposition, sincerity, and the way he treats everybody with undivided attention wins hearts and minds in a flash. In the North there is an expression: "Are you fit?" It means: *are you ready to go* as well as *you look good.* So, whenever we're leaving a pub or a group and I'm ready to go, I say to him:

"Are you fit?"

"Is he fit!" somebody always responds. "Look at 'im? He's fuckin' gorgeous!"

I'm proud to show off. He plays darts in the pub, drinks the warm beer, and even tries to like the food. You'd have to be his bride to see how much of a challenge this is for him. But never a discouraging word from young Mister Aiken.

Of course, Manchester is home to a great music scene. And that's of enormous interest to Bill. One day, as we're sitting around chatting with Me-dad, there's a phone call from the States for Bill. It's MTV asking if he wants tickets and backstage passes to the Rolling Stones concert that night in Manchester!

England, Manchester, even Wythenshawe—they're entirely different for me with Bill by my side.

After a few days at home, we're off to Ireland. Earlier, I asked Me-mum and Me-dad to find a house to rent there. And they did. A cottage on the outskirts of Kenmare overlooking the waves crashing into the craggy cliffs below. It's big enough for Bill and I, for my parents, and—believe it or not—the brother, along with his awful girlfriend and their one-year-old son.

Bill is unfazed by all these people joining us on our honeymoon. But I'm thinking: how, and why, did I agree to this?

Anyway, we convoy in two cars across Wales to Holyhead where we catch the morning ferry to Dublin. From there, we travel the scenic route along the Ring of Kerry south and west to our final destination. We climb out of the cars and look at the Kenmare River and the Atlantic Ocean beyond.

The location is perfect; the weather is perfect; my new husband is perfect; being in Ireland is perfect; Me-mum and Me-dad are perfect. The others in the house with us are not so perfect. But I'm heartened by Bill's laughter, which erupts pretty much whenever Me-dad opens his mouth to speak. He simply adores his new son-in-law and it's like he's never had anyone to talk to before in his life. They take walks along the windy coastal road leading down from the cottage and everything they pass has a story to be told. And Me-dad tells it.

How surreal to see Bill Aiken from work walking alongside Me-dad! On the south coast of Ireland of all places!

Things have indeed moved along pretty fast. It seems like just yesterday Bill and I were sitting for the first time late into the night at the Broadway Diner far away in distant Manhattan. Now, looking out the window, I see Bill and Me-dad returning from one of their evening strolls. Bill looks a little concerned. Apparently, as they were heading down the road, a shepherd came along guiding his flock in the opposite direction and Me-dad said:

"Well, here's ya' man bringing his sheep home for the night."

Bill's never been face-to-face with a large flock of sheep before and he asked, innocently:

"They're not dangerous, are they?"

"Indeed, they are," Me-dad explained. "These here are killer sheep. They don't have much in the way of teeth but they can gum ya' to death."

Bill jumped over a wall and waited for the sheep to pass.

Back at the house, Me-dad laughs himself to pieces as Bill tells us of his narrow escape from the killer sheep of Kincade.

Then, as we sit down to dinner, Bill says he wants to thank everyone for the wonderful welcome he's received and he's thrilled to have this new family to be part of.

"And, soon," he continues, "there will be another member of the family as Moya and I are expecting our first child."

Me-mum lets out a squeal and pumps her fist in the air like a striker for Manchester United:

"Yes! Yes! Yes!"

Me-dad's eyes well up with tears as he stands and reaches across the table to shake Bill's hand. I don't think either of my parents ever thought I'd become a mum myself. So, there's much relief, excitement and wonder.

Back in England, Bill and I visit London. Being in the capital is another first for Bill and it's a thrill to be showing him around. We've been invited to stay with my friend Anne's father, a famous and accomplished actor, whose address is a lovely Georgian brick house close to Hampstead Heath. I've stayed there before and know the old man well. When we arrive, Anne escorts us to the top floor and we pass the great actor's bedroom, the door of which is draped with heavy maroon velvet curtains and is guarded by an imposing suit of medieval armor stationed just off to the side.

We continue up the creaky staircase until we reach our accommodation. We have access to a huge balcony from which we can see all of London, a magnificent view highlighted by the bright lights illuminating Saint Paul's Cathedral. We stand there, taking it all in, breathless, when Bill turns and gasps.

There on the floor is a complete human skeleton.

Anne nonchalantly explains it's just a prop from one of her father's movies. Then, however, in the same breath, she mentions the house was once a lunatic asylum and it's said the voices of the poor lost souls can sometimes be heard as they roam the hallways.

I know this bullshit is meant to frighten the uninitiated so I brush it off as no big deal. We settle in for the night and I'm asleep with Bill's arm around my waist as soon as my head hits the pillow. I wake the next morning with Bill in the same position, only his eyes are wide open. He's as white as a ghost.

"I didn't sleep a wink."

"Why? Is everything alright?"

"There were—noises."

I laugh, thinking he's joking. But then it occurs to me he really does look terrified. We go down to the basement kitchen and discover all six-foot-four of Anne's handsome blue-eyed dad. He leans in to give me a kiss and I say:

"This is my husband, Bill. I got married."

"So, I've heard," he replies, looking Bill over, sizing him up. "Hmm, so you're the fellow who's tamed this one?"

Bill is still a little shaken from his traumatic night. He nervously offers his hand:

"Yes sir. And thank you for gracious hospitality."

"You're very welcome," the older man replies, impressed by this polite, handsome, young American. "Are you going to stay with us for the—"

But before the man can get the sentence out, Bill responds with:

"Unfortunately, we have to head back to Manchester as Moya's parents are expecting us. But thank you so much for your kind offer."

It's news to me that we have to rush back to Manchester. And as I fix us some breakfast, I watch my new husband and think: he believes in ghosts?

I know Anne's father is working on a movie at present and that he's supposed to be picked up at six o'clock in the morning.

Through the little window above the sink, I see his poor driver still sitting outside in the car waiting for him at ten-thirty.

"I thought you were leaving early this morning," I ask. "That poor bastard has been sitting out there in the car for hours."

"Darling," the man explains, "I know, but I had the most frightful night. My poor tummy was terribly upset and I was up and down to the bathroom all through the night. I hope I didn't disturb you as this old rickety house has the water tank on the roof and it does tend to make a bit of a clatter every time the old toilet is flushed."

I glance at Bill but he's unconvinced. We're headed back to Manchester.

I can't believe the whirlwind my life has become. I've never been so happy. I've married the greatest of men, whom my family adores, and I've been accepted into his wonderful family too. And we have a baby on the way!

Bill knows leaving Me-mum and Me-dad is difficult for me. So just as we're packing our bags to head back to the States, he hands me an envelope. Ripping it open, I find two tickets to see Aretha Franklin at Radio City Music Hall.

"Just a little something for you to look forward to when we get back to the States," he says.

Who hit the marriage jackpot? Me did!

33.

Back in America, we settle into our cozy domestic life. Bill and I are still working at MTV when, suddenly, things change. Nan announces to our department that she's leaving her position and moving on to another company. She assures us her replacement is somebody she trusts, who will treat us fairly, and not disrupt the great work environment she herself has nurtured.

Well, she could not have been more wrong about this if she tried. In walks this cocky, aggressive, little man who lets us know in no uncertain terms that he's the captain of the ship now and things are going to run his way and anybody who doesn't like that can leave.

Thus, the nightmare begins.

I pretty much set myself up as a moving target. The problem-child once again with a whole new version of Sister Sheila. From day one, me and Mister Napoleon-Complex butt heads. He has trouble tossing me out, though, because I can draw and have graphic skills, unlike most of my associates who, though computer whiz's, are without any design training. Still, one by one, the graphics department dwindles. Miraculously, I keep my job along with a couple of others who decide their survival is contingent on kissing the little man's arse, which they do—masterfully.

For myself, I know I'll be leaving in a few months anyway on maternity leave and maybe I won't even return. Meanwhile, me and the boss keep butting heads and, probably as a way of getting me out of his hair, he assigns me exclusively to a special program looking back on the 1980s entitled, "Decade."

It's a big project and I'm left to my own devices to come up with a general style and complete hundreds of drawings needed to illustrate the many fashions of the previous ten years. So, day in and day out, I chug away in my own little world, happy to have some distance from our new superior.

And then Bill is hired by HBO to start up a new channel they're launching called, Comedy Central. It's a massive job, starting a network from scratch at the tender age of thirty-one, but he's more than capable of managing it. The hours are long and the pressure intense, but at least he's being compensated well and has a car service at his disposal to bring him home safely on many of his late nights at the office. Friday nights, he arrives home and, the second he walks through the door, raises his two fingers like a peace sign and declares:

"Two days! Two days! We have two whole days together! Yes!"

There are many doctor appointments and tests. Bill is there for every single one. The excitement's building as we await the new arrival. We choose not to discover the sex, even though I'm sure I'm carrying a son. A little Bill—that would be perfect! We go to Lamaze classes and Bill whispers funny observations in my ear as we go through the different exercises, which makes me laugh hysterically and prompts a reprimand from the instructor. Clearly, she thinks, we're not taking things seriously.

But that can't be farther from the truth. Bill reads books and studies everything he can find about having babies. He keeps notebooks detailing everything that will happen, how we should prepare, and what we need to take to the delivery room on the big day. He makes sure I have the best doctors in Manhattan and that our baby will be born at the best hospital, which happens to be Lenox Hill on the Upper East Side. All we have to do now is wait for the big day. I'm determined to work for as long as I can. I want to see my big graphics job on Decade through to the end. And when I do finally finish and prepare to leave, I'm shocked to discover Napoleon is looking forward to my eventual return.

I don't believe it for a second. I'm sure he's happy to see me waddle on out the door for the very last time.

"No promises," I say. "We'll see."

Our first Christmas together I can barely get out of a chair without help. The Christmas tree is enormous but the great height of our apartment allows for such a monster. Bill has to borrow a ladder from the building's super just to decorate it. Christmas morning arrives and I sit trapped in an armchair as Bill brings to me an enormous but beautifully wrapped packager filled with thoughtful gifts, the last being a tiny blue box emblazoned with the familiar Tiffany logo containing a pair of beautiful diamond earrings.

He'd wanted to get an engagement ring, but respected my wishes when I explained:

"That's just not me."

Even so, I'm thrilled with my diamond earrings.

Our due date is December thirty-first and I am so desperate to be done with being pregnant. I'm actually hoping for the first of January, Me-dad's birthday, or January six, Me-mum and Me-dad's fiftieth wedding anniversary.

Bill is hoping for January eight, Elvis's birthday!

"Sweetie," I tell him, "I know he's the king, but I just can't hold out that long."

We pass our due date with no signs of the baby, Me-dad's birthday, my parents' anniversary—nothing.

Will it ever end?

We go for a long walk on the evening of January six, hoping it might stir up some action. But nothing changes until I wake at five in the morning with an unfamiliar sensation. Maybe this is the big day, I think. I wake Bill and he does a vertical takeoff from the bed. He calls the doctor who tells him to wait and see if anything happens before we set out to the hospital. Bill has read that once I'm admitted I'll not have the luxuries of home. So, he suggests a nice bath and helps me wash my hair. Then we sit down and have something to eat as we wait. By now the pain is escalating, so I'm not the most gracious of patients and all Bill's lovely attentions and thoughtful suggestions are met with, "fuck off."

The Doctor checks in from time to time. But seeing as my water hasn't broken, he's happy for us to stay put. Seven hours later, at noon, still nothing is happening other than the most awful pain. We're concerned. Can this be okay? Bill calls the doctor and this time we're told to head for the hospital. Bill has his bag filled with everything we'll need for the day: snacks, fruit, water, and those fucking tennis balls everybody is told to bring.

We leave the apartment and I struggle to the elevator taking us to the garage level. Bill races to bring the car to me, packs our necessities, and off we go.

As we reach Manhattan and head across town, I learn something about myself: I cannot tolerate pain. In fact, I'm a big baby in the pain department.

But I keep this to myself.

Bill is busy driving.

Now we're heading uptown and I'm in complete shock as to how much this hurts and I totally regret venturing into the land of parenting.

"Sweetie," Bill whispers, "you okay?"

"Fuck off."

We arrive at the parking lot across from the hospital and cross to the main entrance. Thankfully, it's Sunday afternoon and the street isn't so crowded. Even so, Bill walks beside me, holding my arm, with his free hand out to protect me from someone bumping into my enormous belly.

"You're doing great, sweetie."

"Fuck off."

Then, to passing strangers, "Oops! Excuse us. Excuse us. We're having a baby. Great job, Moya. Not far now. Oops! Excuse us…"

At last, we're admitted to an examination room with two beds separated by a curtain. The other bed is unoccupied. The doctor arrives and, after a brief investigation, announces:

"You're barely dilated."

"Barely dilated," I repeat, delirious. "Are you kidding me?"

He isn't.

But it hurts so much I'm wondering, what's next? What have I done to deserve this? Still, I'm trying to keep my agony quiet when my new roommate is wheeled in, screaming like a fucking banshee. I almost admire her for her complete loss of dignity. Meanwhile, it's decided we'll be breaking my water ourselves, which seems like a great idea to me until I see the nurse approaching with something like a big crochet needle. Bill is trying to keep me calm and succeeding pretty well until my roommate, in her own terrified drama, yells out: "I'm gonna take a shit!"

My sweet, gentle husband calls the nurse and demands I be taken to a private room immediately. Leaning down to me, he whispers, soothingly:

"Nobody is going to tarnish the most special day of our lives."

He sounds like he's a hundred yards away.

But now we're in a proper room and the doctor says there is still no change.

"You just have to try and relax, Missus Aiken, and stay as comfortable as possible."

Comfortable? Did he actually say comfortable? There is no comfortable when you have what seems like an enormous being refusing to come out of your body. I'm having massive contractions that I'm pretty sure can be detected on the Richter scale. Enough is enough. I want something to stop the pain. A really painful needle in the spine does just that and ten minutes later I'm happily watching the printout on the machine beside the bed showing the variety of contractions I'm having but, blissfully, not feeling.

"Oooo, look," I say to Bill. "That was a big one."

And so it goes. Hour after hour, no change. The only development is that the pain medication is wearing off. So I'm feeling the biggest contractions now. I grimace and Bill strokes my arm, reassuring me.

"You're doing great."

I'm too exhausted and scared to tell my dearly beloved to fuck off again. It's around seven o'clock in the evening and we've settled into a routine with the nurse sitting in a chair in the corner, flipping through a magazine. She looks up and asks Bill:

"Are you hungry? I'm going to order some Chinese food."

"No, thanks," he replies, dividing his attention between me and her. "I have snacks ready to go in the bag there."

Half an hour later, the nurse is happily munching away on her Lo Mein and I'm sucking on ice cubes, the only morsel I'm allowed. Then, done eating, she comes up with a brilliant idea.

"Let's watch a movie."

Now she's watching John Voight in *Coming Home,* giving a running commentary throughout his performance. But her main focus is on how gorgeous Voight is and don't I find him so—

"You know, really sexy?"

But *sexy* is the last fucking word I want to hear right now and I just stare at her blankly. The doctor reappears, sizes up my situation, stands back, and concludes:

"You are going to have a baby today."

Well, thanks Doctor, I think, as he disappears again. Now I know why they pay you the big bucks.

The movie is over and the nurse, bored, decides to start a conversation.

"So, where did you guys meet?"

"At work," Bill replies while mopping my brow. "It's okay sweetie, you're doing great…"

"Where do you work," the nurse proceeds.

"MTV. Easy, sweetie. Deep breath..."

"What!" the nurse exclaims quietly, impressed. She checks the chart at the foot of my bed. "Oh my God, I can't believe this. You're Bill Aiken, *the* Bill Aiken, the comedy guru, Bill Aiken?"

"I don't know about that. But, yes, I am Bill Aiken and, yes, I work in comedy. Okay, Moya, hold on. You're so brave."

At this point, hanging the chart back on the bed rail, the nurse announces:

"I do stand up! I've worked Club Med!"

As bleary and unfocused as I am, I can see Bill sag, like a ton of bricks have just been placed on his shoulders.

She starts performing her standup routine and every time she has to check my pulse or my temperature, she incorporates that into it.

"Did you hear the one about the man whose pulse..."

Meanwhile, the pain medication has evaporated and I am writhing around in agony.

"Excuse me, nurse," Bill cuts in, "Sorry..." and gives me his not undivided attention because this lunatic standing in the room with us thinks it's a great opportunity for an audition. At eleven-twenty that night, the doctor comes to talk to Bill and I.

"I'm concerned about this. Missus Aiken, are you opposed to having a cesarean birth? Would you mind?"

Would I mind? If I could speak coherently, I'd tell him: No, I don't mind at all because right about now I'm prepared to make the incision myself. Doctor, let's get this done, for the love of God!

Bill, whose gotten expert at reading my mind, translates my tortured expressions and I'm prepped and rushed into the operating room.

Eighteen minutes later, our baby is born.

I hear a cry.

This demon from deep inside myself is whisked over to the table to be cleaned up. Then it's brought over to me by Bill. Of course, by now, seeing just a little baby boy, no demon at all, we're both crying like school girls.

"He's a bruiser," the doctor says. "Ten pounds, twenty-three inches long. He'll play for the New York Giants one day!"

I'm surprised I have the energy left to laugh. But I do. "Never gonna happen, Doctor!"

We have a son. The name we already know: Liam Padraic Aiken. Born before midnight on Sunday, January seventh, 1990. The greatest day of our lives.

34.

Immediately after Liam is born, I'm wheeled into a double room. But, mercifully, I'm the only occupant. After making sure I'm as comfortable as can be, Bill goes back to spend time with his newborn baby. I acquaint myself with the button that releases morphine into my body and eases the pain. Another nurse checks in on me and says Bill been outside the nursery holding Liam for three hours, not moving an inch. He only gives the baby up when she says I need to nurse him. I persuade Bill to go home and get some rest. He leaves around four in the morning and, he tells me later, cries all the way to Weehawken.

Liam is a beautiful baby and is quite a draw at the nursery. Apparently, there are several people who want to see, "the ten-pounder."

I'm not doing well in the pain department and can barely get out of bed to sit in a chair, never mind taking a walk. Just to emphasize what an utter wuss I am: I get a new roommate, an Irish woman who's just given birth to twins, both five-pounders. She's sitting in bed, drinking champagne, and chatting with her visitors before getting up to walk over to the nursery.

Not me. I'm completely incapacitated and refuse to even think about getting out of bed. I lie there, watching the clock, and every fifteen minutes I hit the morphine button.

In walks Bill carrying an enormous bouquet of flowers, his head held high. I've never seen such a proud father. He tells me that when he went by to look at Liam through the window in the nursery there were a couple of construction workers pointing at our son:

"Look at that one! He's a big boy!"

While Bill is out of my room, Nurse Standup reappears, meekly, hands behind her back.

"I just went to see your baby. What a beautiful boy. He's gorgeous."

"Thanks," I say, thinking maybe she's not such a looney after all.

"I have something for you," she then says and, from behind her back, reveals a videotape. "It's my standup routine. Can you give it to your husband?"

Click the button. This requires more morphine.

The rest of the day is full of surprises. In walks the sister and her husband, Jerry. My family knows I'll need some help, so they fly over to surprise me. The next visitor is Bill's friend, Lou, who now apparently is willing to give me the benefit of the doubt and accept our marriage. Extremely magnanimous of him. All day flowers and gifts are delivered and all day I refuse to get out of bed. Liam is wheeled in at regular intervals and I can't believe he is ours. He's so alert and tugs at his swaddling blanket—pure genius! So advanced for his eighteen hours! He could easily pass for thirty-six hours old, I think.

In comes the nurse again, insisting I take a walk or I can't be released from the hospital. I'm seriously considering if I can live here permanently. Upper East Side? Not too shabby. But now she won't take no for an answer. I heave myself to my feet, grab the IV pole, and shuffled off down the corridor. I've lost a slipper, my hair's a tousled mess, my gown is wide open at the back. But I don't give a damn. Let's get this over and done with. Just then, Bill comes around the corner and gets the full-page news of his wife's backside, shuffling down the hall, still half out of it on morphine.

"Oh, sweetie, what... Come on. In here. You're all... exposed. Jesus..."

Woozy and irritable as I am, I'm guessing our marriage will last. If we get over this shocking and embarrassing moment, we'll get over anything.

At last, I'm able to go home. I'm wheeled into the elevator with Liam on my lap and everybody saying the same thing: "That baby looks about five months old! You sure it's a newborn?"

I say goodbye to the hospital and, sadly, to my ever-friendly morphine drip. Bill's gone out and bought us a nice new shiny automobile equipped with Liam's car seat. I clamber in, relieved. But every bump in the road on the way back to Jersey feels like a hammer blow. I still ache all over and, I assume, Liam does too. But he's just smiling at the sunlight, the soft rumble of the motor.

As we pull into the underground garage, I see Jerry standing there, patiently awaiting our arrival. He helps us upstairs. Fortunately, the sister is amazing with babies. I'm grateful for her guidance and help. We stay home and just enjoy being together. She and Jerry leave a couple of days later but by then the big guns, Me-mum and Me-dad, have arrived.

"Where is he," Me-mum says as she walks through the door. "I can't wait to hold him. Where is Liam?"

So begins the love fest with Liam and my parents. They're both amazing with him. Seeing them handle this child with such ease and assurance definitely helps Bill and I become acclimated to parenthood. Liam is a good baby. But even if he wasn't Me-mum tells us:

"I love the sound of a baby crying in the house!"

Can't say I agree with that.

We settle into a routine of looking at the baby, feeding the baby, changing the baby, poking the baby if he's been sleeping too long, holding a mirror up under the baby's nose to make sure he's still breathing, and fighting to hold the baby. Then we visit Bill's parents and, as Me-dad is helping Missus Aiken tend her garden, confides:

"If our Moya and Bill lived round here, we would move to America in a flash."

Of course, the Aiken's are delighted with Liam, even though they can't figure out how to say his name. And they're thrilled to see their son so happy and, clearly, a natural in the father department.

Well, it has to happen and after a few weeks everybody's gone. Bill is back to work and I'm left alone all day with Liam. I'm nervous the first day. But eventually I become confident taking care of him.

Of course, plans are being made for the next big event: Liam's christening, which we decide to make a double celebration, tying it in with my parent's fiftieth wedding anniversary. The date is set for July seventh, the venue Manchester, and the Aiken's are onboard to make the trip across the pond. Me-mum is nervous about entertaining the in-laws, especially given the tremendous hospitality they've shown all of us and Me-dad's oft repeated amazement:

"Rita Aiken's a marvel! She can do anything."

No pressure, mum.

Once again, we're fortunate to visit England when the weather is unusually warm and sunny.

"Phew! Sixty degrees England swelters!" runs the headlines.

This time it really is record breaking heat, though.

"I think it might even be hotter than the summer of 1976," you hear in the street everywhere you go. "And that were brutal."

The Aiken's are equally as gracious guests as they are hosts and we try to cram in as much sightseeing and visits as possible. Me-dad's garden is a source of great admiration, as is all the fine produce he grows in his allotment nearby.

Liam's Christening is a typical low-key affair: church followed by sandwiches and cake back at the house. It's held at Saint Peter's, the church I spent, probably, fifty percent of my youth in, where after the pubs closed on Christmas Eve the parade of drunks would pile in as there was nowhere else to go, where on Sundays Me, Me-mum and Me-dad always sat in the same pew; seventh from the front and always on the right. This is where I sat outside the confessional booth, sweating bullets, waiting for my soul to be polished. Where I went to daily Mass before school, hoping it would help me pass my 11 Plus. Where I daydreamed during the homily of living in America...

So many emotions and memories.

And here I am, now, in that same church with my handsome American husband and my son, who will one day have a cool American accent, for whom I'll make peanut butter and jelly sandwiches, waving goodbye to him in the morning as he's driven away to school in a big yellow bus. I'll be shouting, "I love you!" without being embarrassed. I'll have a house with a telephone that sounds like the phone in the movies and I'll carry my groceries home in brown paper bags, struggle to open the door with one hand while balancing the groceries in the other...

This will be my life and I couldn't be happier.

Bill's extremely busy with the new job. I decide not to return to MTV even though *Decade* receives an Emmy in the Graphic Artist category.

Hmm, graphic artist? That would be me, I suppose.

But my heart is no longer there.

I manage to get some freelance work at Bill's new network. Being the boss's wife, I'm allowed to bring Liam with me. So, he's really a media baby. He sits in his little chair, not making a sound, as I work on the Paintbox in a darkened edit suite.

An added bonus is that Bill stops by to check in on us and takes Liam around the offices as he goes about his business. Liam even makes his television debut at the ripe old age of six months in a little promo bit Bill produced.

Life is great. In fact, life can't be any better. I like living in our apartment and we're thinking of buying it. But the price is higher than Bill feels comfortable with and he suggests we look at houses in the neighborhood to see if that's a better use of our money.

Ahhhhggg! First, I am taken out of Manhattan and now he thinks we should buy a house! I'm not convinced. It just seems a bit too grown-up for me. Still, we look at several houses and, as much as I hate to admit it, for less money than the apartment, no monthly maintenance fees, and free parking, we can own a nice home. We settle on an extraordinary, large, detached Victorian house, which is literally 'round the corner! Built a hundred years ago, it still has all the original details: twelve-foot tin ceilings, oak floors, pocket doors, beautiful crown moldings.

I'm all in.

The news from home, though, is not good. The sister's new hus-band, Jerry, has had a little "procedure," and the diagnosis shows he's suffering from esophageal cancer, one of the worse cancers there is, with little hope of a cure. The reports from my parents are sad. Jerry is going downhill fast and we have to prepare ourselves for the worst. The sister, on the other hand, in her weird manner of brushing everything under the carpet, seems oblivious. When I call to ask about Jerry's condition, all I get is, "Oh, ees smashin, doing great! Aren't you, darlin?" Or I'd hear: "Ees just got a bit of cancer in the gullet!"

Finally, we get the call: Jerry's passed on.

Bill agrees I need to go be with my family, but he can't join me because of his current workload. He takes me and Liam to the airport and sees us off.

Me-mum and Me-dad are very upset, thinking Jerry was just what the doctor ordered and that the sister had finally settled on a decent man. They want to see Jerry in the funeral home. And though I go with them, Liam and I wait outside in the car. I don't want to see anybody I care for *laid out*. There is no public viewing, but family members can arrange a private visit.

As we're sitting there, I watch some young lads kicking a ball against the wall of the funeral home. There's no disrespect intended. They just don't realize that on the other side of the wall is a man lying in his coffin.

Life goes on.

I remember when I was young, always being concerned about my parents dying. They were much older than my friend's parents. Me-dad was in his late forties and Me-mum already forty-four when I was born. They were ancient, I thought. My friend's mams and dads wore platform shoes and flared trousers. Their dads had mustaches and their mams had long hair. They were young and I thought they would definitely outlive my parents. I remember thinking all those years ago that if anything happened to my parents, I'd want the world to stop. Everybody would have to be aware that something devastating had occurred, that the world was different now, not just my world but everybody's world.

I wouldn't want young boys playing football a few feet away from my loved one's corpse. It just wasn't right.

But that is what happens, I guess. There's a pause, then everything is back to normal.

I sit in the car playing with Liam when Me-dad comes out and walks over. He opens the door and says, "Ye sister wants you to see Jerry"

"Da, I don't want to."

"There is nothing to worry about, Moya. He looks great. Just like he's sleeping. Go on, Moya. Yer sister needs you to see him. I'll sit here with Liam."

So, reluctantly, I go in.

The only other dead body I've ever seen was Jackie Coonan, laid out in Barrett's funeral home in Hell's Kitchen. This is nothing like seeing Jackie. Jackie was lying in a large mahogany coffin, lined with padded silk, a big fluffy pillow to rest his head on, in a room filled with bouquets and gentle music being piped in. Plus, only half of his mortal remains were on display. All in all, he looked very comfortable.

Jerry, in contrast, is laid out in a box lined with a thin cotton fabric, no padding, the room freezing and austere. He's not embalmed, so the place must be kept cold. His entire suited body is on full display, his feet at unnatural angles. He's wearing his grey slip-on dress shoes. I've always hated grey shoes for some reason. But now more than ever. His mouth is slightly ajar and there's a fly buzzing around him.

The sister has decided not to put on his large framed glasses, which I think might have made him less recognizable—a good thing. She walks around the flimsy coffin, stopping to stroke his hair.

"Ah, doesn't he look gorgeous," she sighs. "I always told him he was very handsome without his glasses." Then she's touching those awful grey shoes, "Look, Mum, he's wearing the shoes you got him for Christmas last year."

All the while, I can hear the thump, thump, thump of the football hitting the exterior wall. The sister continues this macabre choreography, straightening his tie, kissing his forehead, rubbing his hands, talking to him about how great he looks and not noticing the fly buzzing around his open mouth. She tells me that even though Jerry wanted to be cremated, she's going to bury him so she can visit him every day.

That's it for me, I think. Time to go.

35.

Bill suggests I bring the sister back with me to the States so she can get a break. Reluctantly, she agrees. She's exhausted and we're happy to take care of her for a change. By now, we're all settled into the new house and there's plenty of room for guests.

Bill is busy at work but he still comes home on a Fridays with his two fingers up in the air, announcing: "Two days! Two whole days! Two whole days together!"

Whenever I know what bus he's on, I take Liam with me to the corner to see it pull up at the curb across the street.

"Right there," I say, pointing. "Look right over there to that far sidewalk. That's where daddy will appear."

Liam looks, concentrating, alert.

The bus pulls up, blocking our view of the sidewalk. The toddler looks offended. But when the bus pulls away, there is Liam's dad! Bill's face lights up at the sight of us and Liam claps his hands madly at the sight of his daddy magically reappearing as promised.

The long hours Bill puts in are difficult for him as he really wants to spend more time with us. Now, he's offered a position at Nickelodeon, the pay television channel and sister network of MTV. It's a lot more money and a lighter workload. Though he'll have to travel regularly, it will be short trips for only a day or two. It seems like a win-win situation and he takes it. Nickelodeon's work vibe is much different than Comedy Central. If Bill is in his office after six o'clock, somebody tells him to go home to his family. But I never feel he's too far away because from our house in New Jersey I can see Bill's office building way across the river in Times Square on Manhattan.

Liam is growing and growing and every day is a revelation to me. Like his father, he's very polite and his first words are, "thank you." And he's the spitting image of Bill. One day at the park as Bill is pushing Liam on the swing, another young father comes over and says: "Hey, was there an egg involved with this conception?"

We discuss having another child.

"I'm warning you, though," I say, "we've been lucky with Liam. He's exactly like you. The next one might be exactly like me, the Antichrist."

Bill's not worried, though. He's up for it. He's very aware of being a fit parent and cycles for miles with Liam in his little seat attached to the bike. He's also an avid runner and thinks nothing of jogging seven miles a day before dinner or after a stressful day at the office. He's extremely body and health conscious. A snack for me is potato chips. A snack for Bill, a salad.

Bill, I then learn, has never been to Italy. So, I contact a friend with an apartment in Florence who says we could use it anytime. We'll go to England and leave Liam with my family and then head off to Florence for a romantic interlude wherein, hopefully, I'll get pregnant again. Of course, Me-mum and Me-dad are ecstatic we're visiting and that they'll have some time with Liam.

Bill is pretty slammed at work and complains of heartburn; nothing major, he assures me, but he's worried he might have an ulcer. He makes an appointment with his doctor immediately. Doctor Stein doesn't seem too concerned but suggests that once we're back from vacation Bill should have some tests done to be sure everything is okay.

I'm busy organizing, packing, and researching the places we'll visit: Tuscany, San Gimignano, museums, great restaurants! Bill mentions in passing he's concerned the heartburn will interfere with our enjoyment of the great food. So, he calls Doctor Stein purely to get some advice as to what over-the-counter medicines he should pack in case the food bothers him. He speaks to another doctor filling in for Stein and explains his concern. This doctor listens, thinks a little, and decides to speak with Stein.

"We'll get back to you shortly, Mister Aiken."

It's Friday night and our suitcases are packed and waiting in the hallway. Our flight to Manchester is the next day. Bill is still at his office and Liam is playing with his toys on the kitchen floor. The phone rings. It's Doctor Stein calling from his vacation in Colorado.

"Missus Aiken, may I speak with Bill?"

"He's still at work," I reply, glancing out the window to Times Square in the distance.

"Would you have that number handy?"

I give him the office number and continue making Liam something to eat.

Twenty minutes later, the phone rings again. It's Stein.

"Missus Aiken, I just spoke to Bill and advised him against going on this trip."

"Why..." I begin, startled, but then: "What's wrong?"

"Bill doesn't think it necessary to cancel your plans. But I disagree. He really doesn't want to disappoint you. So," the doctor continues, reluctantly, "I've taken the initiative to call again and..."

Now I'm starting to feel cold all over.

"He says he's only uncomfortable when he eats certain foods," I suggest, feebly.

"Citrus, especially. I know."

This doesn't sound good. The doctor is certain of something.

"Of course," I blurt out, "we can cancel our trip if he's..."

"You need to call him and let him know you're okay and that

you're not too upset."

"Certainly. But…" Liam is looking across at me from within his little nest of toys. "What do you think is wrong," I ask the doctor again.

Stein takes a moment to choose his words carefully:

"I think Bill has a tumor."

I fall to my knees. Every part of me slips down into the pit of my stomach and I begin shaking uncontrollably. Liam stands up and comes over, throwing his small arms around my neck.

"It's okay, Mommy," he says, assuming mine and Bill's constantly repeated and tender assurances, "It's okay."

Tumor. Tumor. What kind of tumor? Not all tumors are bad, right? The phone is still on the floor and I hear the beep, beep, beep that a phone makes when it's off the hook. I pick it up and call Bill. As usual, he's his lovely happy self.

"Hi sweetie."

"Bill, we are not going on vacation. Doctor Stein says it's out of the question."

"Moya, I'm fine. Just a little uncomfortable when I eat."

"We are not going. He thinks you may have a tumor!"

"I know. I know what he thinks. But I don't have a tumor. He's just being cautious."

"I'm coming to get you. I don't want you getting on a bus. I'll meet you outside your building." I hang up and call to Liam, "Come on, let's go get daddy at work."

I help him into his little jacket. I look for the car keys. Where are the car keys? I can't find the fucking car keys! Trembling, I open and slam every draw, every cupboard, riffle through every coat pocket, every jacket in the closet. Where are the car keys!

"Liam, have you seen mommy's keys?"

Maybe I left them on my desk. No, not there. Where are the keys? Bill might be standing outside waiting for me and I can't find the damn car keys.

I go back where I started and look again. There they are. Right where I always leave them.

Sure, I'm relieved. But now I also know I'm really shook up and unreliable. I've got to get a grip. I grab Liam, secure him in his car seat, and head into New York City.

Our house is literally two miles from Times Square and, shockingly, on a Friday night the roads are clear. I pull up to the corner of Forty-Sixth and Broadway and park. Within minutes, Bill comes out of the building looking as gorgeous as ever: smart dress pants, crisp white shirt sleeves rolled up, shiny black shoes and swinging his black leather Coach briefcase as if he didn't have a care in the world. He walks over to the car, waving and smiling, opens the door, leans in and kisses me, then turns back to Liam:

"There's my boy! Hello, Haggbagga!"

But he sees I'm a wreck. There are tearstains down my cheek. He reaches over and wipes my face.

"Ah, sweetie," he assures me, sounding just like our two-year-old half an hour earlier, "it's okay. I'm fine. It's going to be okay."

"How can you be so sure? What about the doctor?"

"I don't like Liam seeing you so upset. We'll take care of this. It's going to be okay."

Back at the house, Bill behaves as though everything is normal except that we're calling his parents and explaining that we are not going on vacation after all. I can't call my parents as it's the middle of the night for them.

Bill's parents are worried but they're calmer than I am.

"There is nothing to be done for now," he tells me. "We'll have to wait until Monday and make appointments with doctors and hopefully things will be okay and we can go on our break when I get the all clear."

Finally, when it's morning in Manchester, I call Me-mum and Me-dad to tell them we're not arriving as planned. They're devastated anyway but to hear Bill is *poorly* is almost more than they can bear. I tell them all I know and not to worry.

Not to worry!

Listen to me.

"Bill feels fine and we're sure the doctors are just being overly cautious."

That morning is a grey, cloudy day and our friends' seven-year-old son has a soccer match. So we head down to Hoboken to watch the game. I can't stand still. Everybody is watching soccer and I just keep walking up and down, pushing Liam in his stroller. I look at all these young families without a care in the world. And now Bill's chatting away to friends and neighbors. I have to calm down, I tell myself. But I can't calm down. Two more days of this waiting and I'll be a basket case. The rest of a weekend is just a blur.

Monday morning, Bill starts calling doctor's offices and scheduling tests. His parents come to stay and take care of Liam so we can make appointments at a moment's notice. Firstly, we're back in Doctor Stein's office on Fifth Avenue for blood work. Next day, we're with a top gastroenterologist for an endoscopy. After the procedure, we're told the results probably won't be in for a week.

A week? I'm thinking: that's a good sign, right? If it's such an emergency, they wouldn't want us waiting a whole week for the results, right? In my desperation, I even decide it's another little beam of optimistic sunshine that the gastroenterologist thinks Bill has an ulcer.

Nothing to worry about, then, right? Ulcers we can take care of with diet, rest, medicines—right?

The following afternoon, we get a call from Stein's office. He's seen the results and wants us to meet with another Doctor at Mount Sinai hospital.

"I thought we wouldn't get the results for a week," I say to the receptionist. "Maybe they've got the wrong Bill Aiken."

"No, it looks to be correct."

"Are you sure? Are you sure it's not, say, Bill *Atkin*, Bill *Ahern*, or even Bill *Aken*—A-K-E-N? I've seen that sometimes."

"No, Moya, it's Bill Aiken, your husband." My husband, who

is handling this much better than me.

Wednesday morning, we're in the plush offices of a top surgeon at Mount Sinai Hospital. He's a distinguished looking gentleman, clutching a large manila envelope from which he pulls some photographs.

"Bill," he begins, after a few pleasantries, "you have a fairly serious condition."

All I hear is "fairly." Fairly serious, not really serious, not gravely, not awfully, not incredibly serious, not fatal. The doctor spells out the course of treatment he would suggest: surgery followed by radiation, no chemotherapy…

Again, all I hear is want I want to hear: *no chemotherapy.* That's good, right? I mean everybody knows chemotherapy is for really bad cancer, right? So, no chemotherapy is another good sign. Fairly and No Chemo—I'm liking the sound of this.

Then the doctor asks if we have any questions.

"Will I be able to get life insurance," Bill asks.

Life insurance? Honestly, I don't even realize why he's asking this. But the doctor does. Casting an uneasy glance in my direction and then looking away, he replies:

"No, Bill, you will never be able to acquire life insurance with this diagnosis."

I'm still not grasping the severity of this conversation when Bill calmly takes my hand and says:

"Sweetie, it's okay. God chose me for this because he knows I can handle it."

God what? God knows you can handle it? God chose to let a thirty-three-year-old man get cancer because he knows he can handle it? Well, can you tell God that I can't fucking handle it! And tell God, while you are at it, that we have a little boy back home who can't handle it either.

God knows Bill can handle it!

We leave the doctor's office and walk along Fifth Avenue. We hail a cab and head to the Port Authority bus station. As we stand in line waiting to buy our tickets the light directly above Bill's head goes out. He notices, looks up, and grins at me:

"See, that's a sign. It's going to be fine."

There's a lot of decisions to be made. We need a second opinion. This time one that says: "Oops! Bill, they made a mistake. You don't have cancer after all!

A dear friend, who knows every doctor worth knowing, tells us of a world-renowned gastric surgeon at Sloane Kettering, the world's number one cancer hospital. But he's in such great demand, he's hard to get an appointment with.

I wake in the middle of the night, creep downstairs and sit on the sofa in the living room, watching the sun come up over the city and trembling with fear and helplessness. I run through my mind all the friends I have who might have some weight, some influence. I've met celebrities, I've befriended successful people, I even know some criminals who are well disposed towards me.

And so it goes.

Then Bill gets out of bed, goes to work, calls the world-renowned surgeon and gets an appointment—just like that.

Walking into Sloane Kettering's impressive facility makes you feel like a mind reader because you know that everybody there is dealing with one thing, that big fucking "C" word. Everyone you pass is hoping to beat the odds, even the patient standing outside the entrance hooked up to an IV and smoking a cigarette—even she is hoping to be cured.

We're shown in and the great man himself, the surgeon, arrives. He looks like an American general, like Patton, tall and broad shouldered with his blonde hair in an army buzz cut. He's obviously really fit, judging by the many framed certificates acknowledging the marathons he's completed. He asks Bill what he does for a living.

"Television producer," Bill replies.

"Telephone producer?"

"No," I chime in, "television producer."

Telephone producer? What the fuck is a telephone producer? Somebody sitting in a corner producing telephones? I hope this guy knows what he's doing.

The surgeon acknowledges that Bill does indeed have cancer. But because of its location it's hard to say what kind. It's either gastric cancer or esophageal cancer.

No! Not esophageal! We're sadly too familiar with that demon.

It's explained that protocol for either at Sloane Kettering is three months chemotherapy, surgery, then three months post operation chemotherapy.

Great, I think. That sounds like a plan. I like plans. Then what, doctor? We be all stitched up, sore for a little while, but then we can get on with our lives? Sounds good to me, when do we start? Sign us up!

But sadly, it becomes clear we have a very long and uncertain road to travel. Tests, tests, more tests, blood work, and audiology tests because chemotherapy can damage your hearing. That would be a double tragedy for Bill as his love of music is so great. After that test, the audiologist tells Bill he should go out and buy the best sound system money can buy because he can hear things most people can't.

More tests and more questions. The same questions over and over and over again. Questions about family history, diet, places he's lived.

"Have you ever lived in Japan or any Scandinavian countries as they eat a lot of smoked fish."

"No, no. And I don't eat smoked fish."

Endless questions, enough to test the patience of a saint. But through it all Bill's his usual gentle, considerate, and grateful self. And I wish I could say the same for me. Driving home, my chin thrust out over the steering wheel, glaring at the highway:

"Why do they ask the same fucking questions over and over! Isn't there a print out or a system that can be accessed to avoid all this repetition?"

"Sweetie, easy," Bill says. "Here's the exit on the right."

It's chemotherapy time.

We're told what to expect, what to avoid, and that not all patients have the same side effects.

Bill tolerates his first round beautifully. He's even well enough to continue working. He feels normal and is determined to put on some weight in preparation for the upcoming surgery. We're told he will lose his hair at some point but, so far, he still had his mop of lovely shiny black hair.

Well, the day comes when he does notice small clumps of hair in the shower. Not much, but enough to make him decide to shave his head before he starts looking too mangey. I meet him after work. We jump on the subway and head downtown to the Astor Place Barbers. He sits in the chair and explains to the man there:

"I want my head shaved," he says, adding courteously, "and please don't be alarmed if it just falls out on its own."

I don't think the barber, an immigrant with marginal English, fully understands what's being said. But when he runs his fingers through Bill's hair, a clump comes out in his hand and, shocked, he asks:

"What is wrong with you?"

Bill explains he's got cancer and his hair is falling out because of the chemotherapy. I'm thumbing through a magazine when I look up and I see Bill consoling the weeping barber.

"It's okay, don't be upset. I'll be fine."

With the job done and my husband newly bald, we leave the blubbering man who refuses payment, saying he'll be praying for Bill.

Apart from Bill's shaved head, you wouldn't know anything was wrong. He feels great, he has a good appetite and is gaining weight. We have a lovely Christmas. It's the first time Liam really understands what's going on. Bill films him opening his many gifts and, being his father's son, he takes his time gently peeling back the wrapping. We end up with hours of tape.

The cloud of surgery is always looming and the date is set for February 3rd. Bill wants to have a few special meals before the massive operation. Firstly, he wants to have a steak at the famous Peter Luger's in Brooklyn. Secondly, he wants just the two of us to visit Montreal and check out some of the fine dining establishments there.

Both of his wishes are granted. We go to Peter Luger's with a group of friends and drop Liam off with Bill's parents before boarding a train up to Canada, traveling along scenic Lake Champlain. We enjoy Montreal, but it's bitterly cold. We're not surprised the streets are empty. It's not until the last day of our trip that we discover there's a whole network of underground walkways and shopping centers! We're the only idiots walking around the freezing vacant streets up above.

On that last day in Montreal, we go to Mass at the Basilica and I light candles and pray for a successful surgery.

The surgeon wants to prepare us for what to expect.

"Bill will be prepped and taken down to the theater," he explains. "Missus Aiken, you'll wait in the assigned seating area. After the first incision, if we see any seeding, which means the cancer has metastasized, I will not proceed. We'll sew up the incision and other courses of treatment will be pursued."

He tells me that when the surgery is completed, I will be paged. He warns me the surgery could last up to nine hours and if I am not paged before the second hour that means things are progressing and there is no evidence of seeding.

Bill is admitted to the hospital the night before and shares a room with a middle-aged man who is also having the same surgery but with a different doctor. I assure him I'll be there in the early hours to see him go down to the operating room. His sister, Maryann, and her husband, Mark, are also with me on this nerve-wracking day. Bill's parents stay at our house with Liam.

Bill is fearless as we all see him off to the operating theater, not concerned or worried, just eager to get it over with. We say our goodbyes and off we head to the massive waiting area, which is more like an airport lounge with people nervously waiting for a flight. I see Bill's roommate's wife waiting anxiously. She gives me a little nod. I watch the clock. Two hours, please let's get past two hours! Just two hours.

People are being paged and summoned to the desk where they're given updates.

Please don't page me. Two hours, two hours, the longest two hours of my life. Forty-five minutes in, I hear Bill's roommate's wife paged. She walks over to the desk, there's a little chat, then I hear her wail and turn to see her crying uncontrollably.

Nearly there. Thirty minutes to go to get past the two-hour mark. Twenty minutes, ten minutes, five minutes, bingo! Two hours and no paging of Missus Aiken! Now we can settle down and let the world-renowned surgeon work his magic. Now, it's just waiting, pacing, knowing that the longer it takes the better the outcome. Seven hours, eight hours, nine...

"Paging Missus Aiken," I hear.

I stand straight up and walk over to the desk where I'm told, the doctor would like to see me. I'm told to take the elevator to the OR on the third floor and the doctor will meet there. Just as the elevator doors open, I see the famous doctor approaching. He's in his scrubs and carrying a boom box on his shoulders. The second he sees me he raises his hand and gives me a high five. He's ecstatic:

"Text book! It was a text book case. We got it all. In fact, the tumor was so small I can't believe he had any symptoms. Just brilliant. Fantastic!"

This is the greatest day of my life alongside the day Liam came into our world. I'm delirious with joy and rush to share the news with Maryann and Mark. Then we call the Aikens.

"Thank God," Missus Aiken repeats and bursts out crying.

Thank God, indeed. Maybe I'm not as angry with him as I was a few months ago.

I'm told there's no need to stay at the hospital as Bill will be in recovery until tomorrow. Walking over to Second Avenue, looking for a place to grab a bite, I don't think my feet touch the ground. Grinning from ear to ear, I look at the menu in the diner we've found. I can't get over the excitement: "text book, text book, we got it all!" I choose fish and chips and it's the greatest meal I've ever had.

Back at the house, the mood is celebratory to say the least. Bill's a trooper and has done everything that was asked of him. And look at the result: text book!

The phone rings and I hear a raspy voice saying:

"Hi, sweetie…"

Sounds kind of like an obscene phone call.

"Who is this?"

"It's Bill!"

I'm shocked. He sounds nothing like himself.

"What are you doing! You're supposed to be in recovery. What's going on?"

"I did so well they brought me back to my room. It's better up here. I'm just exhausted."

He asks to speak to his parents and sister, then to speak to me again. I tell him how well he's done, how the surgeon was thrilled, how the tumor was tiny, how he got it all, and how it was "text book"!

Liam is delighted to have his dad home and is very gentle around him, sensing Bill is still fragile. We know it was a big surgery, but we haven't anticipated how tough things are going to be. To make totally sure that all of the cancer is gone, it's necessary to remove a third of the esophagus plus half of the stomach. This means there's no sphincter muscle at the opening of the stomach and with the shortened esophagus food is not massaged into the stomach but just crashes down into it, which is very uncomfortable. Bill can no longer sleep lying flat on his back because the stomach acids will just seep up into his throat, causing a burning sensation. The thought of most food is terrifying. But hunger makes all food seem desirable. Food Bill would never have dreamt of eating becomes: "Maybe I should try that."

Every time an ad comes on the TV, I say: "I wonder if you can eat that?"

For now, the work is all about rest and getting stronger in preparation for the next round of chemotherapy. Then, after that, we'll be home free. Text book.

Throughout it all, Bill's faith never wavers. We attend Mass at our local Parrish church and when people see the dramatic change in his appearance it's not unusual for total strangers to come up and say they're praying for him. When Bill hears a colleague's father has been diagnosed with colon cancer, he writes to her saying he's so sorry and that he's praying for him.

Prayers are a very big part of who Bill is. He's frustrated he can't finish his prayers as he lies in bed because he falls asleep mid-prayer. To combat this, he sits in the most uncomfortable chair we can find. Finally, I wake in the middle of the night to find him slumped over in the chair, all prayed out and totally exhausted.

His hair grows back during the break from chemotherapy, just as thick and shiny as it had been. And, in our naivete and optimism, we're not concerned about him having a rough time moving forward with the next series of chemotherapy. But even though he's on the same drugs, this go round of chemo is brutal: nausea, vomiting, diarrhea—he's hit full force with every hideous and miserable malady known to mankind. He's subjected to prodding, poking, and those fucking questions, the same questions over and over again. Now, too, that he's on the last stage of treatment, he has a stent inserted under his skin to make it easier to administer the poisons into his body.

Never questioning, always a delight, Bill is definitely a favorite amongst the doctors and staff at Sloane. Kettering We no longer meet with the surgeon, as his job is done. We're now under the charge of the wonderful Doctor Christman. Her gentle and patient approach is very much appreciated and I can tell how much she cares about Bill.

Me-mum and Me-dad are anxious to come see Bill. And besides Me-dad's always made Bill laugh. That's got to be a good thing. We pick them up at the airport in our new car. But I'm so used to seeing Bill in his frail state and bald head that I fail to realize how devastating it will be to my parents. They hide their shock well. Bill doesn't see them in the rearview mirror with tears trickling down their cheeks. We try to make their visit as normal as possible. Me-dad buys postcards to send to friends and family back home, and on every one he writes only:

"Bill and Moya have a new car. It has air conditioning."

He just doesn't know what else to say.

Maryann invites us to visit in Pennsylvania for a couple of days, even though she's embarrassed her garden is not up to Me-dad's standards. But gardening is not much on Me-dad's mind these days.

The first night at Maryann's I can see Bill struggling. After taking his temperature, it's confirmed: another fever has come on and now we're hundreds of miles from Sloane Kettering. Doctor Christman advises us to take Bill to the nearest hospital. Fortunately, there is a good hospital nearby. But again, the same questions, but this time there's renewed interest because Bill's a patient of the renowned Sloane Kettering. Every doctor and intern want to check out Bill and discover what his treatment had been so far at the famous institution.

We wait patiently for a room, Bill lying on a gurney in emergency. Next, the curtain is closed around him and I see a doctor go in. I wait a couple of minutes before I enter to check on Bill and see that the doctor is performing a rectal exam.

That's it for me.

"Stop this immediately! This is totally unnecessary. My husband has a fever. He needs to be admitted, made comfortable, and monitored until I can get him to his own doctors!"

"But, Missus Aiken..."

"Nobody is going to touch him and I want him in a bed now!"

Magically, a room becomes available and Bill is cared for without any more interference.

He's released two days later and we head back home. Me-dad, as usual, is chatting away as we drive and keeping everyone's spirits up. Me-mum is looking quietly concerned. About an hour into the drive Bill asks if we can stop by his favorite restaurant, Friendly's.

I'm nervous about this but Bill says he'll be fine. He's hungry and he's got to eat. But he looks so weak. We sit in a booth and try to figure out what Bill can have. Something simple, maybe a sandwich. We all have lunch and, as usual, Bill barely touches his food.

Back in the car, getting ready to pull away and resume our trip, I look over and see him throwing up all over himself. This dignified, beautiful, brilliant man sitting in the front seat of the car in a Friendly's parking lot with vomit all down his clothes.

When will it end? When will we turn the corner?

36.

Back home, Bill seems to rally. He knows he has to take it easy and that his recovery will take time. But he wants to take Me-dad to see the Yankees. He knows Me-dad loves all sports and acquires four tickets for the next home game.

I'm a nervous wreck. But a friend and his son are accompanying them, so I feel better about letting them go. Bill looks like a little boy wrapped up in clothes that are a little too big for him and a Yankee cap on his shaved head.

At home, I'm hoping they're having a good time and following the game on the radio. It's the eighth inning and the Yankees are leading by six runs. "Please God, let everything be okay. Please make sure Bill is managing the stairs. Please don't let anything happen to him."

Just as the announcer says we're in the bottom of the eighth, the door opens and in walks Bill and Me-dad.

"We had a great time," Bill explains, "but I was getting tired. So, we left early and listened to the rest of the game on the car radio."

I hug him and say:

"Well done, Bill. I'm so proud of you." Then, looking aside to Me-dad: "Dad, how did you like the game?"

"Ah, it's a girl's game," he decides. "What a load of rubbish!"

"Okay Dad," I rage quietly once Bill is out of ear shot, "I know it's not darts or sheepdog trials! But honesty is not always the best policy!"

Somebody tells Bill of a nutritionist who is working wonders with cancer patients. So, we immediately jump at the chance to work with him. Part of the regimen is doses of Vitamin C administered through an IV. Then there's a concoction that Bill has to drink five times a day. Plus, he has to eat eight meals consisting of heavy grains. This means I'm cooking at timed intervals, including through the middle of the night. It's not unusual for me to be preparing and serving food at three o'clock in the morning only to have Bill look at it and say:

"Sweetie, I'm sorry. I just can't eat it."

Back to Sloane Kettering again and, though Bill's weight loss is disturbing, the scans show no cancer. So, he takes Liam and I to his favorite beach in North Carolina!

We pack up the car and drive the eleven hundred miles to a little rented beach house we've found. We walk on the beach, make sand castles, Liam chases seagulls while Bill takes photographs of this little boy who is, miraculously, his son. It's the first time in ages we're something like carefree. It seems like we've finally turned the corner. One night, as we're driving along, Bill wonders out loud, a little perplexed:

"Lights don't go off around me anymore."

I flick a switch and all the car's lights go out at once.

"Yes, they do!"

Back home and refreshed, Bill is determined to start going into the office, slowly at first and then gradually settling in to a steady routine. Everybody at Viacom has been great. Bill's boss at Nickelodeon is amazing and thoughtful. Nobody pressures him or makes him feel guilty about being absent as much as he's had to be. Though he tries valiantly, it's too soon. On his first day back, he calls me in tears saying he needs to come home.

Soon, we decide to stop the unrealistic diet regimen. He's losing more and more weight all the time. Somebody in Bill's group at Sloane Kettering recommends yet another nutritionist whose philosophy is the complete opposite of the last one. This one is all about, "pizza, cake, ice cream, anything and everything that facilitates weight gain!"

Bill tries his best to eat as much as he can but it's an ongoing battle. He goes to the supermarket and comes back with food he'd usually never consider eating. But now, contemplating some fattening, starchy, high cholesterol, junk food, he's like:

"Maybe I can eat this."

Every crappy food commercial might have the answer to our quest for something he might be able to keep down. I hear marijuana might help with his appetite and nausea. So, I find a source and procure what I hope might be the answer. But…

Nope.

Bill is finishing the last round of chemo and we feel sure this will help his appetite. He has an appointment with Doctor Christman to have a baseline CAT scan. As we drive across Fifty-Eighth Street, he becomes upset, seeing a colleague heading into work, briefcase in hand.

He begins crying.

"Look, everybody going about their daily routine. I just want to get back to normal."

This is the first time I hear him feeling sorry for himself and I can't bear it. I'm the one who's usually ranting and raving about the unfairness of it all while Bill soldiers on with me crying on his shoulder. Now I find myself dishing out the tough love:

"You don't know," I start, my voice breaking, "how many people are walking around out there with AIDS! Those people have no hope of being cured!" Then I get really carried away: "Look at Magic Johnson! He knows he has a terminal illness! Bill, we have hope you can and will beat this!"

By then, he's consoling me.

Sitting in Doctor Christman's office after his CAT scan, Bill pulls out a list of questions from his briefcase: Can I start riding my bike? When can I lay flat on my back to sleep? When can I travel to Europe? When will the stent be removed? Why am I having so much trouble eating? Why am I still losing weight?

Doctor Christman answers all the questions until she gets to the last one regarding weight loss, which seems to get her thinking about something else.

"Let me just take another look at your CAT scan." She steps out and returns within minutes. "Bill, it appears there are some lesions on your liver."

Liver? Liver? I'm thinking: when did his liver become involved in this mess! But she continues before I can utter my astonishment.

"We need to conduct a biopsy just to see exactly what is going on."

The biopsy is performed and the results are inconclusive. To my wishfully-thinking ears, of course, this sounds positive; *inconclusive* means it may not be cancer, right? Actually, *inconclusive* means some more hope is being held out that will, at the last minute, be ripped out of our hands. That's what *inconclusive* means.

Doctor Christman explains there are treatments Bill will be eligible for. So, here we go back to starting yet another round of chemotherapy. But we will do whatever it takes to beat this thing. So, we start more treatments. There are more fever runs, more vomiting, more nausea, more diarrhea. Through it all, Bill's resolute and we're fighting this sneaky bastard with all our might.

One morning, Bill gets out of bed and his legs give way. He collapses to the bedroom floor. I help him up but again he collapses. I call Doctor Christman who tells me to bring him in. Liam, by now, is in a day care program so we're able to head into the city immediately. As usual, we park in the underground lot at Sloane Kettering and the attendants, who are very familiar with us, are not accustomed to me requesting a wheelchair. I wheel Bill into urgent care and he's put into an examination room where we wait for the doctor. She checks Bill out and says he may have stretched a tendon in his knee.

"Go home and relax," she tells Bill, kindly, signaling for me to go outside. I discreetly leave the room and a few moments later I'm joined by Doctor Christman.

"We're running out of options for further treatment, Moya."

"What do you mean," I ask.

"He's maintaining."

"Maintaining," I repeat, weakening. "Okay, so what does that mean? Maintaining is good, right? It's not failing or, like, slipping, right? If he's maintaining, he's not dying, right?"

"It isn't looking good. He probably has three to twelve months left to live."

I can hardly see anything at this point. But I recall having passed some seats at the end of the hall and I wander towards them and sit. Doctor Christman joins me.

"Don't mention this to Bill," she continues. "In my experience, if a patient is told their time is limited, they just give up and die."

"What am I going to do," I murmur, thinking mostly about how to drive home without sobbing hysterically.

"Moya, I've never seen a couple so in tune with each other as you and Bill. If there's a one-in-a-million chance that this can be beaten, then Bill and you are the ones to do it."

"What will happen? I don't want him to be in pain as the disease progresses. What can I do for him?"

"Just continue doing what you have been doing."

And with that, the door opens across the hall and Bill is wheeled out. I'm grateful to be pushing his wheelchair so that he can't see the look on my face, the tears running down my cheeks. I look at his little fuzz-covered head, the bony back of his neck, and his long, skinny fingers as he waves to the nurses and staff that have come to know him over this difficult year.

One-in-a-million.

Textbook.

That's us.

The next night, I'm in the bathroom fussing around when Bill walks in, shakily, and perches his skeletal frame on the edge of the tub.

"Sweetie," he sighs, "I am so tired."

I look at him for what seems like a whole day, then come down beside him and lean my head on his boney shoulder.

"Bill, if you want to give up, I understand."

"No, no, Moya, I want to fight for you and Liam."

All I can do is hug him and wonder why it's me who's been given the honor of being this man's wife.

The next morning, he collapses again as he's getting out of bed. Doctor Christman tells me, okay, bring him back in. But this time I refuse.

"No, doctor," I say into the phone. "I'm not bringing him in anymore."

Sensitively, she takes her time responding.

"Do you think he's dying?"

"Yes, I do."

"You didn't tell him about our discussion, did you?"

"No, but I know he's dying and he knows it too. And this is what is going to happen—"

Round the clock care for Bill there in his home.

No more hospitals.

Father Vinci is called and a friend drives into the city to pick him up. He forgets to bring the Eucharist and has to go over to our local church and borrow some from our own parish priest. He gives Bill the last rites and spends a little time with him. I call all our family and friends, saying if they want to visit Bill, this is the time to do it.

We set up a bed in the living room and make sure Bill's comfortable. His parents come to stay. For three days, people come and go, family, friends, associates. As weak as Bill is, he manages to lift his head up and thank everyone for coming.

Lou is my rock, taking care of everything we need.

Liam sits on Bill's bed, like an innocent little guardian.

We have two hospice nurses monitoring Bill around the clock. Every night, after everyone has left, I climb into bed alongside him and pray there will be a miracle. And after three nights, I'm feeling sure we can go on like this for a while. But at two o'clock in the morning on that third night, I'm woken by the nurse tapping my shoulder.

"Moya, I think it's time."

It's time.

Time.

"What do I do," I ask, like a child all over again. "I don't know what I should do."

"Tell him it's okay, that he can go now."

But I don't want him to go. What will we do without him?

But I do what she tells me to do. I hold him and say: "Bill, it's okay, you can go now. Don't worry. I will take care of Liam. We'll be okay. I love you."

And with that, Bill opens his eyes and focuses on a corner of the ceiling. He lets out a gentle breath and leaves.

Gone. Just gone.

I hold him for a few minutes, but I know he's no longer there. I know he's moved on. It's two-thirty-eight a.m., September thirtieth, nineteen-ninety-two.

First thing, I go down into the basement where Bill's parents are sleeping and tell them Bill is gone. They come and sit on his bed, his mom weeping, his dad not knowing what to do. I call Lou. He's on his way. I call my neighbors and ask them what should I do. They give me the name of a local funeral home and say they'll be right over.

We're all sitting around the bed when the doorbell rings. It's the funeral director and his crew coming to take Bill. I don't want to see them in case I ever run into them at the grocery store. I don't want to know who they are. I don't want to know they're just ordinary people doing their job. I stay in the kitchen while Lou escorts Bill out to the waiting van. I'm glad it's dark outside. I don't want anybody seeing Bill leaving like that. After a while there's a flurry of activity out in the living room: vacuuming, furniture being moved around. I step out of the kitchen and see the place is all back to normal, as though nothing has happened.

But something has happened.

Bill died.

Now I have to make arrangements. That's how it's referred to. The arrangements. What arrangements? Whatever they are I have to do them. After everyone leaves, I sit on the sofa in the living room and watch the sun come up over the city, just exactly like when this nightmare began. All I can think of now is that there's a little boy asleep upstairs who is now fatherless, who's been robbed of one of the best dad's a kid could have. I hear him stirring and go up to him. I pick him up and hold him tight, explaining as best I can that his daddy was very poorly. But now he's gone to heaven.

"He will always be with us, though, even if we can't see him."

Lou comes back just as Liam and I come downstairs. He looks on as the child walks around the room, looking at the empty space where the bed had been. Seeing Lou in the doorway, Liam stops.

"Lou, my daddy died. I don't have a daddy anymore."

The one thing I know for sure is that there will be no wake. No viewing. Not even I will see Bill again. Nevertheless, a woman from the funeral home explains all the possibilities and decisions I need to make. Bill's mom is with me. This was her boy. She had him for thirty-four years and I only had him for a short while. But she allows me to make the arrangements. She doesn't for one second try to influence or question my arrangement-making skill.

But I know what the arrangements are going to be: No wake, no viewing, and a requiem Mass the day after tomorrow at Saint Patrick's Cathedral, where we were married.

Still, I'm shown towards the casket room.

Since Bill is to be cremated, I'm not sure I need an old school coffin, but what the funeral home gentleman refers to as a vessel.

I'm shown a few appropriate vessels, the first being a blue and white cardboard box with a kind of Laura Ashley print design on its surface. Not Bill, I think. There are a variety of other vessels, none of which are good enough for Bill either.

Then I see the first coffin I like in all my life.

"This one," I say, pointing.

"The coffin?"

"Yes. This one."

"Oh, well, Missus Aiken," the gentleman explains cautiously, "that one is top of the line."

"If Bill was picking out a casket for me, this is what he'd chose," I insist, quavering.

"Of course," the man continues, "but Bill's being cremated."

"I don't care."

"Moya," he continues, trying his best to be tactful, "as your husband is having a Catholic service, the vessel will be covered with a white pall anyway. It won't even be seen."

I could knock this guy's head off his shoulders.

"Excuse me, sir, I am not wanting the best vessel for Bill as a status symbol! I want the best because Bill was the best and I don't care if anybody sees it or not!"

I return to the office with the woman to finalize the payment details and hand over Bills clothes. I've selected his lovely navy-blue suit, white shirt, blue tie, black shoes, and belt; the outfit that made him look like Laurence Harvey in *Room at the Top*. Eventually, they convince me to *rent* the casket temporarily, so it can be repurposed later on for someone requiring a status symbol! I agree, shaking my head, too tired to argue. Who's about the pay top dollar for a used coffin?

Back at the house, the phone is ringing constantly. Food is being delivered, people are stopping by, the doorbell is chiming nonstop.

"Moya, it's your parish priest on the phone," someone calls.

I go over and take the receiver.

"Hello Father, this is Moya."

"Hello, Moya. Can I speak to Bill?"

I lower the receiver and just stare at it.

"Father, Bill died early this morning."

"Oh," the priest grunts. "I guess I'm too late then."

Click. No "sorry for your loss" or even a polite "goodbye." I'm in such deep despair I can't even be bothered to acknowledge this insensitivity.

And I'm so busy! Just as I sit back down at the kitchen table—

"Moya, somebody from the funeral home wants to talk to you."

I grab the phone again and find myself listening to some woman named Janet.

"Hello, Missus Aiken. I'm sorry for your loss. I am the hair and makeup artist and was wondering if I could get a picture of your husband as I will be preparing his body."

"Really? You want a picture of Bill so you can 'fix him up'. Can you put back his beautiful shiny black hair? Can you make his face fuller so he does not look like a child from a famine-stricken nation? Can you make his lovely hazel eyes that sparkled and looked like little crescents when he smiled not look like black holes, can you make his skin not look sallow and translucent? Can you make him not be eighty pounds? Can you make his long skinny fingers back to the loving hands?"

This was all running through my head, so I just explained to Sorry-for-Your-Loss-Janet that we will not require her services as nobody will be seeing Bill, but thank you for the kind offer.

The morning of the funeral the limos line up outside the house. Liam is at John and Lucy's house with their daughter. I don't want him to attend the service. We journey into Manhattan, but I don't see a thing. We pull up outside the Cathedral and somebody's saying, "Bill's here." And for I split second, I think they mean he's standing here waiting for us.

But they don't mean that and he isn't.

People are entering the church. Police are organizing the traffic, policemen on horseback. How odd. Is that normal? Neighborhood people hanging out their windows, looking to see what's going on. The sun shining. I enter the church, thinking about the day we were married and how, back then, the empty cathedral made everybody look so small. But today the church is crammed to capacity and it's the building itself that looks so little. I walk up the aisle behind Bill's casket, propped up by Lou, and sit in the front pew. I look over and wonder if I can reach out and rest my hand on it, just like we were holding hands.

It's the first time in my life I'm not afraid of a coffin.

The service is a blur.

Father Vinci says the Mass. We leave. I stand outside for two hours greeting people.

What do you say?

There's a lot of: "Hi, how are you?"

"Fine. You?"

Then the realization that it is not fine.

The guy from the funeral home comes over and apologizes for not having enough pages in the condolence book. He's getting more paper to add to it now. He didn't realize how big this funeral was going to be and says he's never witnessed anything like it in the forty years he's worked in the business.

"Never saw police having to reroute traffic," he adds, looking around for help. After about an hour, one of his associates comes over to me and asks if it's okay they take Bill now?

I tell him it's fine because I know Bill's already gone.

We all go back to Jersey and, just as we're getting into the house, a town car pulls up and out comes the sister, my older sister, all the way from England. She couldn't make it in time for the service. But she's here now.

And then the phone rings. It's Me-dad calling from Manchester asking how the Mass was. I tell him it was beautiful. And then he asks: "Moya, are you coming home now?"

ACKNOWLEDGEMENTS

In loving memory of Bill Aiken. To everyone who told me I should write a book—I did. To everyone who said I would never accomplish anything—fuck you. To everyone that has helped and encouraged me—thank you. To the most important man in my life, Liam, you gave me strength to carry on. To my incredible parents Charlie and Alice Hession and my selfless brave sister Madeleine—thank you. "I didn't change the world, I just changed my world."

www.ingramcontent.com/pod-product-compliance
Lightning Source LLC
Chambersburg PA
CBHW072047110526
44590CB00018B/3076